Pardon *and Peace*

Pardon *and* Peace

Alfred Wilson, C.P.

Roman Catholic Books
Post Office Box 2286, Fort Collins, CO 80522

NIHIL OBSTAT:
BRENDAN KEIGAN, C.P.
PROVINCIAL

NIHIL OBSTAT:
PATRICIUS MORRIS, S.T.D., S.S.L.
CENSOR DEPUTATUS

IMPRIMATUR:
E. MORROUGH BERNARD,
VIC. GEN.

WESTMONASTERII, DIE 30A SEPTEMBRIS, 1946

ISBN 1-929291-98-0

To her whom, after Mary Immaculate, I owe incomparably more than to any other of God's creatures, I gratefully dedicate this book—my mother.

CONTENTS

Pardon and Peace

I

A Load Off Your Mind

SOME years ago a non-Catholic woman went to a priest to discuss the Faith. She had, like most non-Catholics, a strong prejudice against Confession. To her it seemed a bugbear, an imposition of priests and a torture-process reminiscent of the Inquisition. She could not conceive the gentle Christ imposing so cruel a yoke on unfortunate humanity.

BANE OR BOON?

"You are presuming," said the priest, "that it is a yoke. Are you so certain that it is a bugbear and not a blessing? To me it seems a most convincing proof of the Divinity of Christ and a magnificent manifestation of His goodness and kindness."

She was taken aback. "How on earth do you make that out?"

"Because," said the priest, "it reveals the Supreme Physician of souls, the Divine Psychologist, Who understands human nature through and through."

"How?"

"When you have done wrong," said the priest, "is not one of your first impulses to tell someone about it? You want to get it off your mind, off your chest. Until you do, you know that you will be carrying a heavy burden; you will have something on your mind. You will have no peace of soul."

"That is true," she said.

"Well, then," he continued, "if that is true, would it not be just like Jesus, 'Who knew what was in man,' to institute a Sacrament to enable us to get our sins, our worries, our doubts and fears, off our mind?"

"I never thought of it like that," she said.

"No," the priest replied, "that is the pity of it. Our unfortunate non-Catholic brethren do not know what they are missing, and little realize the blessings that heresy has snatched from them."

It is not suggested that Confession is easy.

Some years ago, when a course of lectures was being given to non-Catholics, this query was found in the question-box: "You said last Wednesday night that confession is most consoling, but I have a Catholic friend who shakes all over every time she goes to Confession and really feels quite ill, and she tells me that she knows ever so many Catholics who feel just the same—how can confession be consoling if it makes people feel like this?"

The question was answered in this way: "You asked your friend how she felt going into the confessional, but did you ask her how she feels coming out?"

Hospitals are useful institutions: all the same, if you were just being wheeled into an operating-theatre for a major operation, that would hardly be the right moment for you to decide what you thought of the value of hospitals. If you came out of the hospital cured, you might have different ideas. It is a pity we need hospitals—but we do. It is a pity we need dentists—but we do. It is a pity that we need the confessional; if we were sinless we should not need it; but we are not sinless and therefore we do need it. Because our bodies get sick, we need hospitals. Because our souls get sick, we need the confessional.

No one goes to the doctor or the dentist for fun, unless he is mad. No one goes to Confession for fun. From the nature of the case, confession cannot be easy. The result, not the process, of confession is consoling.

After serious sin, however, we have no alternative but to confess if we desire to regain undisturbed peace of mind and safeguard our sanity. We must lift the burden from our minds, or become a burden to ourselves and risk becoming a burden to others. Confession is then—if you like to put it that way—the lesser of two evils.

Unforgiven sin, like toothache, places us in a very awkward predicament. From toothache, as we all know only too well, there is no possibility of painless escape. From soul-ache, caused by the consciousness of serious unforgiven sin, there is no possibility of painless escape.

Toothache is exasperating and may induce orgies of self-pity or violent displays of petulant bad-temper. But to give way to exasperation is childish and futile escapism, which neither lessens nor removes the pain, nor solves the problem. After all the distractions, the pain still remains unabated and the problem still unsolved; and the sooner the sufferer faces up to the situation, the better for himself. A person with toothache is faced with a particularly unenviable choice—a choice of pains. If the tooth cannot be filled, he must choose between the sudden sharp pains of extraction or the dull interminable pain of toothache causing progressive danger to general health.

If he wants to be rid of pain, he has really no choice at all. He must either get the tooth out or go on suffering. There is really no other alternative. It is impossible to get out of the difficulty painlessly. Soul-ache, caused by the sense of serious unforgiven sin, places us in a similar predicament from which painless escape is also impossible.

The sinner, in his pride, may give way to exasperation and indulge in the escapism of conscious or unconscious self-deception. He may try to exonerate himself from blame and like the bad workman blame his tools or his neighbours or God. He may deliberately dull his conscience or delude himself by whittling down and explaining away the moral law. He may even succeed in removing the pain by causing atrophy of his moral sense. But he cannot do this without suffering a serious loss of the power of perception of the beautiful, the good and the true. If he faces the facts, he knows that, if he wishes to regain his spiritual integrity, he must make an unenviable choice. He must choose between the shame of telling his sins to a priest or the shame of remaining consciously a sinner, secretly afraid to look his fellow-men in the face and perpetually appalled by the spectre in his own soul. The serious sinner must either put on blinkers or choose between confession and confusion.

Catholics do not enjoy Confession—heaven preserve us from those who do!—but they prefer it, humiliating as it is, to endless, dulling soul-ache and progressive demoralization of character and personality. Kneeling in a confessional to tell a shameful tale is about as attractive a prospect as sitting in a dentist's chair; but it is sometimes even more necessary. Like a bad tooth, sin must be extracted or the consequences are bound to be disastrous, as the average sinner *instinctively* recognizes. The instinct of spiritual self-preservation warns him of the need to find a safety-valve to enable him to "let off steam" safely. He feels a paramount need to obtain relief of mind, to unburden his misery and get it off his mind by telling someone about it. Instinctively he looks around for a prudent friend in whom he can confide.

This instinct often forces a young man to go to an older one and "tell him all about it." "A sorrow shared is a sorrow halved"—we all know the truth of that proverb from personal experience. The same may be said of shame. "A shame shared is a shame halved." Instinctively we feel this. We want to confide in someone; we want and we don't want.[1]

[1] It is humiliating to reveal our shame to another, the words stick in the throat, the disclosure seems too awful and too shocking, we fear the consequences of disclosure, we shrink before the possibility of being despised, and we cannot ignore the risk of breach of confidence. It is unspeakably difficult to reveal our hidden sores to another.

"Tell them out you must, but you cannot tell them to those you see every hour; you want to tell them and not to tell them; you want to tell them out, and yet be as if they were not told; you want to tell them out to one who is strong enough to bear them, yet not too strong to despise; you want to tell them out to one who can at once sympathize and advise; you want to relieve yourself of a load, to gain a solace." Newman, *Present Position of Catholics.*

Yet, in our heart of hearts, we know that no remedy is possible until we do reveal them. A story is told of a certain girl who practically broke in on a parson to tell her sad tale.

"Why did you come to me?" he said. "Have we met before?"

"No," she answered, "but I just had to speak at last. I felt that I had kept it to myself long enough and that unless I told it all to somebody I should lose my reason or die."[2]

Why is this relief necessary? Why must we tell our misery to at least one representative of the human race? Because until we confess we feel hypocrites. We feel that we are being taken for a hundred percent good and we know we are not. We feel that we are obtaining respect and love under false pretences. If, however, we can find one member of the human race who will listen to us sympathetically, who can know the worst and still respect and love us, we feel that our self-respect and social status are somehow restored. We can then reasonably hope for the respect of our fellow-men, despite our fault.

Sin sets up in the mind a conflict between our self-respect and our social sense. That conflict can be terminated only by some form of confession. "Confess, therefore, your sins one to another that you may be healed."

EVASIONS

Confession is the only remedy. It is no use to say, as many non-Catholics do: "I confess my sins directly to God, and that is quite good enough for me." First of all, it is the common experience that confession to God alone does not bring the fullest measure of relief of mind. It is no argument against this to say that it is not your experience. It is the common experience, and it is safe to presume that Christ legislated for the rule and not the exception.

In any case, adequate mental readjustment after sin requires readjustment of our relations with our fellow-men as well as with God. If you insult a friend, it is not enough to

[2] Leslie Weatherhead, *Psychology in the Service of the Soul* (Epworth Press), p. 83.

apologize to God—you must apologize to your friend as well. You have two clear obligations. To claim exemption from the second obligation because you have satisfied the first would be a proud excuse for evading an obvious duty. Sin is an offence against society as well as against God, and for both offences adequate reparation must be made.

Usually those who claim to be satisfied with confession to God alone are very anxious to demonstrate the firmness of their conviction and this attitude makes one wonder whether they are really so sure. If a man is very anxious to assure you that he is not afraid, you have a shrewd suspicion that he is. When people begin to talk a lot about their health, they are generally losing it. One wonders, therefore, if the opponents of sacramental Confession are really as confident of their position as they would like to believe. They would be wise humbly to ask themselves by what right they are so certain that God would not oblige man to confess to his fellow-man. It is a mistake to decide too readily that God's ideas coincide with ours, because "your thoughts are not my thoughts," saith the Lord. In a matter like this, there is grave danger of wishful thinking. A person who does not want to confess may with fatal ease convince himself that he does not need to confess. The wish may be father to the thought and grandfather to the conviction.

MORE EVASIONS

There are some who think that they can evade the odious duty of confession by treating the sense of sin as a phantom of a mind temporarily diseased or as the effect of a narrow education and a puritanical environment. Sin must be pushed out of the mind like a bad dream.

Others go so far as to ridicule the whole idea of moral responsibility and deny that there is such a thing as sin.

All these unrealists (who pout incessantly and suspiciously about their realism) are heading for a nervous breakdown.

THE RED LIGHT AHEAD

Problems of the mind cannot be evaded so easily. The only way to remove a problem, with its tantalizing incidence, is to solve it. We may explain away moral problems, but the snag is that they won't stay away unless the mind has been deadened. The mind is by its nature an inquisitive faculty, whose function is to read into things (*intùs-legere*) and solve problems by getting to the root of them. The mind will not be put off, and if the will constrains it to leave a problem unsolved, it remains restless, peevish and dissatisfied. The seeds have been sown of internal dissension and strife. The mind rests content only in knowledge and in truth.

When a practical difficulty is shirked and we refuse to face up to it, the will tries to push the difficulty "out of mind." The will does not succeed, and merely pushes the problem into the subconscious mind, from which it tends to keep bobbing up. To keep the problem out of the conscious mind requires constant pressure, and that pressure means wastage of mental and nervous energy. We do not rid ourselves of a worry by pushing it below the surface. It merely worries, then, in secret. It acts, and we can no longer check its action. We worry, and we don't know what we are worrying about. Our mind becomes fogged, and we don't know what is the matter with us.

Let me give you an illustration of this. If you have a boil, and, instead of getting the pus out of it, you put on a sticking-plaster, do you cure it? Not at all. You simply drive the poison in, you don't get rid of it. The place may heal in a fashion, but the poison will make its presence felt in some other way and in some other place. Those who try to ignore sin may achieve a surface peace, but underneath there is tumult and mental strain.

It is said that the sea has all its unrest on the surface and that underneath there is an unbroken calm. Many a man's life is the opposite. He preserves in the face of others a calm. But right underneath there is tumult. And what he needs more than anything is to get that tumult to the surface, where it can meet forces which will dispel it and bring the calm of God.[3]

[3] Weatherhead, *op. cit.*, pp. 87-8.

He needs to hear the Master's words: "Be still. . . . Peace be with you. . . . I absolve thee. . . . Thy sins are forgiven thee. . . . go in peace."

Confession of serious sin is necessary for the restoration of health of mind and soul and, redundantly, even for health of body. "Suppressed sin, like suppressed steam, is dangerous. Confession is the safety-valve."[4]

Modern psychologists have rediscovered this. They have found from practical experience that many nervous breakdowns can be traced to a sense of guilt for unconfided and unforgiven sin.

The Reverend Leslie Weatherhead, in an interesting chapter on the "Value of Confession,"[5] gives several instances of this. He tells of one, Dora, who had been engaged to a dentist. The young man fell a victim to an incurable disease and died. Later she became engaged to a young business man. They loved each other deeply. Their prospects were splendid. Dora, strangely, became morose and sad. She gave way to fits of weeping. She complained of insomnia. She even wished she were dead. She was obviously in love, yet she maintained she would never marry. What was the matter? Repeated sins against purity, with the dentist, had led to the fixed idea that she had rendered herself morally unfit for marriage with her present lover. Specialists and holidays were unavailing, until this minister assured her of God's pardon and the possibility of starting again. A good confession and a little elementary advice, such as any priest could give, would have saved all that expense and misery. Weatherhead also tells of a business man who had so completely lost his confidence in business that he was afraid to interview men and was on the verge of a nervous breakdown. He was really brooding over a sin against purity, for which he thought there could be neither pardon nor reparation. Any priest could give scores of such cases if he were permitted.

Is there any need, however, to go further than our own ex-

[4] *Ibid.*

[5] *Op. cit.*, pp. 79ff.

perience to prove the truth of what has been said? Which of us does not know from experience the depressing effect of sin and the harrowing mental torture of the sense of guilt? Sin produces a brooding disposition and unconcealable depression. The sinner may pooh-pooh the idea of sin as much as he likes, yet he cannot stop his natural joyousness from departing with his innocence. Like Cain, the unforgiven sinner develops melancholia, he feels that it is "no use trying," he is "too bad," his past mistakes get between himself and God, and the skeleton in the cupboard of his soul haunts him. Unforgiven sin festers, as it were, in the soul and poisons life and paralyses effort.

Confession is the only adequate spiritual and psychological remedy for unforgiven sin. The remedy may be hard, but the alternative (constant mental strain, spiritual uneasiness and possible derangement) is harder still and infinitely more disastrous.

Intelligent men outside the Church have begun to appreciate this. Modern psycho-therapy has instituted a searching confessional process. The High Churchmen have reintroduced confession, and some Nonconformist ministers openly advocate it. The Oxford Groupists, or Buchmanites, have introduced "sharing," a kind of public confession.

On the merely human psychological plane, confession is amply justified and its necessity proved. But Confession is more than a clinic of psycho-therapy; it is also a Sacrament of Divine Mercy, guaranteeing the pardon of God as well as the pardon of society. It is in no sense an arbitrary imposition, for even the hardest part of it, the obligation of telling out our sins, is medicinal not punitive, and is inspired by mercy, understanding, and a desire to help. The medicine is certainly hard to take and not at all palatable, but it is medicine all the same! A kind Lord could not let us off scot-free—it would not be good for us. In this world, however, all penance is designed to be remedial and is never merely vindictive.

Jesus obliged us to confess our sins for our own sake rather than for His. He took the institution of Confession, which is a natural necessity, and safeguarded, facilitated and elevated it, raising it to the dignity of a Sacrament. He made the inevitably difficult task of confessing *as easy as it possibly could be made*. We confess in secret, to any priest we choose; if we like, to one who does not know us and will probably never see us again. We confess in secret to a man who is bound to secrecy. We confess, moreover, to a man who is trained, not merely to listen with tenderness and sympathy, but to instruct, advise and heal.

In the Sacrament of Penance, Christ Himself is the real priest. There, in His capacity of Divine Physician, He forgives sin, pours grace into our souls, removes the traces of past sins, and gives us a title to actual graces in future difficulties.

Confession is simply a Hospital of Souls, where the Good Samaritan, through the instrumentality of priests, goes about binding up wounds and pouring in oil and wine: a hospital where the Divine Physician displays His healing art. Object to such a Sacrament as too fantastically good to be true, but please don't object to it as a bugbear.

I don't think the majority of Catholics realize how much they owe to the Sacrament of Penance. One of the greatest of Viennese psychologists, a man bitterly anti-Catholic, had the honesty to admit that, among his cases of serious psychological disorder, he had never had a genuinely practising Catholic.

Regular Confession prevents our worries and fears and remorse from degenerating into neurosis and melancholia. Test from your own experience what might have happened to you but for Confession. There are few who certainly retain their Baptismal innocence: few who have not, at some time or other, committed mortal sin or had serious doubts of having committed it. Remember that experience and the aftermath—your worry, misery, joylessness: the joy of others merely accentuated your misery and seemed almost to mock you; praise and approval rubbed in your unworthiness. You went to Confession, you put yourself in contact with the Precious Blood, "one drop of which could cleanse a thousand worlds of sin"; you almost felt "the oil of gladness" being poured into your soul. You came out a changed being. You were free, you were pure, once more a child of God. Others noticed the change and wondered what had happened to you. You simply had to indulge your feelings, you bounded along and almost danced for joy, you felt that you could have jumped over the moon and gladly played the clown in any harlequin show. He had restored unto you the joy of His salvation.

Recall those times of huge relief. That relief is being given daily to thousands. God forbid that any Catholic should come to look on such a Sacrament as a harsh necessity or a cruel imposition.

What would have happened to us had we been forced to go through life without that relief, without a chance of starting again? What morbid neurotics we might have been! Throughout our lives, Confession has been safeguarding us against perils that only recently have we begun fully to appreciate.

Let us make full use of this Divine Sacrament. Let us strive to gain a fuller appreciation of its value and a greater gratitude for its help. Is it not a magnificent proof of the wisdom and love and tenderness of the Good Samaritan, the Divine Physician of Souls? Only on the Day of Judgment shall we know all that we owe to this Sacrament of Mercy: the joy and consolation irradiated from it, the oil of gladness poured into the souls of men, the sins prevented, the weak encouraged, the spiritually-dead restored to life. Was it not just like Jesus to institute, in His infinite Mercy, this Sacrament of pardon, consolation and hope? An imposition? It is a Sacrament of Mercy for which we can never be sufficiently grateful.

NOTE: Soon after this chapter was completed, I came across two rather amazing confirmations of what I have written here.

Samuel Butler would be both surprised and indignant to find himself quoted as having written an excellent apologia for auricular Confession. Yet in the following somewhat harrowing and cynical story, is it not obvious that what Mrs. Thompson both wanted and needed, and what Theobald was unable to give her, was the reassurance of sacramental absolution?

. . . to visit a dying cottager's wife. He takes her meat and wine from his own table, and that not a little only but liberally. According to his lights, also, he administers what he is pleased to call spiritual consolation.

"I'm afraid I'm going to Hell, sir," says the sick woman with a whine. "Oh, sir, save me, don't let me go there. I couldn't stand it, sir, I should die with fear, the very thought of it drives me into a cold sweat all over."

"Mrs. Thompson," says Theobald gravely, "you must have faith in the precious blood of your Redeemer: it is He alone can save you."

"But are you sure, sir," says she, looking wistfully at him, "that He will forgive me—for I've not been a very good woman, indeed I haven't—and if God would only say, 'Yes,' outright with His mouth when I ask whether my sins are forgiven me—"

"But they *are* forgiven you, Mrs. Thompson," says Theobald with some sternness, for the same ground has been gone over a good many times already, and he has borne the unhappy woman's misgivings now for a full quarter of an hour. Then he puts a stop to the conversation by repeating prayers taken from the *Visitation of the Sick,* and overawes the poor wretch from expressing further anxiety as to her condition.

"Can't you tell me, sir," she exclaims piteously, as she sees that he is preparing to go away, "can't you tell me that there is no Day of Judgment, and that there is no such place as Hell? I can do without Heaven, sir, but I cannot do with Hell."

"Mrs. Thompson," he rejoins impressively, "let me implore you to suffer no doubt concerning these two cornerstones of our religion to cross your mind at a moment like the present. If there is one thing more certain than another it is that we shall all appear before the Judgment Seat of Christ, and that the wicked will be consumed in a lake of everlasting fire. Doubt this, Mrs. Thompson, and you are lost."

The poor woman buries her fevered head in the coverlet in a paroxysm of fear, and at last finds relief in tears.

"Mrs. Thompson," says Theobald, with his hand on the door, "compose yourself, be calm; you must please take my word for it that at the Day of Judgment your sins will all be washed white in the Blood of the Lamb, Mrs. Thompson. Yea," he exclaims frantically, "though they be as 'scarlet, yet shall they be white as wool,' " and he makes off as fast as he can from the fetid atmosphere of the cottage to the pure air outside. Oh, how thankful he is when the interview is over!

He returns home, conscious that he has done his duty, and administered the comforts of religion to a dying sinner. His admiring wife awaits him at the Rectory and assures him that never yet was clergyman more devoted to the welfare of his flock. He believes her; he has a natural tendency to believe everything that is told him, and who should know the facts of the case better than his wife? Poor fellow! He has done his best, but what does a fish's best come to when the fish is out of water? He has left meat and wine—that he can do; he will call again and will leave more meat and wine; day after day he trudges over the same plover-haunted fields, and listens at the end of his walk to the same agony of forebodings, which day after day he silences, but does not remove, till at last a merciful weakness renders the sufferer careless of her future, and Theobald is satisfied that her mind is now peacefully at rest.[6]

The second story, which is still more pointed and amazing, is taken from an article in *The Catholic Digest*. The writer, who starts out by saying, "I am not a Catholic," tells how he was on the verge of a nervous breakdown and went to visit an old university friend, who had become one of the best-known psychiatrists of his native city.

After the writer had "told his miserable tale," the refreshingly honest psychiatrist said, amongst other things:

"Do you know what you have just done? Prompted by a deep-seated impulse that lies in the mystic urge to atonement, you have simply gone to confession. You are not a Catholic and neither am I. But if all the people with real or imaginary troubles of a general nature corresponding to yours (in a majority of cases such people are victims not of circumstance but of their own wrong thinking); very well, then, if all such people retained enough common sense"—He waved his hand impatiently—"No I don't mean that. It

[6] *The Way of All Flesh* (Oxford).

isn't primarily common sense that you and the rest need. What you need is faith: 'faith, hope and charity, and the greatest of these,' in cases like yours, is 'faith.'

"And, as I was going on to say, if the thousands of our clients once could gain a deep and abiding Catholic faith, most of us psychiatrists would have to go out of business. Why? Simply because the remedial agency is already at hand in every community and, in terms of money, it costs absolutely nothing."

Later, after having quoted a splendid tribute to the work of the Church, the psychiatrist added:

"People come here in droves and pay me inordinate amounts of money for trying to do what the Catholic Church does for nothing. They do what you have done. They confess their sins, their shortcomings, unscramble their inferiority complexes, uncover their vanities, their prejudices, their false senses of relative values, sometimes their puny souls.

"What does it all amount to? Nothing but the submitting of their sins and problems in confession. Unloading onto someone else in the hope of getting rid of burdens that seem unbearable.

"What do they get in return? Nothing but a scientific solution which falls far short of spiritual absolution. Psychiatry is a comparatively modern remedial agency and, as an honest man, neither I nor the representative rest of my colleagues would keep on with it unless we were convinced we were performing a useful purpose. Speaking as an outsider, corresponding results could be more effectively obtained in the confessional because there the penitent would believe in spiritual absolution.

"The Founder of the Catholic Church, the Church from which all other Christian churches ultimately derive, knew mankind's need for peace of mind and heart, and that same free and simple agency for the relief of all ailing mankind was established by Him as it is today."

The rest of the story can be told in the writer's own words:

"Through my own fault the unexpected help I gained from my friend, the psychoanalyst, was not permanent. I did not act on the suggestion so clearly implied in his nonprofessional counsel. The man who pulled me out of a worse condition was a Catholic priest I had never seen before, summoned to my bedside by a stranger who thought I was at the point of death. Then and thereafter I could not, of course, go to Confession, but I did go through the same story by way, I thought at first, of an obituary. And, because that priest looked on me as one for whom Christ died, he listened to my tale, spoke to me with love and hope, and something of his own peace and security passed over me.

"Sometimes as I pass the open door of his unpretentious little church, I enter and experience a spiritual presence calming a troubled spirit. If I could implicitly believe as a Catholic that 'God so loved the world as to send His only begotten Son,' that He established the Catholic Church to perpetuate His ministry to men, gave to an apostolic priesthood the power of forgiving sin, I am sure that confession would do more for me than innumerable visits to the best of psychoanalysts."[7]

[7] "Confession," Viator: *Catholic Digest,* November 1939 (condensed from *The Missionary*).

II

Easy Terms

MANY non-Catholics cannot see any necessity for confession nor what good it would do God to ask a man to confess to his fellow-man. A question often on their lips is: "Why confess to a man?" Confession, they think, slights the Divine Mercy and makes God appear exigent, hard to satisfy and slow to forgive. When this opinion does not spring from a spirit of arrogant insubordination, but from a sensitive concern about the attributes of God, it is worthy of respect.

Non-Catholics are wrong in concluding that because they can see no need for confession, therefore there is no need. God, Who is infinitely more far-seeing than they, may see reasons where they see none. At the same time, we must admit that if Confession did actually reflect badly on God, it would be proved false. Any sacrament which obscured the Divine Mercy and made God appear an exacting tyrant, would have to be rejected. Our whole point is, however, that Confession proves the exact opposite. Confession is not necessary to appease God's anger and win His pardon. An act of perfect contrition gains us instantaneous pardon and immediate restoration to grace. The truly contrite receive pardon as readily and as quickly as the Good Thief. We must not allow our faith in the readiness of God to forgive to be dimmed or obscured by Confession; otherwise, our attitude towards God will be far more misguided than that of non-

Catholics. They endeavour to honour the Mercy of God; whereas, the Jansenistically-minded dishonour it.

Confession expresses a human need, not a Divine need, and is necessary to satisfy man, not to satisfy God. When our Saviour instituted Confession, He was thinking of us, not of Himself. Whenever there is sincere contrition, He pardons in a flash, and would pardon without more ado, if such an arrangement were good for us. He saw, however, that it would not be good for us to be let off without an apology for serious sin. Parents often insist on an apology from an erring child even when they have long since forgiven it in their hearts. They insist, not for their own sake, but for the sake of the child, whose ultimate good they unselfishly consider. In the same way, God insists on an apology from us, for our sake not for His.

It is evident that penitents often fail to realize this, because if they did realize it, they would not approach Confession as they do. Many of them seem to think that they have no hope of recovering the Divine Friendship until they have been through all the formalities of Confession, and woe betide them if they make any slips. What a complete misconception of the Sacrament! In that case, God is more difficult to propitiate now than He was before the Incarnation. If they are truly contrite, they are already in the grace and friendship of God. Confession is designed not to placate the Divine Justice nor to win a tardy concession of mercy, but to enable us to gain the maximum benefits of Divine Mercy. If you are contrite, He has already forgiven you, and Confession means that He wants to enfold you in His arms and bathe you in His Precious Blood.

The idea of many non-Catholics that our Saviour intends us to confess directly to God in secret is not absurd, but how much it overlooks! Jesus could have been satisfied with that, had He not been infinitely wise and infinitely tender.

After all, the Apostles in the upper room on the first Easter Sunday could have confessed (and presumably did confess) to God their miserable cowardice and infidelity. But they were glad of the reassurance of pardon from the lips of Christ. If we assert that they should have had sufficient faith in the mercy of God to be able to dispense with such a reassurance, the plain fact confronts us that they had not sufficient faith, and that Jesus condescended to their weakness. In like manner, Jesus "yesterday, today and the same for ever" condescends to our weakness, and His condescension is Confession.

If we were angels, we might dispense with verbal and perceptible reassurances of God's pardon. Because we are not angels, the senses must crave for help and reassurance; and we should be humbly grateful to God for all the sense-helps which He, in His mercy, gives us. To talk to God is one thing, but to be *quite certain that God is talking to us* and speaking words of pardon and peace is quite another thing. Those who have tried confession to God in secret admit that it was like "talking to nothing" or like "arguing with yourself on your knees." It might be different with a saint, but saints are few. "Whose sins you shall forgive, they are forgiven them." How reassuring to *hear* the words of pardon from the lips of the priest, speaking in the name and with the delegated power of Christ: "I absolve thee from thy sins, in the name of the Father and of the Son and of the Holy Ghost."

Let us not disdain the extra mercies of Christ. There is no absolute need of Confession as a prerequisite of satisfying the justice of God. Christ could have left us to our own devices and the torturing uncertainties of direct confession to God, but He was too kind. Not merely would He give us Scriptural reassurances of His mercy, He would also leave us a *standing proof*. He saw that auricular Confession would be necessary to give us conclusive proof of pardon and the maximum relief and peace of mind.

Besides being (as we have seen) indispensable medicine for the regaining of perfect spiritual health, Confession is also necessary to intensify our realization of the malice of sin. If we "got away with" sin too easily, we might make light of it. God insists on a formal, penal apology for serious sin to prevent us from confusing His mercy with unconcern.

If He made no fuss about serious sin, we might easily conclude—to our own undoing—that it is not really so heinous and so odious to Him. He has, therefore, obliged us to confess our sins because He is wise and kind.

The Sacrament of Penance was instituted to make reparation for sin easier, not to make it more difficult. The inspiration of Confession is mercy not justice. It is remedial not revengeful. To have other thoughts about it, is to insult the mercy of God and regard Jesus as a task-master. Let us never lose sight of the fact that Confession is meant to be a help not a bugbear.

It is evident that confession to a fellow-man can never be easy, and may be extremely difficult, if there is a shameful tale to tell. From the nature of the case, Confession is a burden. It is unthinkable that our Saviour would add unnecessarily to the natural difficulties of Confession. He was indignant with the Pharisees because they "bound heavy and insupportable burdens and laid them on men's shoulders." It would be implicit blasphemy to presume that He has followed their vicious example.

A law which is too severe for ordinary mortals is no law at all. Instead of being "an ordinance of reason for the common good," which is the definition and purpose of law, an excessively severe law would be a stumbling-block to the common detriment.

If Confession were made too difficult, it would be not a help but a terrifying bugbear. The burden would then be insupportable, and the remedy worse than the disease. It is safe to presume, therefore, that our Saviour has not added to the inevitable intrinsic difficulties of Confession. It is impossible to visualize Him piling on the agony. Better for Him not to have instituted Confession at all than to have done that. Better to have left us free to confess directly to God in secret. He would defeat His own purpose if He made Confession unnecessarily difficult. The burden was imposed to be a blessing in the long run. Unnecessary requirements would be unnecessary sources of anxiety and insecurity, tending to make Confession a sacrament of strain and worry instead of a sacrament of peace.

Let us not defeat our Saviour's merciful designs by approaching Confession as though it were the imposition of a prosecuting-attorney anxious to trap us into further mistakes. We must be careful not to hurt our Saviour by want of trust. If we make Confession a botheration, we are not using it properly, because we are not using it according to the mind of Christ.

Civil authorities set up courts of justice, where strict justice is meted out. Our Divine Saviour has set up instead a Court of Mercy, and its name is Confession. The difference between the two courts is admirably illustrated by a story told of Father Henry Day, S.J., whose father is a judge. One day a penitent was seen coming away from Father Day's confessional, obviously very jubilant. Her friend noticed it and remarked on it. "Why shouldn't I be?" was the decided retort. "He has only given me three Our Fathers and three Hail Marys and his father gave me three months."

We must never lose sight of the fact that Confession is prëeminently a sacrament of mercy. Jesus comes to us as our merciful judge on the Way, that He may not have to be a stern judge at the Journey's End. If we treat Him as a taskmaster, we completely misunderstand Him. It is no excuse to say that we want to be on the safe side. We do not put ourselves on the safe side by insulting Him and nursing heretical ideas. Not merely need we not, but we *must not,* make Confession a worrying nerve-straining effort. Straining is *prohibited* not commanded.

Because Confession is not meant to be a bugbear, all theologians teach that *no one is obliged to put himself to serious inconvenience when he goes to Confession.* This is a principle of great importance, which should be well pondered and never lost sight of. If we act on any other principle, we are guilty of obstinate pride by constructing our own practical theology in direct opposition to the teaching of Christ and His Church.

All Our Lord demands is that we take enough trouble to

make our confession sincere. When we have confessed sincerely, there is absolutely no need to worry because we did not confess with the greatest possible earnestness and intensity. We are bound to do our best; but we are not bound to do our bestest-best (if I might be pardoned the ugly phrase).

If penitents remembered this, they would save themselves much entirely unnecessary worry and nervous strain. It is a patent fact that many Catholics go infrequently to Confession because of a false notion of its requirements. They imagine that they must make a super-effort every time, and naturally they cannot make such an effort often, because it takes too much out of them. Even some of those who go frequently to Confession find it a strain, and are relieved when they have got Saturday night over.

To act like this is to play into the hands of unbelievers. At the Reformation, Confession was called a "butchery of consciences," and Catholics were accused of leaving nothing to the mercy of God. Over-anxious penitents might profitably ask themselves what they do leave to the mercy of God.

It is unfortunately true that some penitents find Confession a source of serious nervous strain. The mere thought of the approach of Confession day causes them to become nervous and preoccupied; and for days beforehand they are recurrently spring-cleaning their consciences. After Confession they never feel satisfied that they have done enough; perhaps their examination of conscience was not sufficiently thorough, perhaps they should have given more time to preparation, perhaps their sorrow was not what it ought to have been. They keep going over their examination of conscience in case they left out something, they multiply acts of contrition and scheme to test the sincerity of their contrition, they try to work themselves up to a fakir-like frenzy of fervour and devotion. How insulting all this to the merciful Christ! What sort of a Master do they think they have? A single, simple, straightforward effort is enough. He who has done his best, with moderate diligence, has done all that Christ demands. If a penitent wants to do more than is *demanded,* he should examine his motive. If the motive is love, well and good; if the motive is fear, it is cowardly distrust and far from good. If he thinks a nerve-racking effort necessary, he insults Jesus by implying that He intended to make Confession a botheration. If he does not think all this fuss necessary, he condemns himself as ridiculous and his conduct as dishonourable to God. If Jesus is satisfied, there is no reason why anyone should worry.

Let us hope that the scrupulous will not approve this doctrine as consoling theory and then do nothing to reduce it to practice. Those who are inclined to go back on past confessions, and have repeatedly done so despite explicit prohibitions of the confessor, could profitably change the direction of their scruples and examine themselves instead of their confessions and—confessors! They suspect, perhaps, that the confessor is lax and taking a risky course of action—which, besides being a rather serious rash judgment of the priest, amounts to an obstinate refusal to submit to any judgment but their own. Obviously, in their own conceit, they are wiser and more prudent than the confessor. Not realizing how meticulously exact they are, he is dispensing them from an obligation, and they want no dispensations. He is doing no such thing. He is not dispensing them from anything but simply declaring that the law no longer obliges, because they have already done more than the Lord demands. Further effort would imply self-will, secret pride, want of trust and an appalling misconception both of the nature of the Sacrament and of the goodness of God. An illustration should make this clear.

Suppose I lost a small sum of money and asked you to look for it for me. Suppose I said: "If you don't find it within a quarter of an hour, don't look any longer." If you did not find the money in the stated time, and did not look for it any longer, obviously I could not blame you; and if I did blame you, I should be both unreasonable and unjust. Our Lord tells us to use moderate diligence in preparing for Confession, and if we do no more, He cannot blame us without being unjust.

Let us study the kindly, helpful intentions of Jesus in

obliging us to confess serious sins, and we shall be saved from forming a distorted idea of this Sacrament of Mercy and from approaching it in fear and trembling.

THE ACTUAL TERMS

It is surprisingly easy to fulfill the task set in Confession, because amazingly little is absolutely demanded. God's terms are the easiest possible. It is child's play for a sincere person to secure the valid reception of the Sacrament of Penance.

The three indispensable acts of the penitent are confession, contrition (which includes purpose of amendment) and satisfaction. The essential requirements for the validity of these acts are amazingly light; the rigorist would probably say—scandalously light.

For the sake of clarity, let us consider the various kinds of confession which our Divine Saviour *could* have imposed. We may reduce them to four heads:

1. A general accusation of sin, such as, "I have sinned." This is called by the theologians generic confession.
2. An indication of the theological species of sin. "I have sinned mortally or venially."
3. The accusation according to number and kind of *all sins,* whether mortal or venial.
4. The accusation of *all mortal sins* according to number and kind.

Generic confession—"I have sinned"—is obviously demanded from the nature of the case. Unless confession of some sort were prescribed, there would have been no point in instituting the Sacrament. Our Saviour was not obliged to institute the Sacrament, but once He did so, He was obliged to insist on generic confession.

As regards the other forms of confession, He was perfectly free to choose. This is a point of great importance. In making His choice He acted as a legislator. His choice represents positive law; and positive law, as we have seen, does not oblige with serious inconvenience.

We should not allow ourselves to have any doubts whatever as to what our Saviour *has chosen to oblige* us to confess. Ignorance on so vital a point is lamentable and must lead to confusion of thought and endless perplexities.

THE EXTENT OF THE LAW OF CONFESSION

Jesus has obliged us to confess *mortal sins* according to their *kind* and *number*. There is never an obligation to confess venial sins, unless we have no other matter; in which case, we must confess *at least one venial* sin for which we are truly sorry.

A law to confess all sins, mortal or venial, would be extremely onerous and worrying, and it was to be expected that our kind Saviour would not impose it.

Confession of only the theological species of sin, "I have sinned mortally or venially," would, by its vagueness, destroy to a great extent the efficacy of the Sacrament. A vague confession would not induce adequate relief of mind, and would deprive the Sacrament of much of its satisfying and therapeutic value. It is not surprising, therefore, that our Saviour did not choose that form of confession.

The actual obligation of confession is surprisingly easy and should reassure those who are inclined to make examination of conscience a fierce, nerve-racking ransacking of the soul. We are obliged to confess only mortal sins. Now even a very ordinary Catholic would not need to *look* for mortal sin. The thought of the sin would have been torturing him ever since the time it was committed, and the difficulty would be to forget rather than to remember. As soon as he knelt down to prepare for Confession, his sin would be nagging at him, and would, so to speak, give him a knock-out blow between the eyes. No need to find out the sin; it will find him out and, like an unwelcome guest or a bore, will introduce itself. A sincere person can, therefore, find necessary matter for confession in a split-second.

There is never any obligation to make a complete catalogue of venial sins, and it is seldom or never wise to try. If some venial sins are omitted, it does not matter; because, provided we are sorry for them (there's the rub!), they are forgiven by the absolution. It is a mistaken policy to rake up forgotten venial sins at the next confession. There *never was any obligation* to confess them, so there is no need to make so much fuss about them. They are forgiven already, no extant obligation to confess them remains, so there is absolutely no reason why we should not be done with them.

It is pathetic to find people harrying themselves to a state of stupor by excessive concern about the confession of venial sins. Penitents with a haunted look about them, will say anxiously: "But suppose I leave out some venial sins?" Well, if you do, it is no great matter. Inform yourself about the Church's teaching, and you will cease to be your own unlawfully appointed inquisitor.

When theologians say that our sorrow must be *universal,* they mean that it must include *all mortal sins,* not that it must include all venial sins. Similarly, when they speak of the necessity of safeguarding the *integrity of confession,* they mean that, in ordinary circumstances, we must never omit to confess a mortal sin. In extraordinary circumstances, when it is morally impossible to make an integral confession, the obligation to do so is for the time being suspended; because our kind Divine Legislator does not wish even this law to oblige with serious inconvenience which arises from unusual and accidental circumstances. Applications of this law are rare and best left to the confessor, so it is hardly necessary to treat of them at length here. The law is of practical application, however, in cases of scrupulosity.

Thus a scrupulous person, for whom examination of conscience is a nightmare, may be dispensed from the obligation of integral confession, and should have no hesitation in restricting himself to generic confession at the request of the confessor.

The obligation of confession has been made as easy and worry-proof as is consistent with the purpose of the Sacrament. The same is true of the second act of the penitent—contrition.

CONTRITION

It is presumed that you know the distinction between contrition and attrition. Contrition is sorrow for sin because we have offended God's infinite goodness. Attrition is sorrow for sin for some less noble and more selfish supernatural motive, for example, that we have lost heaven and deserved hell.

In the Sacrament of Penance attrition is enough to obtain the pardon of the most heinous sins. The implications of this doctrine are a startling manifestation of Divine Mercy, meriting prolonged and grateful meditation. This teaching means that if we take the trouble to go to Confession, God is willing to forgive us our sins, even our mortal sins, just because we have turned to Him with a feeble incipient love, which is still largely selfish and occasioned principally by a prudent regard for the security of our own skin. Even though we are still much more concerned about ourselves than Him, He forgives us because we are back once more on the road that leads to Him. Only God would forgive on such terms. One wonders how He can, how such easy forgiveness is consistent with His dignity. Who said that we leave nothing to the Mercy of God?

Outside the Sacrament of Penance attrition is not enough to restore the mortal sinner to grace; inside the Sacrament it is enough, and this is a very powerful reason for confessing to a man if that man happens to be a priest. Forgiveness is very much more certain in the Sacrament of Penance than it could possibly be elsewhere; in fact, when we have done what Our Lord demands, forgiveness is morally certain. Penance may be called the Sacrament of easy forgiveness.

Another startling aspect of the sufficiency of attrition is that all that is absolutely required for the validity of the Sacrament of Penance is attrition for mortal sins.

If we are not sorry for some venial sins, even if we are not sorry for any of our venial sins, the Sacrament is not invalidated provided we have attrition for mortal sins, even past and confessed mortal sins. Needless to say, such imperfect dispositions diminish the grace received from the Sacrament, but they do not nullify it.

Mere humans could never be so merciful. The implications and significance of this ready forgiveness should inspire the most absolute confidence in the Divine Mercy. Consider one parallel case and see how you would act.

A former friend has robbed you and made an attempt on your life. Afterwards he comes to you and expresses his regret for the attempted homicide and restores his ill-gotten goods; but adds that he is not in the least sorry for a succession of petty slights and pin-pricks spread out over years. You might forgive him his major offences, but would you readmit him to your friendship? Yet that is what God does for us. Provided we are sorry for our major offences, He tolerates our minor ones and receives us back to His friendship. His kindness is amazing and should be most reassuring.

Whenever we go to Confession honestly determined to try to avoid all mortal sin, it is almost impossible not to have the required minimum of attrition if we have any faith at all, and are not quite asleep. Could He have made things easier?

A word about purpose of amendment, just to emphasize the easy requirements of the Sacrament. Suppose you went to Confession in a hurry. You made definite acts of contrition, but you cannot recall having made any explicit acts of purpose of amendment. Was the Sacrament validly received? It was. Genuine contrition implies hatred of sin, which, in turn, implies a determination to avoid it in future. This is not a wise procedure, but it is enough to secure validity. Failure to make clear-cut explicit acts of purpose of amendment is one of the major reasons why the Sacrament does not produce more fruit (as we shall see later), but for the moment we are discussing what is absolutely necessary, not what is advisable. If we see how easy it is to lay the necessary foundations, we shall, to our own great benefit, approach the Sacrament with confidence and tranquillity of mind.

SATISFACTION

With regard to satisfaction, the essential requirements of the Sacrament are that at the time the penance is given, we are willing to accept it. If we changed our mind afterwards and refused to say the penance, we should, needless to say, commit a sin; but even then the Sacrament would not be undone. If the penance was a grave one imposed for mortal sin, refusal to perform it would constitute a new mortal sin. If the penance was a light one, refusal to perform it would amount to a venial sin.

If *deliberate* refusal to say a penance does not invalidate the Sacrament, it is perfectly clear that *indeliberate omission* of the penance through forgetfulness does not invalidate it. If the omission is due to a bad memory, there is no sin at all; but only a regrettable loss of grace and sacramental satisfaction. Say your penance reverently and earnestly, because it has a double value and works *ex opere operato* as well as *ex opere operantis* (i.e. its efficacy is partly due to the sacramental operation of Christ and partly to the virtuous activity of the penitent); but do not say it anxiously, as though indifferent or distracted saying of it would ruin the Sacrament.

Our Divine Saviour has obviously done His best to make Confession as fear-proof as possible, so let us not frustrate His merciful designs by introducing unwarranted fears based on ignorance. It is possible to commit a good many sins in the actual act of Confession and yet not nullify the Sacrament. He demands the very minimum. It is not for a moment suggested that we should be content with the minimum. All the same, it is a great advantage to know the minimum requirements of Confession, because such knowledge enables us to appreciate how easy it is to lay the sure foundations; and when we have done that, we can go on tranquilly to raise a noble superstructure, which we cannot do if we spend all our time worrying about the foundations.

Why is Confession so easy? "Because by His bruises we are healed. The chastisement of our peace was upon Him. The Lord laid on Him the iniquity of us all." The blows that were aimed at us fell aslant across His bruised and battered Body and He broke the force of the blows. That is why we get off so lightly. "He took the handwriting that was against us and nailed it to the Cross in His own Body." He made the supreme sacrifice and perfect satisfaction for all the sins of all the world.

Moreover, in the Agony in the Garden, He made a perfect confession and a perfect act of perfect contrition for *all* the sins of the world. "Him Who knew no sin He hath made sin for us." His confession was absolutely accurate: His contrition, His sadness, was of infinite intensity. Remember that, when you go to Confession. He has already told those very sins you are about to tell, He has sorrowed for them. Your task is to supplement His perfect confession and perfect contrition as best you can.

Naturally, you feel that your effort is hopelessly inadequate. Of course it is. His will supply. Think more of His confession and you won't be so worried about your own. You never approach Confession alone. He is always by your side, ready and anxious to help; and He will never fail you nor allow you to fail Him, if you do your honest best. Remember that Confession is a Sacrament of Mercy and approach it with childlike trust. He wants our trust and is pained when we do not trust Him. And, after Calvary, the Mass and the institution of this Sacrament of Mercy is it surprising?

III

Tonic: Penance as a Keep-fit Sacrament

THE statement has already been made that there is no obligation to confess venial sins. This statement deserves to be underlined and its practical implications drawn out, because experience teaches that it is news to some Catholics and that many others regard it as a truth to be stored away in an attic of the mind and not allowed to have any practical influence on conduct.

There seems to be reluctance to teach this truth; or, at any rate, reluctance to emphasize it. It is considered more prudent to let people take the impression—the false impression—that they are obliged to confess every venial sin which they can remember. Whatever may be said in theory, to confess every venial sin is the only *safe* course in practice. The idea is—as statements in question-boxes have often made clear—that penitents might become slipshod and superficial if they realized that they are not obliged to confess venial sins.

Let us beware of presuming that the clear teaching of the Church requires the corrective of our more factual and practical prudence. The suppression of any part of the Church's teaching, however wise and justified it may seem at first sight, is always, in the long run, disastrous; and the attempt to make the confession of venial sins seem obligatory is largely responsible for the ineffectiveness of the Sacrament of Penance as a constructive instrument of virtue.

For the present it will be sufficient to indicate some of the evil consequences of this mistaken policy. Here are a few of them:

1. It is partly responsible for the undue concentration on confession described in the next chapter.
2. It creates at least a subconscious idea of God as a task-master.
3. It makes confession a torture to pious souls. Earnest souls (and are they not the majority?) are "put through it" and their efforts misdirected in order that the minority (the laxer folk, who won't be cured in any case) may not let themselves off too easily.
4. It causes the very defect which it is designed to obviate, namely, superficiality. If our energies are spread out over a wide field, it is impossible to put much drive into our efforts. An attack along a whole front is less likely to make a deep penetration into the enemy's position than a concentrated attack at one given point. The false prudence of rigorism prevents concentration. Other unfortunate consequences of it will be described in the remaining chapters of this book.

Before we go any further, let us briefly review the official teaching of the Church on this matter.

The Council of Trent is very clear and explicit: "Venial sins may without guilt be omitted in Confession and expiated by a variety of other means."[1]

Canon 901 of the Code of Canon Law states that all who have committed mortal sins after Baptism are bound to confess them. Canon 902 says: "Sins committed after Baptism, either mortal sins already confessed or venial sins, are sufficient, but *not necessary*, matter for the Sacrament of Penance."

This clear and repeated teaching of the Church will be confirmed and illustrated by a short review of the history of devotional Confession.

For the first four centuries of the Christian era (according

[1] Sess. XIV, C. 5, *De Confessione.*

to some, until the seventh century), it was the universal practice to employ Confession only for mortal sins. Many of the faithful never received the Sacrament of Penance at all, and it seems fairly certain that we must include in this number some of the saints, e.g., St. Ambrose, St. Cyprian, St. Augustine and St. Jerome.[2]

"With many of the saints of the first centuries, there is no evidence that they ever thought of receiving what we call the Sacrament of Penance, whose necessity, in any case, was much diminished by the delay in the reception of Baptism."[3]

For the deleting of venial sin, the early writers recommend "prayer, almsgiving, a forgiving spirit, daily acts of mortification, the word of God, the Holy Eucharist"—but never Confession. In all of the early Christian literature there is not a single sentence which clearly states that the Christians of those days went to Confession solely for the purpose of obtaining forgiveness for venial sins.[4]

From about the fifth century onwards, and largely as an outgrowth of monasticism, the confession of venial sins became common. In the thirteenth century, devotional Confession was recommended two or three times a year. In the fourteenth century, St. Catherine of Siena recommended it once a month, more often if possible, never less often.

After the council of Trent, frequent Confession was encouraged by all spiritual writers, and it became the practice of many of the saints to go to Confession daily.

In modern times, and especially since the reintroduction of frequent Communion, there has been a tendency to exaggerate the necessity of frequent Confession. If present-day Catholics were asked if it would be wrong deliberately to omit to confess venial sins, some would reply with an emphatic "Yes," whilst others would be uncertain how to answer.

The differences in the Church's devotional practice will

[2] Phillip Scharsch, F. A. Marks, Ed., *Confession as a Means of Spiritual Progress* (Herder), pp. 22-4.

[3] Paul Galtier, *Sin and Penance* (Herder), p. 208.

[4] Scharsch, *op cit.,* p. 40.

surprise only those who are unfamiliar with the theology of the development of doctrine. The official teaching of the Church remains unvaried, but the grasp of it varies from age to age. The early Christians had the full revelation, but not the full understanding of revelation. Divine Revelation was more than the human mind could take in all at once, and only gradually has the complete harmony and profundity of it become clear. Moreover, spiritual writers, who are not guaranteed infallibility in their expositions of revelation, tend to be unconsciously influenced by the ideas prevalent in their day; and in consequence, popular theology does not always attain the perfect, delicate balance of the Church's official teaching. In controversy there is always a danger of swinging from one extreme in the direction of the opposite extreme, or of neglecting any truth which is being exaggerated by one's adversaries.[5]

The official teaching of the Church about the means of deleting venial sins is perfectly clear, and may be summarized thus:

1. Venial sin "may be expiated by a variety of means."
2. Of all the means of expiating venial sin, sacramental Confession is eminently the most effective; and, therefore,
3. The confession of venial sins is highly advantageous and much to be encouraged, but must not be considered rigorously necessary.

However favourably the practice of frequent confession or devotion to absolution as it may be called, is viewed by the Church, and in spite of any obligation that may have been imposed upon certain classes of the faithful—priests, religious and others—by laws and regulations that particularly concern them, it remains true that according to the common law and general teaching, there is no universal divine obligation to submit venial sins to the power of the Keys. There is no obligation even to do penance or seek forgiveness for them before death. Venial sins, however

[5] Cf. Watkin, *The Catholic Centre* (Sheed and Ward). A most thoughtful and useful book.

numerous, cannot deprive us of the friendship of God, and therefore can be no obstacle to our salvation; it only remains, before being admitted to the enjoyment of Heaven, to be purified of their stain and to suffer a penalty for them in Purgatory. However, the spirit of penance conspires with considerations of personal interest to urge us to be freed from them without delay.[6]

The early Christians were so well aware of the multiplicity of ready-to-hand means of deleting venial sin that they overlooked the benefits of devotional Confession. The attitude of the early Christians seems to have been something like this: "You *can* confess venial sins if you want, but we don't see why you should." Confession as a tonic sacrament was practically unknown to them.

The modern attitude is the exact opposite and may be summed up like this: "You can confess venial sins, and we don't see any reason why you should not." Modern Catholics have lost sight of the truth that venial sins may be deleted without Confession. It would be interesting to trace the causes of the smoke-screening of this truth. Perhaps it is due to a lingering shadow of Jansenism, or to an excessive reaction against Protestantism. If it is stated that *no sins* need be confessed, there is an obvious danger of going to the opposite extreme and insisting that *all sins* must be confessed. Whatever may be the explanation of our mistaken notions, there is no doubt that they are widespread. Let us integrate our doctrine by learning from the mistakes of others, so that we may be able to utilize *all the means* of deleting venial sin from our souls.

It is easy to see why the confession of venial sins is not necessary. Among friends, little slights are not magnified into great wrongs, and are soon repaired and cast into oblivion by a few little extra attentions. Why should it be different with the Divine Friend of Friends?

Moreover, venial sin does not destroy the supernatural life of the soul. No matter how many venial sins we have committed, the soul still lives. Now living things can throw

[6] Galtier, *op. cit.*, pp. 247-48.

off minor ailments by increasing their own vitality. Venial sin decreases the fervour of charity; any act of virtue, therefore, which restores our charity undoes the harm caused by venial sin.

Possibly the reader thinks that this is a matter of no great practical importance, which hardly deserves so much insistence. It is a matter of vital importance. There is at stake the rectitude of our idea of God and His Christ. If venial sins can be remitted only with comparative difficulty, the logical conclusion is inevitable that our Divine Friend is touchy and slow to forgive injuries and not "a gracious and merciful Lord, patient and rich in mercy and *easy to forgive injuries*."[7]

I am not suggesting for a moment that any Catholic will draw such conclusions consciously and deliberately. That is the very point of danger. He may draw them unconsciously and be unaware that he has drawn them. If he saw where his ideas led, he would reject them at once with horror. If he does not see where his ideas lead, he may draw false and disastrous conclusions—*unconsciously*. It is a well-known fact that our activity is often inspired by unconscious motives. How many scrupulous and timid souls are tortured and paralysed by unconscious false ideas of God. "Something tells them that they ought to do this or omit that." The "something" is probably a false idea of God, which, because it is unrecognized, cannot be dealt with and removed.

We cannot be too careful not to store our minds with erroneous notions from which we may unconsciously deduce disastrous ideas of God. One such idea is that it is difficult to repair the damage done by venial sin. The implication of that idea is that God is less forgiving than human parents. Earthly parents do not demand a formal apology for every peccadillo of their children. If the child shows sorrow and tries to make amends, is not the fault immediately forgiven and forgotten? "If you, then, being evil know how to give good gifts to your children: how much more will your Father Who is in heaven give good things to them that ask Him?"[8]

[7] Joel 2:13.
[8] Luke 11:13.

"For you have not received the spirit of bondage again in fear: but you have received the spirit of adoption of sons, whereby we cry: *Abba* (Father)."[9]

"Our Father Who art in heaven." If any idea threatens to obscure the fatherhood of God, let it be anathema. The paternal kindness and tenderness of God are infinitely greater than the combined tenderness and love of all parents of all time. It would be an implicit surrender to ghastly heresy to drift into an attitude of mind which implied that we thought God less forgiving than human parents.

There is another very important practical aspect of this question. If a person decides that God "keeps things up" and that once a venial sin has been committed nothing effective can be done about it until the next confession, it is morally impossible for that person to preserve a joyous, unclouded peace of mind.

If God "keeps things up" our plight is indeed pitiable. None but the greatest saints can persevere for long without committing some semi-deliberate venial sins. Must those sins, once committed, overshadow and darken the soul until the next confession? Is there no other way of removing the blight? If there is not, the conclusion is inescapable that it is morally impossible for the devout, unless they become callous to venial sin, to maintain a joyous peace of mind and an intimate sense of close union with God. The very first sin after Confession starts a subtle process of gradual estrangement from Christ. As the sins multiply—and alas they do!—the sense of estrangement grows; the clouds darken and deepen and produce a spiritual black-out; the soul is oppressed with a depressing sense of sinfulness, and becomes nervous of our Divine Saviour and almost afraid to think of Him.

Whilst the soul lives in such a spiritual atmosphere, it can have no sense of the indwelling of the Blessed Trinity, and must tend to become servile and lose the liberty of the children of God. The divine Friend of Friends is relegated to the position of a task-master or slave-driver. Instead of

[9] Romans 8:15.

enjoying the friendship of Christ and delighting in the Lord, the soul lives in an almost unbroken state of spiritual uneasiness. When people think that Our Lord is so "difficult to get on with," it is not surprising that they give up trying to cultivate His friendship and content themselves by doing only what they consider rigorously necessary. Confession must be an ordeal for anyone who approaches it without confidence in the mercy of Christ, based on personal experience.

The Jansenistic attitude towards the forgiveness of venial sin has done enormous harm to souls. It has such a speciously pious and safe look about it that it deceives many, even the elect. The devil is always most successful when he appears as an angel of light. False rigorism prevents Our Lord from "being friends with us," and deprives us of the greatest of all blessings—the intimate, secure, experimental knowledge of the personal friendship of Christ.

Sensitive souls are rightly distressed when they feel that a barrier has been placed between themselves and God. They must be taught to remove the barriers at once, or it is good-bye to holiness. Obviously they will not remove the barriers unless they realize the possibility of doing so. No one will attempt what he considers impossible.

If venial sins are repaired quickly, they may ultimately become occasions of gain. Consider attentively what Our Lord said to St. Gertrude:

> When anyone perceives a dirty spot on his hand, he washes it away at once; after washing, however, not only has the spot disappeared, but the whole hand is clean. Thus it happens that if a person commits a slight offence, but makes an act of contrition, he thus, by humility, becomes more pleasing to Me. Greater humility, more interior attachment to God: this is the only conclusion you should draw from your failings.

If that is not done, what was only a scratch is allowed to fester and become a real sore. Too much fretting over minor faults wastes time, depresses the soul and makes the remedy worse than the disease. "If you have a vase," says the Curé of Ars, "and it receives a slight stain, you don't get the scrubbing brush to it." If you did, you would not have the vase for long. It is not necessary to use the scrubbing brush of Confession for every venial sin. Perhaps the importance of this doctrine will be made still clearer by a homely illustration.

There were two housekeepers, one of whom had the strange notion that it was not permissible to do any cleaning or dusting except on Saturdays. Her home was always dirty and unsightly, and she was confronted with a formidable task every Saturday morning. Because of the untidy state of her home, she was ashamed to invite friends to visit her and full of apologies and excuses if someone dropped in on her, uninvited. The other woman wisely did some cleaning, dusting and polishing during the week, as need arose. Her home was always neat and clean and Saturday was an easy day.

If we restrict spiritual housework to one day per week or per month, it will hardly be surprising if we find the task dismaying and laborious. Worst of all, we shall be ashamed to invite our Divine Friend into our dirty and disorderly home. Not unnaturally we shall feel that a spiritual spring-cleaning is necessary before we can respectfully issue such an invitation.

Let us repair venial sins at once, and aim at keeping our souls spotless, so that there may be nothing in us to impede the operation of grace or to make Our Lord look upon us with less pleasure. The habit of deleting venial sins, as soon as we become conscious of them, will conduce to peace of mind and sensitiveness to sin.

WAYS AND MEANS

Sacred Scripture praises many works of virtue as means of expiating sin, notably almsgiving, the corporal works of mercy, prayer and fasting. "Numerous," says Galtier, "are the ways by which pardon for venial sin may be obtained. As a general rule, it may be said that to seek it is to obtain it, provided always that sorrow is there. . . . It is possible, therefore, to speak of the ease with which the remission of venial sins may be obtained from God by one who is in the state of grace."[10]

[10] *Op cit.*, pp. 249-50.

Venial sin may be expiated by a quick trusting return to God with humble acknowledgment of the fault and protestation of undaunted trust in His mercy; by devout use of the sacramentals, e.g., holy water; and by any act of virtue, especially by acts of fraternal charity. Sacred Scripture makes it clear that an act of perfect contrition instantly obliterates the guilt of mortal sins, *a fortiori* the guilt of venial sin. Theologians teach that venial sin may be expiated by acts of attrition. In the present state of human nature, it is easy to fall into semi-deliberate venial sin; and it is unlikely, to say the least of it, that our Saviour would have allowed it to be easy to fall and difficult to rise.

No suggestion is made here that we should think lightly of venial sin. On the contrary, our precise point is that because venial sin is a horrible and disastrous thing, we should do our best to expiate it at once, so that it may not continue to damage the soul and obstruct our union with God. In any case, we are speaking here of souls who are anxious to obviate venial sin, and are depressed and discouraged by an apparent impossibility of doing so without disproportionate difficulty.

A person who has acquired the habit of instantly expiating venial sin may approach the Sacrament of Penance with great tranquillity of mind and without any constraint and worry. He is in need of a tonic rather than of medicine; for him Penance is a sacrament of prevention rather than of cure. Unless he approaches in that spirit, Confession will do him more harm than good.

Confession may be compared to a very complete hospital, with three departments—a medical and surgical department, a convalescent home and a health clinic. To which department a penitent should go depends on his spiritual condition. If he has committed mortal sin, he must go to the surgical department. He will need the X-ray of a very close examination of conscience and a major operation. His thoughts will be more of sin than of grace and virtue; because until he is cured of his disease, health is for him out of the question.

If the penitent has no serious ailment, that is, if he has only venial sins to confess, it would be a mistake and waste of time to go to the surgical department. Unnecessary fussing about minor ailments would tend to produce a spiritual hypochondriac. In that case, a visit to the surgical department would do far more harm than good. A penitent who is spiritually "run down" should go to the convalescent home, or his treatment will generate more ailments than it cures. Many pious souls are actually harmed by the way they approach the Sacrament of Penance. A penitent who has no unexpiated venial sins to confess should go at once to the health clinic, and should think in terms of health and virtue rather than of disease, and approach Confession as a tonic sacrament.

TONIC SACRAMENT

We know from experience the beneficial "tonic" effect of devotional Confession, which has an effect on the soul similar to that of a hot bath on the body. It renews our vigour and enables us to keep spiritually fit. It is sun-ray treatment for the soul.

If we neglect frequent Confession our spiritual life soon begins to languish and decline. Bad habits gain renewed strength, temptations are harder to conquer, spiritual truths seem unreal, and we lose our sense of contact with the Master. Quite rightly we make a great point of keeping physically fit; it is infinitely more important that we should keep spiritually fit. Spiritual fitness is as essential for spiritual health as physical fitness is for physical health. If we keep in training spiritually, we shall be able to take in our stride obstacles which prove insurmountable to the spiritually flabby. If you have not already done so, join the "keep-fit" movement of frequent devotional Confession.

For brevity's sake, I can do no more than give a list of some of the reasons why devotional Confession has such a beneficial tonic effect on the soul. Each point deserves attentive consideration.

1. It deletes sin. The Sacrament has special efficacy for this.

2. It remits the temporal punishments due to sin, and does this more effectively than ordinary acts of virtue because of Sacramental efficiency.
3. It heals the soul from the evil effects of sin.
4. It has an incomparable power of restoring peace of soul. Making a clean breast of things gives us the maximum relief of mind and powerfully restores our resolution.
5. It gains us a right to actual graces for future combats and supernaturally strengthens our purpose of amendment.
6. It is a powerful moral and educational force, which fosters self-knowledge and self-control, gives insight into human nature, and makes us more sympathetic and understanding and therefore more helpful to our fellow-men.
7. Confession to a fellow-man helps to knock the conceit out of us and nullifies a grave danger to personality and salvation.
8. It enables us to get useful advice and surer guidance.
9. It increases sanctifying grace and the fervour of charity.[11]

These reasons have been summed up admirably by Pope Pius XII in his encyclical on *The Mystical Body of Christ.* "To hasten daily progress along the path of virtue, we wish the pious practice of frequent confession to be earnestly advocated. Not without the inspiration of the Holy Spirit was this practice introduced into the Church. By it genuine self-knowledge is increased, Christian humility grows, bad habits are corrected, spiritual neglect and tepidity are countered, the conscience is purified, the will strengthened, a salutary self-control is attained and grace is increased in virtue of the Sacrament itself."

[11] Cf. Francis M. de Zulueta, *Letters on Christian Doctrine,* II (Benziger), pp. 243-4; Scharsch, *op. cit.,* pp. 40 ff.

A SACRAMENT IN ITS OWN RIGHT

From all this it should be evident that Confession, even when it is approached without rigorous necessity, is a great Sacrament in its own right and not, as many seem to think, a mere appendage to Holy Communion.

Many Catholics never dream of going to Confession unless they intend to go to Holy Communion; and if something turns up to prevent them from going to Holy Communion, they abandon immediately the intention of going to Confession. This is lamentable logic. The fact that they are prevented from receiving the Bread of Life should be an additional incentive to go to Confession. If one channel of grace is closed to them, all the more reason for using the one which still remains open to them. Perseverance and immunity from sin may depend on this. Many people, especially those in the Forces, who on account of circumstances are seldom able to receive Holy Communion, would receive invaluable help from frequent Confession. Probably they are struggling against new, strong and insidious temptations; and precisely because they are deprived of the graces of the Blessed Sacrament, they have imperative need of all the graces and helps they can get. A frank exposure of their difficulties would take the sting out of them. "A temptation revealed is half-conquered," says the wise St. Philip Neri. The moral support of the confessor will give them confidence; and the feeling of solidarity with the good will be a powerful antidote to the herd-instinct. The grace of the Sacrament itself will transform them into spiritual athletes and enable them to stand the pace.

No one will go far wrong if he devoutly approaches the Sacrament of Penance every week. Of course, this habit will take a good piece out of his time and force him to curtail many pleasures. Pleasure, however, is of little use if there is torment in the soul. If we want to keep our souls pure and in the grace and peace of God, we must seize *all* the available means of spiritual self-preservation. Many people will not take the trouble and then wonder why they fall into sin. When they have fallen into sin, through not using the means of grace at their disposal, they exonerate and console themselves with the thought that religion is impossible in this busy work-a-day world of ours. Of course it is, if we put this world first. If we have not got time for necessary religious duties, we must *make time* and not treat religion as a side-issue. Many people seem to expect heaven for a song and see nothing shameful in their attitude. "The kingdom of heaven suffereth violence and the violent bear it away."

CONFESSION AND COMMUNION

It is dangerous to get the habit of regarding Confession simply as part of our preparation for Holy Communion, because such a habit of mind may lead to an unconscious limiting of our purpose of amendment. We must not fix time-limits to amendment.

After Confession, some people seem very anxious to avoid all sin until they have been to Holy Communion, in fact they make themselves slightly ridiculous and are afraid to laugh heartily or play cards or pay the marriage debt; but they are not nearly so anxious to avoid sin afterwards. They remind one of a certain Irishwoman who replied to an insulting neighbour: "It's well for you, Biddy, that you insulted me now, when I'm in the grace of God. But beware! I won't always be in the grace of God."

We must not limit our resolution to the interim between Confession and Communion. "Whoever, in going to Confession," says Scharsch,[12] "limits his attention to the approaching Communion and loses sight of the future, will not only make very imperfect resolutions, but also logically arrive at a stage where he no longer thinks of carrying them out as soon as Holy Communion is over, and makes no further efforts to correct his faults." Such an attitude of mind is an impediment to permanent reform, perverts the main purpose of Confession, and involves self-deception. People *feel* pure when they have been to Confession, but if they

[12] *Op cit.*, p. 231.

are secretly clinging to their faults and determined to make only a temporary effort to avoid them, they are not really as pure as they feel. Probably the majority intend to make a permanent effort, but are prepared to relax somewhat when they have received Holy Communion.

Another common mistake is to regard Confession as a *necessary preparation* for Holy Communion. Not a few Catholics will never go to Holy Communion unless they have received absolution almost immediately beforehand. They put off absolution to the very last moment, for fear they might commit a venial sin if too long an interval elapsed between absolution and Communion. If they did commit a venial sin after Confession, they would either refrain from approaching Holy Communion or receive it with misgivings and principally out of human respect. People of this type often make a nuisance of themselves by trying to go to Confession on Sunday morning during Mass, or by invariably turning up on Saturday night at the very last minute before closing-time.

Confession is, of course, an admirable preparation for Holy Communion, and it would be a sign of an unbalanced and slovenly spirituality to go frequently to Holy Communion and seldom to Confession. But Confession is *not* a *necessary preparation.* After all that has been said, it should not be necessary to insist on this. Fussy, over-anxious and scrupulous prospective communicants say: "I don't want to go to Holy Communion with sin on my soul." Naturally! On that we are all agreed. But you are presuming that you must inevitably approach Holy Communion with sin on your soul unless you go to Confession; and in that you are quite wrong. You can obliterate venial sin without Confession, and you ought to have done so long ago.

You should not be hugging venial sin like this. You should have thrown off the guilt as soon as you became conscious of it. These mistaken notions about Confession are poisoning your spiritual life and making impossible habitual union with God. If you do not feel fit to go into Our Lord's sacramental presence as you are, you cannot have been living in

His spiritual presence. "Know you not that you are the temple of God and that the Spirit of God dwells in you?" If your relations with the indwelling Christ are more or less habitually strained, you will hardly be able to approach Him with confidence in any case, even after Confession, and your periods of complete peace and conscious union will at the best be of very short duration and restricted to brief periods after Holy Communion.

In any case, it is permissible to approach Holy Communion when we are conscious of the guilt of venial sin on our souls, even when we are conscious of attachment to a habit of deliberate venial sin. Most of us are always in this boat, and if we think we are not, it is a hundred to one that we are self-deceived. One of the purposes of Holy Communion is to free us from these faults. Pope Pius X speaks of it as a "Divine Drug" (*Divinum Pharmacum*), and the Roman Decree on Frequent and Daily Communion (December 20th, 1905) says: "Although it is *most expedient* that those who communicate frequently or daily should be free from venial sins, especially from such as are fully deliberate, and from any affection thereto, nevertheless *it is sufficient that they be free from mortal sin,* with the purpose of never sinning in future; and if they have this sincere purpose, it is impossible but that daily communicants should *gradually emancipate themselves* [N.B., gradually] even from venial sins, and from all affection thereto."

Let us not base our right to receive Our Lord on make-belief and a weekly or monthly process of kidding ourselves that we are better than we are. Anxious communicants and nervous penitents have yet to realize the plenitude of significance of the title of Divine Physician, and that He is still the friend of all publicans and sinners who are willing to try again. "If He washes us not, we can have no part with Him."

Behind the fussing of Jansenism lurks an odious pride and self-sufficiency, or, at any rate, irritation at one's insufficiency, which obviously presupposes a latent desire to be self-sufficient. The Jansenist is unwilling to put himself under a compliment to the Lord. He wants to approach the Lord purified by his own devices so that he may have to rely in nothing on the mercies of God.

"If you have sins on your conscience," says St. Augustine, "as long as they are not mortal sins, do not hesitate to come. But be careful first to pray: Forgive us our trespasses as we forgive them that trespass against us. If you forgive, you will be forgiven. Come, therefore, it is food for you, not poison."[13]

If you are in a state of grace, never refrain from going to Holy Communion merely because you have been unable to go to Confession. "His delight is to be with the children of men." Don't deprive Him of the satisfaction of coming to you. Allow Him to do for you what you cannot do for yourself. It is a thousand pities needlessly to miss such a precious opportunity of grace. God alone knows how many graces have been lost in this way and how much harm has been done to souls. Remember that for centuries Christians, saints included, *never* went to Confession in preparation for Holy Communion. If you are distressed about certain venial sins, offer up fervently the Holy Sacrifice in expiation for them. The Mass is the sacrifice of expiation *par excellence* and has spiritual efficacy to destroy sin. If your attempts at expiation are inadequate, His expiation is most definitely not inadequate.

A less respectable variety of the reluctance to go to Holy Communion without previous Confession is sometimes expressed like this: "I should not *feel* happy . . . right . . . safe . . . if I did." Think what He feels for a change. Is how *you* feel all that concerns you? Think less of your badness and more of His goodness, and the result will be beneficial for your spirituality. You may even begin to see and feel the sunshine of His love. It is a disastrous mistake to make feelings and vague fears the laws of spiritual conduct. Jesus invites you, He wants you to come to Him. "Compel them to come in that my house may be filled . . . the blind, the halting, the lame." If you will not take Christ at His word,

[13] Tract *In John*, 26; Cf. Scharsch, *op. cit.*, p. 24.

you are not reverent but unbelieving and encrusted with spiritual egotism.

It is a matter of supreme importance that the last traces of Jansenism should be eradicated from our devotional life. Far too many souls still resemble those of whom Our Lord complained to St. Gertrude: "Some souls tie the bandage of their unworthiness so tightly over their eyes that they cannot see Me and My love."

Excessive fussing about venial sins is a distressing symptom of spiritual hypochondria. Approach the Sacrament of Penance frequently, but approach it with tranquillity and peace of mind and imperturbable confidence in the readiness of the Mercy of God. May you never have to go to the X-ray department or the operating theatre, and seldom or never to the convalescent home. May you be able to go at once to the health clinic to take a tonic and come away spiritually refreshed and happy in mind, singing the mercies of the Lord.

THE DISTINCTION BETWEEN MORTAL AND VENIAL SIN

In human friendship there are certain faults which, much as they may regret them, friends are nevertheless prepared to tolerate, and there are other faults incompatible with friendship which destroy it at once. Exactly the same holds good with the Divine Friendship.

Mortal sin is an offence against God's law which "destroys divine friendship, robs man of sanctifying grace and the right to eternal happiness, and so kills the spiritual life of the soul. Venial sin is an offence against God which does not destroy Divine Friendship but leaves grace and the right to eternal happiness substantially intact, does not imply complete aversion from God, and is more easily pardoned than mortal sin."[14]

Mortal sin implies the practical preference of some created good to the friendship of God by breaking His law in a serious matter and defying His sanction of eternal damnation. To prefer the creature to the Creator (and the mortal

[14] Henry Davis, *Moral and Pastoral Theology,* I (Sheed and Ward) p. 204.

sinner does this since he knows that he cannot have the two together and that it is therefore a question of either—or) is a supreme defiance of God which makes farcical any profession of friendship with Him.

It is immediately obvious to common sense that certain sins are, of their nature, serious; e.g., murder, suicide, adultery, robbery with violence; and that other sins, e.g., white lies, are not serious. In between the obviously serious and the obviously not-serious sins, there are other sins whose gravity it would sometimes be impossible to decide without the help of revelation and God's infallible Church.

In discussing the gravity of sins we must bear in mind:

1. The importance of the law, and
2. The wilfulness of the offence.

A venial sin cannot destroy God's friendship, no matter how deliberate it is. On the other hand, even a serious offence will not destroy God's friendship unless it is committed with full deliberation. Before a sin can be mortal there must be:

1. Serious matter, i.e., question of an important law;
2. Full advertence of the mind to the gravity of this matter; i.e., we must *know and recollect* its gravity at the time of acting; and
3. Full consent of the will in the act of sinning; e.g., if we were hustled by spontaneous and indeliberate passion into acting before we had had time for sufficient deliberation, there would be no mortal sin.

If any of these conditions is not verified, the sin is not mortal. It is extremely important that these distinctions should be understood. We must beware of a pharisaical mentality which would make all sins mortal and the friendship of God almost impossible to preserve; and, on the other hand, we must beware of whittling down God's law and deluding ourselves that hardly any sins are mortal. In practice the laws of God and His Church are made known to us individually by our minds. Conscience is the final, intimate promulgator of law; and, therefore, it is of the utmost importance that conscience should be rightly informed and register law as it really is. To disobey a law which conscience proclaims serious (even if it isn't) is a mortal sin, because such conduct reveals a person prepared to forfeit the friendship of God rather than restrain his self-will.

Theologians distinguish three main grades of sins:

1. Sins which are, of their nature, light; e.g., lies. A lie is never a serious sin unless it involves serious uncharity or injustice.

2. Sins of their entire nature grave; e.g., murder, impurity.

3. Sins which may be mortal or venial according to the gravity or levity of the matter; e.g., uncharity, injustice, immodesty, gluttony, drunkenness, pride.

If a sin is of its nature light, only a false conscience can ever make it serious. If a sin is, of its nature, grave, only incomplete wilfulness, due to imperfect advertence or only partial consent, can make it venial.

IV

Topsy-turvy Tactics

ANY Catholic of average instruction who was asked which is the more important, confession or contrition, would answer without the slightest hesitation: "Contrition, of course." Were he then asked to which he devotes more time and attention, it is extremely doubtful if he would be able to answer without hesitation: "Contrition, of course."

The majority of penitents give to examination of conscience considerably more time than they give to exciting contrition and securing amendment. This is a topsy-turvy procedure. It is evident that what is most important should be given most attention. And contrition, which determines the reality of our repentance and the amount of grace received from the Sacrament, is admittedly the most important disposition of the penitent. Strange, then, that it should be scamped in favour of confession and become the Cinderella to the less important, and even less attractive, sister.

Let us consider how the average Catholic prepares for Confession. That the following description is substantially correct has been proved by the giggles and open admissions of members of various kinds of audiences.

After a preparatory prayer for light, she begins her examination of conscience, which is indeed a formidable task. (I say "she" because women are more addicted to these mistaken methods than men, though "scrapism" has plenty of clients among the men-folk too.)

The examination of conscience has three distinct parts, three torturing rackings of the unfortunate memory. Part one consists of drawing up the inventory of faults. The penitent ransacks her memory and turns the house of her soul upside down and inside out, hunting for every peccadillo. They are as evasive as fleas. She hunts and hunts and hunts, until her nerves are in a state of quasi-prostration. She scrapes and scrapes and scrapes until the poor soul is raw. She tries to recall everything she has done since her last confession, everywhere she has been, everyone she has met; and it is not surprising that she finds herself distracted and chuckling over the latest joke or fuming at the impudence of the newcomer at work. She reads through lengthy lists of sins and gets together a worth-while budget of "possibles" and "probables" and "certs." After an orgy of fault-finding, she finishes up discouraged, mentally muddled and unable to see wood for trees.

Then starts process number two—checking up on the budget. She has to recall her sins (and, will-o-the-wisps, they keep escaping!) and label and learn them by heart. Her memory is on the rack again. By this time, she is thoroughly miserable and ready for a pick-me-up. The long inquisition is followed by a few sentimental acts of contrition and hardly a thought about amendment; and then at long last she goes into the confessional, terrified that she will leave out something, which means that almost infallibly she will. She is scared that the priest will butt in before she has got through her precious list, and put her out of her stride and upset everything. In her worry she is often unwittingly rude and will not let the priest get in a word edgeways until she has had her say.

Confession over, she flops down on her knees and the inquisition starts all over again. She reviews her precious list to make sure that no item was omitted, she recalls what she said and how she said it; and if she finds that she has omitted something, even a "possible" or "probable," immediately she is in a state of quasi-panic and the Sacrament is deprived of its peace-giving quality.

How pathetic! How absurd! No wonder many penitents dread Confession and "tremble all over" at the thought of it, if that is their method of preparation. A small boy told of the sky-scrapers in New York, remarked: "I didn't know the sky needed scraping." Neither does the soul need scraping.

Some penitents suffer from a delusion, common among preachers, that to be effective they must be prolix. They seem to imagine that the essence of a good confession is the compiling of a satisfactory budget; and in consequence of this delusion, they never progress beyond the spiritual development of the boy who said that he was not ready for Confession because he had not made up enough sins. They cannot understand why nuns go to Confession so frequently; to them it is a mystery what they find to confess. A request that they themselves should go to Confession is regarded as an insinuation that they have been misbehaving; and, somewhat aggrieved, they will reply that they have not done anything wrong. Not a few people think that they will be wasting the priest's time, as well as disappointing the poor man, if they are unable to tell him something that will make him sit up and whistle. Supreme optimists!

MISSING THE POINT

Whoever gives a disproportionate and unnecessary amount of time to examination of conscience misses the point of the Sacrament.

"We remark," says Blessed Eymard, "that those who give themselves much trouble in preparing and confessing, do not ordinarily amend their faults."[1] This is not surprising, since they are misdirecting their energies.

"He is not going to forgive you your sins," says Father Considine, "because you are clever at remembering them or ex-

[1] *The Eucharist and Christian Perfection,* IV (Sentinel Press), p. 538.

pressing them or marshalling them, but for one reason only, because you are sorry for them."[2]

God wants sorrow in the heart, not sorrow on the lips. It would be no use whatever to make a strictly accurate confession, if there were no sorrow in the heart. A confession of that sort would be an annoying piece of humbug and hypocrisy. It is not much use to make a strictly accurate confession, if there is very little sorrow in the heart. Such a confession is only one remove from humbug and hypocrisy. Better far to say little, provided we say enough, and have keen sorrow in the heart. In the confessional, God sees through us. It is an awful thing if our fellow-men see through us and discover that we are not genuine; it is far worse if God sees through us and finds that we are not genuine. God judges an apology, just as we do, not by its length or polish or glibness or gush, but by its sincerity. God "needs no prompting" from us, and provided we tell a sincere tale, accuracy of statement is not essential. The grace given at Confession is not proportioned to knowledge of sins in the mind but to sorrow for sin in the will. God proportions His grace, not to the *number* of sins remembered and confessed, but to our real detachment from them. The Sacrament of Penance is not a revelation of God's interest in mathematics.

Contrition is absolutely indispensable for the forgiveness of any sin. God could forgive us without demanding confession; but even God could not forgive us without demanding contrition. A dispensation from contrition would imply a logical contradiction. The mortal sinner turns his back on God; the venial sinner turns aside from God. Only contrition or a violation of free-will by God can make the sinner turn back to God. A dispensation from contrition would imply a sinner turned to and from God at the same moment of time; which, of course, is a sheer impossibility. Contrition is absolutely indispensable for the forgiveness of any sin, and, therefore, on no account must it be given a secondary place in our preparation for Confession.

[2] *Virtues of the Divine Child* (Herder), p. 102.

The tactics of topsy-turvydom, because they are so prevalent, are worth closer analysis. They are constructive neither in outlook nor in method.

BULLDOZER TACTICIANS

There are two aspects of Confession, which might be called the *destructive* and *constructive* aspects. The destructive aspect of Confession is restricted to the ridding ourselves of sin. To do this it is not necessary to ride through the soul with a bulldozer. Bulldozer methods merely tear and hack the soul and do about as much good as a typhoon or an earthquake. Merely to root out and trample on sin is not enough. That is only the beginning, and if we do no more than that, we merely create depression and a vacuum; and the devil comes and finds the house of our soul empty, swept and garnished, and taking unto himself seven other devils more wicked than himself, he re-enters there and our last state becomes worse than the first.

The constructive aspect of preparation for Confession is by far the more important. Merely rooting about among the tangles of sin is likely to do nothing except get us entangled. We can acquire a real hatred of vice for the right reasons, only by learning to love virtue. Only when we have seen the perfect can we properly assess the tawdriness of the imperfect. Merely *natural* concentration on sin cannot give us a *supernatural* horror of it. We must take care not to make our preparation for Confession depressing and discouraging. *Sursum corda!* Raise up your hearts! Cultivate the practice of virtue rather than the avoidance of vice. Study what you should *do* rather than what you must *not do.*

Don't exaggerate your own importance! Everything does not depend on you. There are several factors which will make Confession effective; on the natural plane, sincerity and correct technique; on the supernatural plane, grace and the love of God. Correct technique is important because grace does not dispense us from the obligation of using our common sense. God helps those who help themselves. Grace is a *co-operating* force and presumes *operation.*

Nevertheless, our activity is only preparatory, because "Unless the Lord build the house, in vain do they labour who build." "Our help is in the name of the Lord." Our preparation for Confession must not be self-reliant and self-centred but God-centred, and nothing can take us out of ourselves except the contemplation and love of God. "It is God Who works in us both to will and to do." Our task is to go on, as it were, patiently pressing down the switch, waiting for the electric current which will produce the light of grace to expel the darkness of sin. It is a capital mistake to prepare for Confession as though everything depended on us. We should come to Confession to get help from God, precisely because our own efforts are insufficient and unavailing. Grace will purify, strengthen and divinize us, and therefore we should concentrate on grace rather than on sin and human weakness. Grace will be proportioned, not to the length of our confession, but to the strength of our contrition. Let us strive, therefore, to get all the grace we can, by using all our endeavours to intensify our contrition.

Love of God is the most effective antidote to sin. If we love God intensely, we shall hate sin effectively. If you desire to hate and conquer sin, try to forget all about yourself for a time, and study instead and ponder the goodness and lovableness of God, so that your soul may be refreshed by basking in the sunshine of His love. Get out into the fresh air of God's love and away from the fetid atmosphere of the repulsive and depressing dungeons of self and sin.

Do not look upon Confession as a *departure* from sinfulness to nowhere in particular, but rather as an *approach* to sinlessness and the God of immaculate purity and perfection "in whose sight the angels themselves are not pure." The soul, which is capable of infinite progressive refinement, can never be too pure and therefore may always derive advantage from Confession. Go to Confession to bathe your soul in the Precious Blood, so that it may become white as snow and ready to stand unabashed in the Divine

Presence. Console yourself with the thought of what you are after Confession, and do not depress yourself with the thought of what you were before. The doleful dumps are as useful to God as they are to man.

Confession is not merely a *putting-off process*, but also and principally a *putting-on process*. We "put off the old man, that we may put on the New Man, Christ Jesus." Our task at Confession may be compared to that of a man who has been asked to paint a door. The painter will not attempt to put on new paint until the old paint has been removed. If the old paint still adheres to the door, it must be burnt off. If the old paint has been worn away, it would be worse than folly to do any burning, because the sole effect of unnecessary burning would be to damage and mark the door. In the same way, when we approach Confession, we must burn off the old paint, which is sin, before we put on the new paint, which is grace. If there is no old paint to be burnt off, so much the better: we may then quietly thank God and proceed at once to put on the new paint. If we insist on doing some burning when there is no need, we shall foolishly damage our own souls. If we cannot find much to say in Confession, so much the better, for then any sin for which we are certainly sorry will do for absolution; and there is absolutely no need to start a fierce and anxious inquisition. Let us get on, instead, with the real work of putting on the new coat of paint.

LESSONS FROM THE SURGERY

We might learn some useful lessons by comparing our technique when we go to an ordinary doctor with the technique of our approach to the doctor of souls. The physician expects us to use our commonsense, and usually we do. He expects us to be precise in our statement of symptoms, to put first things first, and deal with one thing at a time.

If you told the doctor that you were suffering from every conceivable complaint, he would decide immediately that your mind needed attention not your body. It is not unheard of for penitents to confess almost every conceivable sin, under the absurd impression that God obliges them to this nonsensical recital.

A sane doctor does not try to cure *all* your ailments at once. If you went to him suspect of tuberculosis, he would not want to hear about irrelevant details. If you talked irrelevantly, he would soon ask you not to waste his time and tell him at once your major relevant symptoms. The doctor treats one or two complaints at a time. It would be a decided advantage if the confessor were allowed to do the same. If it were not just pathetic folly, one would be obliged to accuse some penitents of outrageous presumption in expecting to cure all their faults at once. A long vague confession of venial sins is a sheer waste of time. If definite resolutions are not made against the venial sins which are confessed, there is no point in telling them. If you can hardly remember your budget of sins, you are not likely to remember a budget of resolutions to match, and resolutions which are not even remembered can have no effect on conduct. To draw up a big budget of resolutions (in the unlikely event of such a task being attempted) would take at least half a day. It is useless to find out what you have done, unless you also decide what you are going to do about it.

REMEDIES

After the analysis of the disease must come the study of remedies and the prescription. Imagine what you would say to a physician who made a clever analysis of your disease and then confessed that he had not the foggiest idea how to set about curing it nor the slightest intention of trying. It is to be feared that your language would be unparliamentary, and possibly unprintable, and that you would call him other names besides "doctor." "What earthly use is it to me," you would say, "to be told what is wrong with me, if you can't tell me how to put it right?"

In your dealings with your own soul, don't imitate the imaginary doctor, or the net result of your folly will be to add to your misery and despair. Instead of giving most of your time to the study of disease, concentrate on remedies and the *causes* of your complaints. Ask yourself why you did wrong. If, for example, you are inclined to tell lies, lying is not your fundamental trouble, but only the rash on the surface. Why do you lie? Perhaps cowardice is the cause; perhaps pride, a desire to pose as a wonderful "guy." A vague resolution to avoid lies will get you nowhere. It is pride, cowardice, some deeper vice at the root of the lies, which you ought to ferret out and tackle. If it is pride, you should concentrate on the study and practice of humility. Our methods should always be positive not negative. God grant that our preparations for Confession may not be summarized in the Book of Life as "Much Ado about Nothing"!

WHY SUCH TOPSY-TURVY TACTICS?

It is a matter of no small importance to decide why the tactics of topsy-turvydom are so prevalent, to the immense harm of souls. The main cause is ignorance of the fact that venial sins are optional matter for Confession. (Cf. Chapter III.)

A contributory cause are the examinations of conscience sometimes given in prayerbooks. Many of these examinations of conscience are *misleading* and inaccurate and sometimes even imply unsound doctrine; they mix up counsels and precepts, imperfections and sins, and inordinate natural tendencies and sin. They ask, for example: "Was I angry?" instead of: "Did I give the rein to anger unreasonably?" "Did I have bad thoughts?" instead of "Did I consent to impure thoughts?" "Did I have distractions during a Mass of obligation?" which might be taken to imply either that such distractions were of peculiar enormity endangering the fulfilment of the obligation or that distractions during Mass are of no concern unless the Mass is of obligation.

Father Considine is very severe on these examinations of conscience. "I am reminded," he says, "of the well-known story of a Carmelite novice going to St. Teresa with great glee to tell her that she had discovered a new kind of sin hitherto unnoticed in the books. 'My dear daughter,' the Saint replied, 'have we not only too many sins already?' "[3]

Besides being misleading, the prayer book examinations of conscience are *distracting*. They will take you through long lists of unnecessary queries—"the duties of masters and servants, when you are neither one nor the other, the nine ways in which we may share another's guilt, and make us wonder how our friends avoid them."[4]

Prayer book examinations of conscience lead us to examine *everybody's* conscience not *our own*.

Probably you have heard the story of the Irishman who went to Confession one Saturday night. After a long silence, the priest said, "Well, what have you done?"

"Everything," said Pat.

"Have you committed adultery?"

"Father, what sort of a man do you think I am?"

"Have you committed murder?"

"Father, have a heart," said Pat.

"Look here," said the priest, "have you examined your conscience?"

"No, Father."

"Well, go and examine your conscience and don't come back until you have examined it properly."

As Pat came away from the confessional, he met a friend who was making his way towards it, so he said to him: "If you are going to Confession, don't be after bothering yourself, he is only hearing murder cases tonight!"

Possibly you are wondering what is the relevance of that story and why I have introduced it here. The point is that the priest wisely concluded that Pat had not examined his conscience at all because he confessed everything. In the same way, when a penitent trolls out a lengthy stereotyped list of sins, obviously culled from a prayer book, the confessor knows that he has not examined his conscience at all. He has examined everybody's. The lengthy recital gives

[3] *Op. cit.*, pp. 100-01 and 198-9.
[4] *Ibid.*, p. 101.

the confessor no clue whatever to the real spiritual condition of the penitent. Many of the accusations are probably lies occasioned by panic. The penitent sees the sin in the book. "Yes," he says, "I must have done that. At any rate, I'd better confess it to be on the safe side," and then proceeds to add the imagined sin to his already considerable budget. Probably he has not committed the sin at all: at any rate, he has no recollection of having done so. The only basis of his accusation is a vague, uneasy feeling that he might have sinned in that way. Such accusations, which are neither healthy nor helpful, are a very irritating and nonsensical waste of time.

Reading through examinations of conscience is as much use for enabling us to find out our spiritual condition as reading through the *Home Doctor* for finding out our physical condition. A man who regularly read through descriptive lists of physical ailments would be liable to become a confirmed neurotic and imagine that he had every complaint to which human nature is heir. No wonder, then, that the examination-of-conscience readers become disturbed and scrupulous and imagine that they have all the faults in the catalogue. Let us not confuse and distress ourselves to no purpose. Examinations of conscience seldom help us to know ourselves better, nor does a lengthy recital help the priest to know us better. When people say, "We haven't examined our consciences yet," they usually mean that they haven't examined the corporate conscience of mankind.

So be quick about examination of conscience. Time spent in examination of conscience that is not rigorously necessary is time mis-spent. A pious penitent can sufficiently guarantee the confession part of the Sacrament in a few seconds. In fact, anyone who habitually tries to avoid sin could walk into the confessional without any immediate preparation and not endanger the validity of the Sacrament (N.B., "could" not "should"). More time given to unnecessary examination of conscience means less time given to essential contrition and amendment.

Let us sum up. A soul is never too sinless to approach

Confession with profit. "He that is just, let him be justified still: and he that is holy, let him be sanctified still."[5] A lengthy budget of sins is by no means an indispensable requirement for the fruitful reception of absolution. When we have little to confess, Confession is more effective not less effective. Be no longer than is strictly necessary about examination of conscience, be briefer and more precise in your confession, concentrate on contrition, love and Divine Grace; and give grace a chance to become operative by making a wise, well-directed, concentrated purpose of amendment. Do not spend all your time bemoaning your defects, crying, "Lord, Lord," and possibly, "Oh! Lord," but see what you can do about it; because "not everyone that saith to Me, 'Lord, Lord,' shall enter into the Kingdom of Heaven; but he that DOTH the will of My Father Who is in Heaven, he shall enter into the Kingdom of Heaven."

[5] Apoc. 22:11.

V

Preparing the Brief

After all that has been said about examination of conscience, it only remains for us to sum up and consider a few practical rules.

The catechism says that "we must carefully examine our conscience." Carefully, but not too carefully. Examination of conscience can be overdone as well as underdone; and, as we have seen, is very often overdone. We must avoid the two extremes of defect and excess. At one extreme, there is danger of carelessness, routine, indifference and presumption. At the other extreme, there is danger of anxiety, excessive care and quasi-panic.

Anything that disturbs calm judgment, muddles the mind or disturbs the nerves, is obviously not from God; because God would have nothing to gain by causing such upset. Confession is not a trap set by God for the unwary or for those who are not a hundred-per-cent wary. There is no prosecuting attorney to try to upset you. The counsel for the prosecution is also the counsel for the defence. The confessor is bound to believe you both when you speak *for* yourself and when you speak *against* yourself. The tribunal is one of mercy not justice. The real judge is infinite Mercy Incarnate.

You will save yourself unnecessary anxiety and misdirection of effort if you keep clearly in mind when and why you must examine your conscience. Examination of conscience is absolutely necessary only when it is possible or probable that you have committed *mortal* sin. If it is *morally certain* that you have not committed mortal sin, there is no strict obligation to examine your conscience at all. Examination of conscience is not an end in itself, but only a means to an end. We examine our conscience so that we may be able to confess sufficiently.

Examination of conscience is necessary when we have *necessary matter* to confess, for we must make certain that we do not omit to confess mortal sins.

If we have no *necessary matter* to confess, examination of conscience is, in a sense, *optional.* If we have not committed any mortal sins since our last Confession, we are obliged to confess, and therefore to find out, *at least one venial sin or one sin of our past life* for which we are *certainly* sorry. This is the full extent of our *obligations* in devotional confession. If we have discovered one venial sin for which we are truly sorry, we have sufficient matter for confession. There is no *obligation* to search for *all our venial sins* or even for any more venial sins. Further efforts to enlarge our budget are a matter not of obligation but of *counsel and zeal,* to be regulated by the virtue of *prudence.* If we have no mortal sins to confess, *one* venial sin *must* be told; other venial sins *may* be told.

One clear implication of this doctrine is that pious people, who go frequently to Confession and do not normally commit mortal sin, are under no strict obligation to examination of conscience. If they had committed a mortal sin, there would be no need to look for it. It would be *"on their mind,"* nagging with monotonous and torturing insistence. Neither do they need to look for venial sins, because a few old favourites will generally present themselves without introduction. In a minute, therefore, and without difficulty, pious souls can find *sufficient matter* for Confession. It is not quite true to say that they do not need to make *any* examination of conscience—since they must find some matter for confession; but it is true to say that their conscience will sufficiently examine itself without prodding or prompting. The process of sufficient examination will in their case be almost automatic. Acting on these principles, Father W. Doyle wrote to a pious "worriting" soul: "Don't examine your conscience. If there is a big fault, it will stand out and show itself; if not, any sin will do for absolution."

The point of insisting so much on the strict limits of obligation is not to encourage carelessness, but to reassure penitents and safeguard them against disturbing anxiety and nervousness. When they have discovered one venial sin for which they are *certainly sorry*, they are already sufficiently prepared, so further efforts can be made with great peace and tranquillity and complete absence of strain.

HOW LONG?

It is impossible to lay down fixed rules as to how much time should be spent in examination of conscience. The time-factor will be determined by the type of life the penitent has been leading, the length of time which has elapsed since his last Confession, the degree of his spirituality, the tendencies of his personality. Hitler or Goebbels, in the unlikely event of their having gone to Confession, would have needed somewhat more time than a St. Aloysius or a Carmelite nun. A penitent who has not been to Confession for sixty years will not find examination of conscience as easy as one who went six days ago. An old man who had been sixty years away from Confession remarked to the priest as he was leaving the confessional: "I won't leave it as long again, father." To which we could all add a devout "Amen!" If he did leave it as long again, his examination of conscience would be no easy matter and would require considerable time.

Father Scharsch says very wisely that examination of conscience should never take up more than half the time devoted to preparation. (Never more, generally considerably less than half the time. "Give *more time* to contrition than to the examen," says Blessed Eymard, "The examen shows the wound, contrition is the remedy.") "For weekly Confessions, examination of conscience need not last longer than five or six minutes. When one is very busy, it may be even shorter. In very urgent cases, when our conscience is in good order and only a few faults come to mind . . . it is permitted to go to Confession without examination of conscience."[1]

Modern authors are fairly agreed on the five-minute rule for devotional confessions. Father Walshe[2] suggests four to five minutes; Father Kearney,[3] five minutes; Father Lord says: "Perhaps three minutes . . . at longest five. If he goes often, he can do it in less. If he makes an examination of conscience at night, as he should, it may not take more than a minute."[4] Father Considine contents himself with repeating, and with the words in italics: *"Be quick about it."*[5] Even for those who have been a long time away from Confession, an examination of from ten to fifteen minutes is sufficient.[6]

METHOD

In speaking of examination of conscience for Confession, it is presumed that the penitent is making regular examens and occasionally giving himself a thorough spiritual overhaul. The self-analysis required for Confession is not sufficient for the spiritual life.

Anyone who has difficulty in finding matter for confession should read Chapter VIII.

Many penitents seem to think that the application of the commandments is limited to telling lies, missing or being late for Mass, being disobedient, and impurity. Do not omit to examine how you have fulfilled the *duties of your state of life.*

Blessed Claude de la Columbière says that neglect of the duties of their state of life is the commonest sin among pious

[1] *Op cit.*, p. 113.
[2] Nicholas Walshe, S. J., *Practical Advice on Confession*, p. 7.
[3] *My Spiritual Exercises*, p. 192.
[4] *Confession is a Joy*, p. 18.
[5] *Op. cit.*, pp. 101-2.
[6] Michael Quinlan, S. J., *How to Make a Good Confession*, p. 2.

people. A courageous confessor once interrupted the confession of the Emperor Charles V and said to him: "Thus far your Majesty has confessed the sins of Charles; let us now hear the sins of the Emperor." How often we hear the sins of the individual, but not the sins of the employer, employee, husband, wife, trader, et cetera!

Be very punctilious about charity. Pious people often cause serious scandal by glib uncharity, which has its root in spiritual pride. When there are no serious sins since your last Confession, it is a good plan to start the examination of conscience by recalling the sins you specially proposed to avoid in your last confession. If your resolutions have petered out and sins recurred, you have quite enough to go on with and need examine no further.

Don't—If you have kept your resolutions and no old favourites present themselves, do not make examination of conscience a *memory test*. It is a mistake to try to recall all that has happened since your last confession. This is simply asking for distractions and the strain involved in such an effort tires the head and freezes the heart.

Do—A better plan is to run quietly through the ordinary duties of everyday, for then extraordinary faults will stand out of themselves, e.g. rising—lazy?—a nuisance? late for Mass or work as a result? Prayers, duties, charity and courtesy at home and abroad, et cetera?

Once a few outstanding sins have been collected, it is a mistake to go on examining. Instead of ferreting out more sins, we should then find out and, as far as possible, obviate the *causes* of the sins to hand. "Lay the axe to the root of the tree." Uproot the weeds and do not be content to continue merely chopping off the tips of the weeds. Quality not quantity, intensive not extensive search—these should be our mottoes.

Do not use prayer-book examinations of conscience except perhaps for a periodical overhaul apart from confession. Examine *your* conscience and your symptoms, not everybody's.

We should completely finish with examination of conscience before we go into the confessional. Anxiety to "check up" on our confession afterwards and reassure ourselves that we have not omitted anything, is a *temptation not a grace.* Surrender to this urge implies doubt of Our Lord's effectual co-operation and a sneaking fear that perhaps He has "let us down."

After confession keep your soul in peace and be on your guard—this is a point of cardinal importance—against giving access to any fear about the validity of the Sacrament, either as regards the examination of conscience, the contrition, or anything else whatsoever. These fears are suggestions of the devil, whose aim is to instil bitterness into a sacrament of consolation and love.[7]

After confession is not the time to examine ourselves to find if we have told all our sins. We should rather remain attentively and in peace near our Lord, with Whom we have just been reconciled, and thank Him for His great mercy. Nor is it necessary, subsequently, to search out what we may have forgotten. We must tell simply all that comes to mind; after that we must think no more about it.[8]

Remember, in conclusion, that according to the common opinion of the saints, the fear of sin is no longer salutary when it becomes excessive.[9]

If examination of conscience is a torturing process for us, it is our own fault. Anxiety and worry do not spring from sensitiveness of conscience but from temptation, ignorance, obstinate self-reliance or defective hope. Let us not sin against hope under false pretences. In preparing the brief against yourself, be brief and leave something to the Mercy of God.

[7] Charles J. Quadrupani, *Light and Peace* (Herder), p. 47.
[8] St. Francis de Sales, quoted by Quadrupani, *ibid.*, pp. 47-8.
[9] *Ibid.*, p. 61.

VI

Letting in the Light

MANY earnest penitents are genuinely distressed because they can find so little to say whenever they approach the Sacrament of Penance. It seems absurd that they who have an almost habitual and cloying sense of sinfulness should not be able to put their finger on definite sins, and they find it hard to reconcile such a purblind inability with sincerity and earnestness.

NOTHING TO TELL

Inability to find matter for confession may be due to a bad memory. It is one thing to have committed sins and quite another thing to be able to remember them. It is consoling to find that St. Gertrude complained of inability to recall her sins. Inability to remember sins is an inevitable consequence of a bad memory, which could not be obviated without miraculous intervention by God.

The real trouble with most penitents, however, is not so much that they cannot recall their sins as that they cannot detect them. They know that they are suffering from self-deceit, and it seems a shameful mockery to carry this self-deceit into the confessional; yet, no matter how hard they try to unmask themselves and how carefully they prepare, they never seem to be able to focus the searchlight of truth on their souls. In consequence, they are never satisfied with their preparation, and never feel ready for Confession. If they go to Confession in this mood, they come away dubious of their own sincerity, discouraged and dissatisfied. If they defer Confession, in the vain hope of being more successful next time, they become even more dissatisfied.

The earnest desire to be absolutely sincere may make examination of conscience a positive agony. For the comfort of souls who suffer in this way, I want to make it clear in this chapter that the acquiring of self-knowledge is the work of a life-time—not the work of ten minutes or half an hour before confession. As well expect to explore a continent in half an hour as expect to explore the unexplored (and without Divine Light—unexplorable) continent of the soul in the same time. Self-knowledge can be acquired only gradually and by degrees. At each confession we must do our bit to acquire it, but a bit is all we can do.

"The harder we sweep," says the wise St. Philip Neri, "the more dust we raise." Complete self-analysis, made at one session, would imply a moral miracle, and would prostrate us. God cannot allow us to see how bad we are, until we have begun to see how good He is. To cope with comprehensive and vivid self-knowledge, we should need a very outstanding development of the virtue of hope. Vaguely we suspect this, and hence we have a certain misgiving about praying for self-knowledge.

> O wad some power the giftie gie us,
> To see oursels as others see us!

If we adopted the words of Burns as a prayer, we should have a sneaking hope that the Lord would not take us too literally. Naturally we are puzzled and dismayed by the contradictions and apparent insincerity of our attitude. We want to be sincere and yet we fear to be sincere. It may seem a melancholy satisfaction to be told that this conflict of desires is inevitable; but it is a real satisfaction to those who have been hoping, and yet not hoping, to do too much at each Confession.

> To know ourselves is the hardest thing in the world . . . A truthful man is the rarest of all phenomena. . . . The fact is, we are all of us thoroughly untruthful, those of us most so who think ourselves least so, those of us least so who think ourselves most so. . . . It is worth spending two-thirds of our life in doing this work alone, trying to be less of liars than we are.[1]

Two-thirds of our life! Not ten or twenty minutes, or even twenty hours, before Confession! Effective self-analysis is the work of a life-time. "Perfect self-knowledge stands not at the beginning, but at the end of the path of virtue."[2]

The comprehensive self-knowledge which we expected to acquire at each Confession cannot be attained all at once without a very exceptional grace. *"Ad impossibile nemo tenetur"*—"no one is obliged to the impossible." If such a self-analysis were an essential requirement of the Sacrament of Penance, we could never approach it. Let us not expect too much. There is a latent pride and impatience in expecting to take the kingdom of heaven by storm at one attack. We can never be perfectly satisfied with our preparation for Confession until we realize how much (or, if you like—how little!) we can expect to do. *Sufficiently prepared* we can easily be; *fully prepared* we shall never be.

When it is insisted that a brief and relatively cursory self-analysis is sufficient for Confession, there is no intention of proclaiming emancipation from the laborious and insistent task of keeping a close watch on our motives and of striving to attain self-knowledge. All that is asserted is (1) that at Confession there is not sufficient time for adequate self-analysis, as there are then other more important things to do; and (2) that excessive self-analysis obscures the purpose of Confession.

The purpose of Confession is not so much that we may attain self-knowledge as that we may lovingly and trustingly

[1] Frederick W. Faber, *Spiritual Conferences* (Murphy).
[2] Scharsch, *op. cit.*, p. 112.

place our souls in the Master's Hands that "His mercy may pardon and His grace help us."

One might compare our souls to motor cars, and Our Lord to a perfect motor mechanic. In our examens we are expected to overhaul the car ourselves, while the Divine Mechanic stands by and helps us with His suggestions and His grace. At Confession the Divine Mechanic Himself takes over and, as it were, says to us: "Leave the car to Me! I'll give it a look-over." He wills to do for us what we cannot do for ourselves, and if we have opened all the compartments, as far as we can, and kept nothing locked, He will give us a thorough overhaul. But He will not force the locks, because He has too much respect for the car.

It would be a pity to overlook this consoling aspect of the Sacrament of Penance. We can never be emancipated from the labour of trying to understand and overhaul the car, but we have every right to be thrilled and consoled and rest awhile if the Divine Mechanic comes to give us a hand with the work. Excessive anxiety about our preparation implies that the *ego* has figured too prominently in our thoughts, and that we have overlooked the part the Divine Mechanic wishes to play, and by our foolish fussing have impeded His co-operation. We should be glad of this "breather" called Confession, when the work of overhauling is done for us; and we should gladly, gratefully and wholeheartedly let Our Lord take over. It would be foolish to worry because we cannot make the overhaul, when we are not asked to make it. All we are asked to do is to take the car back to the Maker's, where, and where alone, the engine is perfectly understood. Once we have taken that much trouble, He will do the rest.

How much He does for us in those regular sacramental overhauls, we shall know only in eternity. Let us spare an occasional prayer of thanksgiving for the unobtrusive and mostly unrecognized labour which the Divine Mechanic puts in on our souls. If regularly we place the car of our soul in His omnipotent Hands, we need not be unduly preoccupied about the working-condition of the engine. Our Confessions would profit us more if we spent less time worrying about the car and our defective workmanship, and concentrated instead in loving amazement on His staggering goodness. We could profitably meditate on the *reality* and efficiency of His Divine Workmanship, for then we should suffer far less from discouragement and dismay at our own utter incompetence. Let us leave something not merely to the Mercy of God but also to the sacramental operation of Christ. The help we shall receive will be proportioned to our faith. Expect Him to do great things for you and He will do great things.

Worry about our sincerity is not altogether a bad thing, provided we deal with it wisely. "The knowledge of our self-deceit," says Father Faber, "is the nearest approach to its cure." To admit our self-deceit is to take the first step towards curing it. It should be a source of consolation and reassurance to know that the acquiring of self-knowledge is difficult and slow work. "We cannot trust much to ourselves," says the *Imitation*, "for grace and understanding are often wanting to us. There is in us but little light, and this we often lose by negligence. Oftentimes we are quite unconscious how interiorly blind we are."[3]

On the difficulty of acquiring self-knowledge all spiritual and psychological writers are agreed. Why it is so difficult we shall discuss in the next chapter; in this chapter let us confine ourselves to discussing why self-knowledge is so essential.

WHY WE MUST PUT OFF BLINKERS

1. Self-knowledge is necessary because self-deceit undermines peace of mind.

Self-deception, whether deliberate or indeliberate, is fatal to peace of soul. It is evident that our real motives do not cease to be there (any more than the ostrich's attackers cease to be there because it buries its head in the sand) because we choose to ignore them. Neither do they cease to influence us. We become blind to their influence—that is

[3] Bk. II, Ch. 5.

all. We work in the dark and become subject to all the terrors of the night. We do not know what we really want, and therefore cannot satisfy our most real wants, and the result is a vague feeling of dissatisfaction and frustration. We are vaguely conscious of a sense of unrest, insincerity and unreality. Life seems to be cheating us, and we tend to become cynical and bored and like the bad workman blame our tools, our neighbour, the clergy, the local administration —anything but the real culprit, ourselves. Civil war rages within us, we have conflicting wishes and desires, one part of our nature is at war with another, and because of our deliberate self-deception, we cannot recognize the adversaries, much less effect a reconciliation between them.

The result is unhappiness, and the outcome may be dissipation, a vain attempt to escape from the battleground, or morbid and excessive introspection. Probably we shall alternate between the two moods and become weather-cock personalities. In all our moods, we shall be fundamentally unhappy.

We must establish harmony between the conscious and the subconscious, if we want to maintain peace of soul. Subconscious motives of which we are sublimely unconscious will not worry *us*, but they will cause annoyance to others. Subconscious motives of whose reality and influence we have a vague suspicion will continue to tantalize us until we bring them out into the open and subject them to control. Subconscious motives are like steam, useful, if controlled; decidedly dangerous, if allowed to get out of control.

2. Self-knowledge is also necessary because self-deceit impedes growth in holiness, occasions loss of grace, and causes spiritual ineffectiveness.

Allers, speaking of sins and broken resolutions, says:

> Of these things we know sometimes; but there are others we never really know, though their presence is not absolutely hidden from us. There is the vanity which pervades all our actions, the egoism mixed up with our most unselfish intentions, the pride which will boast secretly even of humility and sincerity, the ambition which is never satisfied by

any success whatever, the unruly longing for praise, the ingrained tendency for envy—all those attributes of average human nature which are the powerful agents of most of our troubles.[4]

The merit and value of our actions consists in our *real* purity of intention. It is of little avail to delude ourselves that we are acting solely for the love of God, if the real motivation of our actions springs from self-love. God is not deceived by our make-belief. "You are they who justify yourselves before men, but God knoweth your hearts."[5] What is essential is that we should be justified before God. Whilst our motives are a polyglot of vaguely recognized, instinctive, selfish urges, we cannot act solely for God. And until we act solely for God, we cannot become saints nor make the best effective use of our time.

To control and subordinate our natural and *inevitably selfish* urges, we must first have the honesty and courage to admit and face up to them. Until we face the facts, our love of God is bound to be, in part at least, more fictitious than real.

It is not asserted, be it noted, that the element of vaguely conscious selfishness in our actions deprives them of all merit, but simply that it decreases their merit and makes perfection impossible. If natural imperfections completely destroyed the merit of our actions, it would follow that no one could merit unless and until he became a saint; in fact not even then, since even the saints are constantly finding in themselves new and unsuspected roots of selfishness.

Self-knowledge is necessary to make us less of a nuisance to others.

Self-deceit, which is only another way of saying want of humility, poisons life and causes most of our social troubles. We are startled by the blindness of others. The contrast between what they are and what they think they are, is so patent that we are amazed they cannot see it. Sometimes, perhaps, we are tempted to believe that their blindness is wil-

[4] *Self-Improvement* (Benziger), p. 74.
[5] Luke 16:15

ful. Probably we cause them a similar amazement and similar suspicions. If our friends could hear us making our confessions, they would probably have difficulty in believing in our sincerity. How easily the wife could make her husband's confession, and how easily the husband could make his wife's! Yet how difficult they find it to make their own confession.

Our apparent insincerity, even if it is indeliberate or only semi-deliberate, often makes us a scandal to others and a poor advertisement for the Church. Even indeliberate insincerity tends to nullify the power of example.

How many of the troubles of life have their origin in self-deceit! "A man goes to church and believes himself religious, whereas, if he honestly examined his motives, he might find that it is his honour in the community more than homage to God that prompts his Sunday devotion."[6] He deceives himself but he does not deceive others. Some find themselves tempted to rash-judge him, others definitely judge him and are embittered by his conduct and "put off" religion.

"A person accredits himself with a delicate conscience or a keen desire to advance the interests of an organization, and retails to authority all the gossip that he happens to hear about this or that member: his real purpose in the matter being to start a wave of misunderstanding and to ride on the crest of it to importance."[7] How many organizations are upset in this way! How often the earnest and talented are broken on the wheel of uncharitable criticism and mischief-making and depressed into the rut of mediocrity.

"Again, here is the individual that thinks he is making sacrifices for a cause, while in reality he is having an excellent time expressing himself and, moreover, is seeking that he himself, rather than the cause, be crowned."[8] Here we have the reason for the feuds which often arise in choirs, altar-societies, confraternities; for the frightful jealousy of stall-

[6] Edward F. Murphy, *New Psychology and Old Religion* (Benziger), p. 81.
[7] *Ibid.*
[8] Murphy, *op. cit.*

holders at bazaars; for accusations and altercations among the pious, often resulting in their "not speaking" for months or even years.

Prudes, who join vigilance committees and get sexual licence "on the brain" and are fond of retailing salacious gossip in detail, are probably convinced that they are actuated by the highest angelic motives, when in reality they are merely expressing sex in a morbid way.

This list could be prolonged indefinitely. An adequate discussion of the ways and means and results of self-deception would require a complete treatise on psychology. What has been said should suffice to show how important it is for the common good that all should strive earnestly to acquire self-knowledge. All the people mentioned above "keep their less respectable psychology in the sub-cellar of their consciousness, where they need not be bothered with it nor ashamed, and they live on a level to which they are not entitled."[9]

To safeguard ourselves, as far as possible, from all these disastrous self-deceptions, it is an excellent practice periodically to subject our soul to a thorough and searching examination. This could be done once a week, say on Sunday morning, or once a month during a regular day of recollection. This examination is, as we have seen, better separated from Confession; first, because it takes too long; and secondly, because if it is connected with Confession, it may obscure the consoling purpose and significance of the Sacrament of Penance. It is hardly necessary to insist how much such a practice will facilitate and enrich our confessions.

It may be objected that a regular searching examen will tend to cause depression and excessive introversion. Try it and see. This is a practical matter which can best be tested by practice, just as the pudding can best be tested by the eating. Depression is not caused by facing our faults but by refusing to face them. We shall not be able to face our faults realistically and optimistically, however, until we rid our minds of some prevalent childish illusions. Examens must

[9] *Ibid.*

not be allowed to diminish either our confidence in God or our self-respect.

CONFIDENCE IN GOD

It is a childish illusion to imagine that because we shut our eyes to our faults, God does not see them. By blinking at our faults, we try to bolster up our confidence in God; which means that our real trust in God is almost non-existent, and our spiritual life based on make-belief. We trust in God because we have bluffed ourselves that as we are not really so bad after all, there is no unsurmountable obstacle to prevent God from loving us. In other words, our confidence is based on *our* goodness not on *His*. No wonder it is a very uneasy confidence and soon upset.

God's knowledge of our faults is independent of our knowledge or ignorance of them. Whether we know them or not, God knows them always. It is childish to presume that new knowledge of our faults on our part implies new knowledge on God's part; yet that is what we often do presume unconsciously. We are prone to imagine that new knowledge of our faults, which has made us seem very objectionable to ourselves, has suddenly made us very objectionable to God. Why should it? Those faults have been as clear as daylight to Him all along. Before we discovered our faults, we believed and trusted in His goodness (or thought we did!); there is absolutely no reason why we should cease to trust Him now. The only change on God's side (if one can speak of change in God) is that He recognizes that we are now less of liars that we were, and so loves us more because we are becoming more honest.

Such childish mistakes show that we have seldom looked out of the windows of our soul at the sky of God's immensity, and, in consequence unwittingly apply to God's immense, limitless love the span-measure of our own very limited love, and become guilty of some childish fallacies and *non-sequiturs*.

Here is a specimen of our logic. "I find myself unlovable, therefore God finds me unlovable." The unconscious assumption is that God's love is on a par with our own and that because finite love is upset, therefore infinite love must be upset. It would be far more logical to argue that because a baby cannot lift a fifty-pound weight, therefore the strongest man could not lift it.

We must try to *realize* the *practical* implications of the fact that God's love is infinitely greater than our own. We must also try to appreciate the practical implications of the Incarnation and Redemption. That fault, which has suddenly upset us, was foreseen by Jesus and, instead of being embittered by it, He actually made atonement for it in advance. Such is our faith. By childish worry about our fault, we are implicitly saying: "But, surely, He didn't *really* know how bad it is?" Let us not imply by our conduct that we think that our Saviour did not know what He was doing when He redeemed us. Let us not fix limits to the infinite mercy and goodness of God. If we are to face our faults with tranquillity, we must dig deep and real foundations for our hope.

We cannot make ourselves safe by our own devices and become independent of the Mercy of God. Oftentimes scrupulous people and "safe-siders" are really proud, independent characters who are willing to accept God's help as an *additional security*, but only when they have first secured themselves. They are unwilling to be forced to trust solely to the Mercy of God, and because they cannot make their position safe without God, they fret and fume, and, as the ancient philosopher said, spend one part of their time in doing wrong, another in doing nothing at all, and the rest in doing the contrary of what they should do.

We have not, and cannot have, assets with God; none whatever, only liabilities. Our confidence, however, should be based on our liabilities and helplessness. If we could manage by ourselves, there would be no particular reason for God to help us. Because we are helpless and hopeless "of ourselves, as of ourselves," He is bound to help us, provided we do not obstruct Him by pride; otherwise He would not be giving us a square deal. Our title to His help is that, by His ordinance, we are helpless.

One claim I have upon Thee,
Which Thou wilt ne'er deny,
In the bounds of Thy creation,
No one needs Thee more than I.

Misery is the lodestone of mercy. The saints were actually glad when they discovered a new fault in themselves, because they believed that they had found a new claim on God's help.

Alack, thou knowest not
How little worthy of any love thou art!
Whom wilt thou find to love ignoble thee,
Save Me, save only Me?[10]

Because He loves us *infinitely more* than we love ourselves, He can be patient with us even when we find it impossible to be patient with ourselves.

SELF-RESPECT

Many people are afraid to face their faults because they imagine that self-knowledge will destroy their self-respect. This fear is not altogether unreasonable, because, unless we take an *optimistic view of human nature* our defective tendencies will tend to destroy our self-respect.

This optimistic view of human nature is unfortunately not very common. Many people, for instance, who have strong sexual tendencies are afraid to admit the fact even to themselves for fear that they will lose caste in their own eyes. They develop a prudish, easily shockable disposition, which is designed (probably unconsciously) to convince themselves that they are not really strongly sexed; if they were, they surely could not react like that. All the innate tendencies and instincts of human nature are God-designed and God-given, and are therefore good. There is no need to be ashamed of any instinct that God has given us. "All things work together for good for those who love God." Abuse of our instincts is the only thing we need be ashamed of, not the fact

[10] Francis Thompson. *The Hound of Heaven.*

of having them; and we begin to abuse them immediately we begin to deny their existence.

A strong tendency to impatience, for example, is not a shameful liability. It may be only an inherent and inevitable tendency of a forceful personality who likes to get things done and is therefore irked and irritated by slow-moving and slow-witted people.

If this tendency to defect is viewed constructively, it may become a very real asset. If it is curbed and controlled, it may exercise and strengthen our character and be the occasion of the gaining of innumerable graces. When you have failed, remember this. The one defeat may have been preceded by many victories. If we can see some possibilities of good in our defective tendencies, we shall not be ashamed to admit them, and we may then get some good out of them. Otherwise they will lie like so much lumber in the mind, a constant source of irritation, rebellion and loss of self-respect.

One aspect of our instincts is *danger*; the other aspect is *opportunity*. If God had not planned to give us grace to seize our opportunities, He would not have allowed them to occur. The innate tendencies of our nature, whatever they are, cannot make God love us less, for the very simple and obvious reason that He is responsible for them. If He did not love that queer mixture of good and bad to which we correspond, we should not exist. "For He did not make anything hating it." "For Thou lovest all things that are, and hatest none of the things which Thou hast made: for Thou didst not appoint or make anything hating it."[11]

INTROSPECTION

Contrary to what a superficial person might expect, regular honest and prolonged examens will save us from the pest of morbid introspection. Introspection is morbid when we are "always at it." Introspection, like everything else, must be kept in its place. Morbid introspection is an outcome, not of excessive, but of defective self-knowledge.

[11] Wisd. 11:25.

Worry is caused, not by facing a problem too squarely, but by putting off facing it. When the mind is not allowed to tackle a problem and sort it out, the problem remains "on the mind." The mind will not be put off, hence the urge to keep reopening the discussion. Morbid introspection is the result of an attempt of the will to put the mind off by endless discussion in place of a decision. Every confessor is familiar with the type of penitent who talks and talks and talks and goes over the same ground time and time again. Let the confessor give clear-cut definite advice, and he will soon find his penitents going elsewhere for spiritual consolation. The last thing they want to do is come to a decision. Morbidly introversive people suffer from the same malady.

We must learn to detect and eradicate our faults without becoming self-centred introverts. Perhaps an illustration may help us to devise a correct technique.

A motorist does not normally trouble about the working-condition of his car unless it is giving trouble. As long as the car is running well, he takes it for granted that the engine is in good order. It is always possible that engine trouble may be developing, but he has to risk that. If he were always stopping to make sure that the engine was in good order, he would waste so much time that he would never be able to go anywhere. Periodically he hands over his car to a mechanic for a thorough overhaul, and then considers that he has taken sufficient precautions and does not concern himself about the engine until the next overhaul, unless something has gone wrong in the meantime.

The morbid introvert is like a foolish motorist who is always wanting to reassure himself about the running condition of his car, even when it is running. In his anxiety to have his car running perfectly, he stops it from running at all. He is so anxious to be able to go anywhere that actually he never does go anywhere. The cowardice involved in this foolish "safism" is evident. The man might as well never have a car, for all the use he makes of it. Because he will risk nothing, he makes obvious and *certain* mistakes. "Safe-siders" who inhibit their talents through excessive fear could profitably make a prolonged meditation on the parable of the talents. "Trade till I come." Trading implies risk. The narrow, selfish safe-sider risks nothing except final condemnation out of his own mouth and on his own principles.

A man of sound spirituality tries to concentrate all his *conscious* life on God and the love of God. He never thinks of himself and tries to forget himself, unless self has somehow got in the way of his union with God. As long as the car is running well, he lets it run. Periodically, however, like the wise motorist, he gives the car of his soul a thorough overhaul to prevent the surreptitious insinuation of bad habits into his soul. The best way to safeguard ourselves against self is to forget self and live always in the presence of God.

A modern saint was puzzled by what spiritual writers say about self-deception. To her God's love was so real that she could not conceive how anyone could act from any other motive. The best way to empty ourselves of self is to fill our minds with the knowledge and our wills with the love of Christ. If we never think of ourselves but only of Him, we cannot act for self. A loving soul has no time to heed the wounds it receives in battle, and this saves it from self-pity; no time to consider its own interests, because it is concerned solely about His interests; no time to consider its own ease and comfort, because it is anxious to do in all things the Holy Will of God. Such a soul is as nearly an impossible subject of self-deceit as can be found among poor self-loving, self-seeking creatures.

"In His light we shall see light." The nearer we approach to God, the viler shall we become in our own eyes. Spiritual writers use a well-known analogy to illustrate this. A ray of sunshine shot suddenly into a room reveals tiny particles of dust and small hairs which were not apparent in ordinary light. In a similar way, the light of God shining in our souls unmasks our self-love and reveals imperfections and unrecognized selfishness which could not be detected by the ordinary light of self-analysis. The best way to learn to know our faults is to try to know God. Mere self-analysis cannot reveal our buried motives, and even if it could, would be incapable of correcting them. To be able to face our faults without discouragement, we need the illumination of the "Light that is Life," the Light which simultaneously *warms* and enlightens. We shall eliminate our faults best by developing the good in us and starving the bad; that is, by striving in all things to know and love God and ignore self.

Let us strive then to acquire self-knowledge so that we may not secretly put obstacles in the way of God's work in our souls. It will be a consolation to the earnest to know that the work of self-enlightenment is slow and difficult. No need, therefore, to worry because you find progress slow, because you are still a mystery to yourself and full of self-deceit, because you experience a certain reluctance to unmask yourself. You would have far more reason for surprise and concern if you found in yourself no evil nor self-deceit.

> There is hardly a man or woman in the world, who has not got some corner of self into which he or she fears to venture with a light. . . . We prophesy to ourselves that, if we penetrate into that corner of self, something will have to be done which either our laziness or our immortification would shrink from doing. . . . Almost everyone has some woeful uncertainty resting on his conscience about some part of his conduct . . . a suspicion that investigation will compel them to commit themselves to God or deny Him something, both of which they are equally anxious to avoid.[12]

Understandable as these tactics are, they are, nevertheless, penny-wise and pound-foolish. The lazy man always does most work in the long run and never has the satisfaction of acquiring efficiency. The bluffers buy a very uneasy, insecure and unreal peace.

Magnified personal goodness plus minimized Divine Goodness = false peace. "Peace and there is no peace."

Minimized personal goodness plus magnified Divine Goodness = real peace, "the peace of God which surpasses understanding, the peace which the world can't give and can't take away."

[12] Faber, *op. cit.*

We cannot have it both ways. Let us reflect seriously what we lose by cowardice and want of sincerity. For a few clinging attachments, which we refuse to admit or only half-admit, we are sacrificing perfect peace and the intimacies of Divine Friendship. Well may we pray with St. Alphonsus: "Lord, help me to strip myself of all affection for things of earth (i.e. all excessive or inordinate attachment), that I may place *all my love* in Thee, Who art so worthy of my love." Divine love is cheap at any price, and we cannot have it unless we sell all that we have to buy it. "He that shall lose his life for My sake, shall find it."

No harm can come to us if simultaneously we study the bad in ourselves and the good in God. Let us open our minds to the light. "*Veni lumen cordium, consolator optime*"—"Come, Thou Light of the Heart, true Consoler." We must value the natural light of reason, but above all the true light which enlighteneth every man that cometh into this world. May the light shine in the darkness, and may the darkness comprehend it. "May the God of hope fill you with all joy and peace in believing; that you may abound in hope, and in the power of the Holy Ghost."[13]

[13] Rom. 15:13.

VII

Blinkers

SELF-LOVE," says Monsignor de Ségur, "is a fool; like a peacock, it struts about imagining that it attracts every eye, whereas, in reality, it is generally its sole admirer." The cure for self-love is self-knowledge, which acts on vanity like a cold-douche. Self-knowledge, however, as we have seen, is difficult to acquire, and the main difficulty is that our worst faults are the very ones we are least likely to admit.

A review of a few of the kinds of blinkers we are accustomed to use, and why we use them, should help us to devise a wise method for our examens and enable us to find matter in plenty for confession.

Since self-deceit is obviously very foolish (at least in others and more especially in So-and-So!), a tantalizing question arises why we are so addicted to it, so self-satisfied about it, and for the most part, so sublimely unconscious of it.

WISHFUL THINKING

One cause is that our nature disposes us to wishful thinking. A glance at the arrangement of our faculties will enable us to understand why this is the case. The table should explain itself.

			Reaction	Controlling Virtue
Human Nature	*Soul*	*Mind*	*Satisfaction of knowledge*	*Prudence*
		Will	*Spiritual Desire*	*Justice*
	Body Senses	*Unattractive Object*	*Desire to avoid*	*Fortitude*
		Attractive Object	*Desire to obtain*	*Temperance*

The desires of the senses are instinctive, not free, automatic, irrational and irreparably selfish.

The desires of the soul are indicated, but not controlled, by reason.

A glance at the scheme will show that, apart from the mind, all our faculties are faculties of *desire*. Reason, therefore, is encompassed by untrustworthy counsellors. Desire is a bad adviser because, as we know from sad experience, the wish (or desire) is very often father to the thought. Whenever we badly want something, we are inclined to dispense with enquiry about the legitimacy of satisfying our desire. We turn a blind eye on our real motives and focus our attention on plausible pretexts which will give us a specious justification for doing what we want to do.

From the nature of the case, therefore, reason is exposed to grave danger of wishful thinking. The danger is aggravated by the fact that, since all our life begins in the senses, the senses always get the first innings. If desire is allowed to rule us, our conduct is bound to become progressively more and more unreasonable, and as a result of the blacking out of reason we shall live in spiritual darkness.

Self-deception is a device for enabling us to be selfish

without remorse or loss of self-respect. Such veiled selfishness is often glorified by the moderately respectable title of thoughtlessness. We may be too busy satisfying our desires, our whims and inclinations and passions, to have time or inclination to try to understand our real motives. We just feel that way about things and that's that. To act like this is to live "like the ass and the ox which have no understanding." Impetuosity, frivolity, whimsicality, superficiality, may make our rational life negligible. The ways of self-deception are innumerable, but the essence of them all is an attempt to camouflage and whitewash our real motives.

Desire is the major difficulty in the way of self-knowledge. Whenever, therefore, our desires have been aroused or frustrated, we should spare no pains to keep reason in charge of the situation. If our feelings have been excited, we should keep a close watch and a stern grip on ourselves. How many bad matrimonial matches are made because this is not done! If we are "hurt," or if we are violently attracted or repelled by someone, we shall be hard pressed to remain entirely reasonable in our conduct. As soon, however, as reason loses control, we begin to make fools of ourselves, no matter what the world may say. Let us, therefore, carefully review our desires; desire to have our own way, stubbornness, impetuosity; desire for revenge, perhaps only in a petty mean way; desire for our own ease causing us to fear any form of sacrifice, to neglect duty, to be selfish; desires for sex gratification; desires to shine and be outstanding, et cetera.

Wishful thinking causes us to become experts at disguising our motives, which the modern psychologists call—rationalizing. The fat woman going up a hill sits down half-way to admire the view, so she says; the real reason is, of course, because she is "puffed."

St. Thomas says that "*omnis peccans ignorat.*" Every sinner acts in ignorance, though his ignorance is voluntary. Before acting we always try to justify our conduct to ourselves, and there is an obvious danger that we may be too proud to admit our voluntary self-deception even when we have cooled down from our fit of passion; or too lazy and weak-willed, because we shirk the labour involved in self-correction; or too full of human respect and so unwilling to admit our fault before others.

HOME-MADE COMMANDMENTS

Another very common reason why people cannot find matter for confession is because unconsciously they have adapted the commandments to their own convenience, and whittled down their obligations to more sizable proportions.

Some people seem to think that the only serious sins are impurity and Mass-missing. It is significant, as Dorothy Sayers points out, that the word "immorality" has come to mean one thing only, whereas it was made to cover the whole range of human corruption. "A man may be greedy and selfish; spiteful, cruel, jealous and unjust; violent and brutal; grasping, unscrupulous and a liar; stubborn and arrogant; stupid, morose, and dead to every noble instinct—and still we are ready to say of him that he is not an immoral man."[1]

Sometimes one finds Catholic maids in non-Catholic households, who are lying, immodest, lazy, dirty, dishonest and mischief-making; but they go to Confession and Communion once a month, and never miss Mass, so they are obviously in a position to look down superciliously on their irreligious employers. Oftentimes oldish people, whose passions have cooled down, will say that they no longer have any occasion of serious sin. Obviously in their minds the only serious sin is sexual sin. If they thought again, it might suddenly occur to them that there are ten commandments, not two, and that breaking some of the other commandments is more serious than breaking the sixth and ninth. A modern version of phariseeism—which is the religion of the minimizers—is sometimes summed up like this: "I don't harm anybody, and though I don't go to church, I'm as good as those who go," and, therefore, we are left to conclude, they are quite justified in being very smug and self-satisfied and in tearing their church-going neighbours' characters to bits. Probably they

[1] *The Six Other Deadly Sins* (Methuen). (Cf. Newman's masterly sermon, "The Religion of the Pharisee, the Religion of Mankind": *Sermons on Various Occasions*.)

are practising birth-control, approving, if not practising, abortion and euthanasia, hardly ever doing an honest day's work, sailing very near the wind in business and completely ignoring the first and greatest commandment—but, of course *they* have decided that these things are not sins! That they should set themselves up as pontiffs in Israel and echo their pontifical locutions from the abysses of their ignorance does not strike them as insufferable pride.

If we do not trouble to find out what God really wants, naturally we decide that He wants what we think He wants; or, at any rate, what we think He ought to want, what would content us if we were God.

If we are self-righteous and inclined to be very self-satisfied about our conduct, or addicted to making such pretty little speeches as: "I may be . . . but, thank God (shudder!), I'm not. . . ."; or if we make a fetish of certain practices, mostly external, or bitterly censure certain types of delinquents whilst we are very tolerant of others—in any, or all of these cases, we convict ourselves of phariseeism. Pharisees are also fond of priding themselves on their *practicality* in religion; which means in all probability that they have neither piety nor devotion and very little faith, hope or charity, and practise a merely natural religion which aims at satisfying social conventions rather than God.

FADS AND FASHIONS

What the moderns call the herd-instinct is responsible for much ignorance of our faults. We are by nature social beings, and therefore we are inevitably, and rightly, but dangerously affected by what our fellows think of us. Fear to lose caste is one of the most powerful motives of human conduct.

The desire for esteem is a powerful urge, and, provided it is regulated by reason, a good and constructive urge. It may lead, however, by:

EXCESS *to self-assertiveness, vanity, showing-off; fear to be odd, singular, different, etc;*

DEFECT *to excessive self-esteem. A man may react too vigorously against the desire for esteem and strive to acquire an odious self-sufficiency.*

The social instinct disposes us not to think at all but simply to accept blindly the prevailing ideas and fashions. Ideas which are taken for granted by our neighbours easily come to be taken for granted by us, for we imbibe them unconsciously and acquiesce in them indeliberately.

Fear to be thought odd, narrow-minded, old-fashioned, out-of-date or ignorant, has a powerful influence on our opinions, our sentiments and our conduct and is one of the major causes of the spiritual blindness and inefficiency of the Catholic body. In a world which is organized on God-less principles, it is inevitable that a Catholic who has the courage of his convictions should often seem odd and unreasonable. To be true to his principles in the modern world, a Catholic must be mentally alert and vigilant and full of moral courage. Because of insufficient spiritual reading, thought and prayer, many Catholics accept without challenge the world's standards and values and become infected with its spirit. As a result, they are indistinguishable from others of their class except on Sunday mornings, and as Christians exercise no influence on society.

What the world needs today are other-Christs, men and women not merely Christian in name and devotions but Christian also in their outlook and principles, and different, fundamentally and obviously different, from others. To endeavour to be Christ-like is an *obligation* not a presumptuous pious eccentricity. "So let your light shine before men that they may glorify your Father Who is in heaven. I have given you an example that as I have done, so do you also." If we are not attempting to become Christ-like, we are failing in our *duty*. To be a Christian in reality, not merely in name, means to be an imitator of Christ. We can't have it both ways. "He that is not with Me, is against Me." If we are not drawing others to Christ, we are alienating them from Christ and ruining his work. Our own masses must first be leavened, if the rest of the world is to be affected. Because of worldliness many Catholics couple all the faults of their class with a sublime unconsciousness of infidelity.

Our modern benighted education has, for example, almost expunged the words "reverence" and "respect" from the dictionary, and often no attempt is made to practise these virtues—even by Catholics: to show, for example, respect and reverence for parents, priests and superiors as enshrining God's authority, and respect for one's social inferiors as children of God. The world would consider such conduct old-fashioned and spiritless, so even Catholics are sometimes off-hand, blasé, and reverent neither in manner nor in speech. Reverence is reserved for those who have achieved notoriety or got on, or made money, or are useful to know, or who wear fine clothes and have an affected accent. To show respect to a tramp or the charwoman would be a social impropriety bordering on an unforgivable sin. The canons of the worldling's moral code are "what is done" and "what is not done." He does not think, he imitates, he follows fashion, he is a perfect marionette. Each class has its own conventions, which are frequently not those of Christ.

Unworthy conduct may be due to abuse, probably unconscious abuse, of our faculties.

ABUSE OF THE IMAGINATION

Mr. A. has a vivid imagination. Every minor happening in his life sets his imagination working and evolves into a thriller. Result, he becomes a first-class liar, impractical and unreliable.

Mr. B. also has a vivid imagination and a tendency to self-pity. Result, he broods over every slight or imagined neglect, makes mountains out of mole-hills, and becomes moody, melancholic and a bitter critic.

Mrs. C. lives in a make-belief world of heroic sanctity. Her make-belief is so real to her that she fancies herself something of a saint. Really she is lazy, self-indulgent, negligent about household duties, proud and condescending to others and merely sentimental in her devotions.

ABUSE OF THE INTELLECT

A. has an ingenious mind, which he uses to explain away any duty he does not wish to honour, and justify any shady affair which he has decided to promote.

It is inevitable that we should all tend to misuse the mind when we are dealing with our own affairs, in which we are interested parties and therefore prejudiced. "No one is a judge in his own case." Let us, therefore, submit to our confessor affections, friendships or conduct, if we are uneasy about them and find that they are disturbing our peace of soul and diminishing our sense of union with God. It is a wise plan to listen attentively to what others say about us, even enemies. Others are no more infallible in their judgment of us than we are in our judgment of ourselves; but friends are likely to be right, and even enemies are not certain to be wrong. "Hatred has keen eyes, and its malicious tongue often speaks truths which our friends do not dare to utter because they are bitter."[2]

Examination of our faculties on similar lines might bring home to us a crop of faults.

In the following cases, there is obvious need for thorough self-examination:

1. If we are in the class of the old woman who said to her friend: "All the world's queer save thee and me—and thee's a bit queer." If we are the only ones in step, if we get into persistent difficulties with others, there is obviously something wrong and seriously wrong with us.

   The world is usually what we make it. If others constantly get on our nerves, obviously we have nerves. It takes two to make a quarrel, at least as a general rule (there is, of course, such a thing as "picking a quarrel," but such obstreperous conduct is rare), so if we are seldom at peace with our neighbours, we cannot be at

[2] Scharsch, *op. cit.*, p. 109.

peace with ourselves. If all the world seems black, we must be wearing black glasses.

Those who are constantly at loggerheads with parents, superiors or associates, should engage in humble self-examination. They are certainly failing in humility and are probably making no attempt to curb a natural defect of character, e.g., moroseness, stubbornness, melancholy, et cetera.

2. *When fervour seems to be abating*—Perhaps it is only our sensible fervour, our "ginger-beer" fervour, that has gone, as sooner or later it must go if we are to progress: but let us make sure, or the doubt, even if it is no more than a doubt, will constantly tantalize and discourage. The only remedy for doubt is solution of the doubt.
3. *When we suffer from aridity for long periods or almost unintermittently*—Aridity may be a purifying trial or a punishment for habitual faults.

   If aridity is a punishment for habitual faults, e.g., uncharitable gossip, toying with temptations, dangerous curiosity or familiarity—the aridity will be liable to continue until the fault is amended.

   Whether aridity is a punishment or a trial, we must submit to it with patience because in either case it is a manifestation of mercy.

In making our examens we should not try to X-ray the soul and read it like a book. Our examen should start *out* of self in the consideration of external ideals and norms, e.g.:

1. *Habitual recollection*—What prevented me from maintaining it? Laziness? Want of faith? Excessive desire to succeed?
2. *Daily duties*—Have I done any of them badly or omitted them altogether? Why?
3. *Moods*—What put me in that black mood? That dissipated one?
4. *Temper*—Why did I get into such a vicious temper? Why do I find it so difficult to recover my balance?

And so on, indefinitely.

The clues to our interior defects will be furnished from without. These few suggestions will, it is hoped, make clear several points:

1. That if we want to acquire self-knowledge and progress in holiness, we must be in earnest. Casual spirituality allows our souls to "become an unweeded garden that grows to seed; things rank and gross in nature possess it merely."
2. That if we examine our conscience with method and insight, we shall find more than enough matter for Confession.

May the Holy Spirit enlighten and strengthen us: *"Domine noverim me, noverim Te!"*—"Lord that I may know myself and know Thee."

VIII

Sidelights on Self

TO HELP in the work of ambushing self-deceit, an examination of conscience has been compiled. It is by no means exhaustive and is meant principally as an indication of the type of things on which we should examine ourselves. In our examens we should definitely get down to brass tacks and not content ourselves with reading through a list of abstract nouns and phrases. If we conduct our search wisely, we shall probably find more than enough matter to engage our attention. It would be a mistake to read right through this list at one session; the reader should stop as soon as he finds enough to "go on with" or the result might be discouragement or scrupulosity. "One thing at a time" is a safe rule and the only safeguard against superficiality.

The examen is intended for use in the periodical overhaul, not in preparation for confession, unless the penitent has difficulty in finding matter.

We have a duty to conform as far as possible to the *real* (objective) law of God, not to what *we think* is the law of God. Many of the faults on our lists may not hitherto have seemed wrong to us, and we may have fallen into them without consciousness of sin. In that case, we did not sin against God, though we transgressed against the letter of the law. However, we must live and learn. Even unconscious faults harm us and scandalize others, so it is our duty to try to eliminate them. Conscience is one of the greatest of mysteries and it is for each individual, and no other except the confessor, to try to determine his (or her) exact culpability before God. Whether our faults have been indeliberate, semi-deliberate or fully deliberate, we must do our best to combat them.

Even though this list is not exhaustive, if anyone can read through it without finding matter for confession, he must be a great saint or spiritually purblind.

LIES

In recounting an argument or a quarrel was I strictly truthful and just; or did I make deliberate omissions which threw everything I said out of perspective?

Were the brilliant retorts I narrated suggested by after-wits, what I should like to have said, not what I actually did say?

If so, do not simply confess lies, but lies occasioned by vanity and a desire to "show off."

Did I pretend to have read a book, when in reality I had read only a review of the book?

Have I made statements as "gospel," of which I was not certain or which I had at third or fourth hand?

In relating my own sayings and doings, have I exaggerated my success and minimized or explained away my failures?

One can act as well as tell a lie.

Have I feigned intense welcome or friendship for someone I really detested? (To show a genial charity is virtue, to pretend special friendship or pleasure is hypocrisy.)

Have I developed a habit of dissimulation, making mental reservations not only without sufficient reason but almost without any reason?

Have I been affected and put on airs?

PRIDE

Has my spirituality been merely a quest for personal excellence?

Am I seeking a reputation for humility rather than the reality of humility?

Have I failed to take leadership or strong action for fear of being thought proud or ambitious? In other words, do I prefer to be proud rather than to be thought proud?

Have I fished for praise with the bait of false modesty?

Have I refused responsibility for fear that prominence might reveal my limitations?

Are the main causes of my joys and sorrows the gratification or frustration of vanity?

When anyone is praised, is my first impulse always to belittle; in other words, do I suffer from jealousy based on pride?

Have I boasted of my achievements, wealth, et cetera? Dressed ostentatiously?

Have I been too proud to accept well-merited correction, even from my confessor? When I have been corrected have I sulked and adopted the pose of the misunderstood injured-innocent? Have I dispensed myself from heeding a correction by presuming that my superior or confessor was merely depressed or liverish and that he will get over it?

Is my neighbour a darling when he agrees with me, and a pig-headed egoist when he doesn't?

Am I something of a "private pontiff"?

JUSTICE

Have I stolen other people's books by borrowing and not returning them?—a particularly mean thing to do if the book is out of print. Lapse of time does not give the borrower-thief a prescriptive right to possession: "*res clamat domino*"—"the book calls for its owner"—indefinitely.

Have I owned and paid up if I have broken or damaged

anything belonging to another—or allowed someone else to be blamed?

Have I driven my housekeeper, wife or mother to distraction by hopelessly regular irregularity, e.g., by coming in late for meals?—and then added insult to injury by complaining about the cooking?

Have I caused small tradesmen inconvenience and possibly fairly serious financial embarrassment by endless delay in settling accounts?

Have I forgotten that charity is of *obligation* in business relations. Have I stopped short at a dubious justice, always driving the hardest bargain, taking advantage of the necessity of others to pay scarcely equitable prices or starvation wages? Has my comfort been bought by blood money?

Have I gained a reputation as a generous benefactor to the church with money that was not my own, money due in justice to my employees, defrauded money crying to heaven for vengeance?

Have I taken advantage of the minimum wage to do the minimum of work?

Have I been seriously unjust to my employer by creating dissatisfaction or grossly exaggerating minor grievances?

Have I subscribed to the false doctrine of inevitable class-warfare?

Have I shown grave irresponsibility by advocating or supporting strikes, without sufficient reason and before amicable attempts at a settlement had been made?

Have I smoked to excess, to the detriment of my health, my family, my honesty?

Am I incurring debts which, if I maintain my present rate of expenditure, I shall never be able to repay? That is, am I stealing under false pretences?

Does my addiction to the cinema amount to a mania, undermining my self-control? In order to go to the cinema, do I neglect my duty, half-doing housework, leaving the children to roam the streets, and failing to prepare proper meals for my husband?

Am I careful about the films I allow my children to see,

or have I packed them off to anything just to get them out of the way?

Am I a snob? Do I believe in a caste-system? Have I failed to show respect to my social inferiors as children of God? Have I treated servants or the working-class as though they were unworthy of a refined charity? Have I exacted overtime without paying for it? Have I expected servants always to be at my beck and call, and chosen to forget that they have need of and a right to decent recreation? Have I paid wages with a lordly air, as though I were doing my servants a favour?

CHARITY

Have I sometimes laboured the good points of my adversary or enemy a little more than usual in order to emphasize my impartiality and so enhance the value of my indictment?

Have I displayed an unctuous, whitewashing, untruthful charity, motivated by a desire to increase my own reputation, rather than by a desire to safeguard my neighbour's?

When uncharitable things have been said of us or done to us, we are not thereby justified in broadcasting the fact. Theology allows us to relieve our minds by talking of the injury to *one* intimate, who can be relied upon to maintain a discreet silence—no more. When *one* injury has been done to us, have we not often retaliated by inflicting *ten* injuries on our offending neighbour, and still continued to broadcast our misfortune and nurse the idea that we are the *injured party*? "It was unfair," "it was unjust," "she shouldn't have said it"—these and suchlike excuses are no justification for uncharitable broadcasts.

Have I repeated things which might cause mischief? Have I, out of jealousy, vindictiveness or ambition, maliciously tried to create misunderstandings and ride on the crest of them to prëeminence? Have I distorted what was said by inventions, innuendo or studied omissions?

Am I a destructive, carping critic, spreading discontent and disseminating gloom?

Am I well disposed toward *all*? If to love does not mean

this, it is an empty sham. Have I been unforgiving? Do I habitually "cut" certain people? This is a serious matter. If we harbour an unforgiving spirit, we have no right to go to Holy Communion, Confession is a mockery, and whenever we recite the "Our Father," we invoke upon ourselves not a blessing but a curse.

Has my charity to individuals been limited or paralysed by excessive nationalism? Have I hurt and scandalized my neighbour by habitually "running down" his country or by refusing to accept or admit my responsibilities as a citizen of his country? Have I shown favouritism to compatriots? Have I adopted the my-country-right-or-wrong attitude?

Do I gossip? Do I constantly give inside information prefacing my remarks with the rhetorical question: "Have you heard?" and obliging my neighbour to inviolable secrecy?

Is my conversation almost invariably about persons, scandals? Is my conversation limited to personalities because my head is empty? An idle mind exposes us to greater danger than idle hands. If "the devil finds work for idle hands to do," how much more easily does he not find work for idle minds!

Is my mind empty because I am too full of myself? Have I ever tried to store my mind with suitable matter for conversation? The conversation of the empty-headed must be limited to puerilities—"she said to me" and "I said to her," and suchlike fooleries.

Am I habitually disagreeable and discourteous at home? Do I make no serious attempt to be otherwise? Generous abroad, mean at home?—in other words, is my generosity merely thinly veiled vanity?

Have I been wanting in charity by neglecting to answer letters or by answering only after an unnecessarily long delay?

Am I touchy and hypersensitive? Have I magnified the least oversight or thoughtlessness into an insult or deliberate slight?

Do I make a habit of righteous indignation and continually use strong and bitter language? Am I more concerned to punish and humiliate offenders than to repair and obviate the offence; in other words, are my righteousness and zeal merely camouflaged vindictiveness and bad-temper?

Am I morose? unsociable? always complaining? haughty? contemptuous?

Am I always boasting about my principles and consistency?

Am I too rigid in enforcing my *rights*, careless about my duties? especially the duty of patience and long-suffering?

Irritability? To feel irritable is no sin, but it is sinful to give way to it deliberately. Don't be content to confess irritability, find its cause. Nerves? Get a tonic and practise patience. Anxiety? Practise trust in Divine Providence, et cetera.

Have my charities been nothing more than investments, designed to bring in a regular income of praise, gratitude and esteem?

Have you had a "row" with someone? Of course, he or she was *entirely* to blame! Are you *quite certain* that the Divine Judge thinks so? What is the use of bluffing yourself and others, even at Confession? What have you done to put things right? What are you ready to do? How many people have you told about it?

It will be amazing if there is no fault on your side. If you cannot get rid of a certain soreness from your *will* (N.B., I do not say "feelings"—time alone can heal them), you are definitely not blameless.

When you were beaten in argument, did you cling obstinately to your own opinion, even though you knew it was wrong, because you were too proud to admit your mistake or afraid that your antagonist might think himself intellectually superior to you?

What were your thoughts about him afterwards?—"He thinks himself a very smart chap, doesn't he?" How do you know?

Irritation will continue until you admit your share of blame. Quite possibly you are the only one to blame!

Have you made impossible demands on others and then lamented *their* selfishness because they could not accommodate you?

PURITY

Have I realized that, if I do not see the facts of life from God's point of view, I must inevitably see them from the devil's point of view, since it is impossible completely to ignore them and maintain a merely negative attitude?

Have I a reverent attitude towards sex, or do I implicitly indict the Creator by dubbing sex "not nice"?

Do I realize that sex is a God-given talent to be *used*, either in the normal way of marriage or at least by *sacrifice* outside of marriage? To sacrifice sexual desires and give them back to God, we must first have the sincerity and humility to recognize that they are there to be offered.

Have I tried to convince myself that I am "above that sort of thing" and so unconsciously adopted a pharisaical pose: "O, God! I give Thee thanks that I am not as the rest of humans"?

Has this pose led me to become a prude or a perambulating purveyor of salacious gossip?

Has my attitude to sex been cowardly and talent-burying, and so stunted and warped the development of my personality?

On the other hand, have I been careless about holy purity? Gone into *avoidable* occasions of sins? Allowed myself to be *engrossed* by human affections and lawful pleasures to such an extent as to acquire a distaste for the things of God, or merely to lose my spiritual freedom?

Is there anything I dare not discuss even with a broad-minded, kindly, reliable and experienced friend? Is there anything I tend to gloss over in Confession? When one is driven to secrecy, there is usually something wrong. A person with no guilty suspicions would not be afraid to discuss his conduct with a prudent confessor.

Are you allowing your moral fibre to be weakened and endangered by inordinate affections? (*N.B.* Inordinate is not a synonym for intense. An affection may be very intense without being inordinate. An affection is inordinate and a danger to chastity when "for no apparent reason, one wants to be in the presence of another and is unhappy in his or her absence.")

Conversation? reading? amusement? reveries?

Sensuous idleness, e.g., dawdling in bed? softness? excessive love of comfort?

Kissing, embracing? There are, of course, kisses and kisses. Kisses are permissible when they are not inspired by mere sensuality and selfishness and when there are sufficient safeguards, no scandal and no undue clandestinity; otherwise, they are a danger to chastity and therefore wrong. Prolonged petting is cheapening and dangerous and therefore wrong.

AUTHORITY

Have I exerted authority without accepting responsibility?

Have I given a reasonable freedom of action to subordinates with delegated authority?

Have I confused authority with personal infallibility and divine inspiration, and so made authority an excuse for autocracy?

Have I deliberately surrounded myself with mediocrity, toadies and lick-spittles, and done my best to repress the talented and keep them in their place?

Have I shown abnormal care to safeguard the humility of brilliant subjects who might put me in the shade?

Have I resented humble, honest, face-to-face criticism and been vindictive towards those whose good advice I was too weak to follow?

Have I realized that no one can undermine authority as effectively as a superior who abuses it?

Have I posed as *personally* superior to my subjects and expected them to bow to me, not to the divine authority in me? And by so doing, have I done my best to destroy their virility and spirit?

Have I mistaken obstinacy for firmness and fatuous narrow-mindedness for love of law?

Have I been fatuous enough to imagine that a multiplication of rules and petty restrictions will make people holy, and paid little or no attention to the cultivation of the interior spirit? Instead of leading, have I tried to drive people to God?

Have I been a coward in my exercise of authority? Have I been exigent and possibly harsh and unjust, with the weak and obedient; and falsely condescending to the forward, obstreperous and bitter-tongued? Have I bullied the weak and fawned on the strong?

Have I realized that my own authority is limited and to be exercised according to law?

Have I forgotten that with the Christian there is "no distinction of the Jew and the Greek"? Blinded by national prejudice, have I given preferment to compatriots irrespective of merits?

Have I reflected that for every abuse of authority I shall have to give a very strict account on the day of judgment?

OBEDIENCE

Is my obedience natural or supernatural?

Do I play up to, blarney or try to engineer my superiors?

PARENTS

Have you spoiled your child by selfishly considering your own feelings, not the child's good?

Have you nagged? Have you got a "boss-complex"?

Have you attempted to keep your child's confidence and form its mind? Have you considered your duty done when you have clothed and fed your child and seen that it goes to church?

Have you stunted your child's growth to maturity by making it too dependent or by selfishly trying to keep it a child when it was no longer a child?

Are your hot-house methods responsible for your child's shyness and awkwardness?

By not allowing your child to mix sufficiently with other suitable Catholics, have you made yourself, in part, responsible for a mixed-marriage?

Have you driven your children into lanes and back-alleys by not allowing them to bring their friends home?

Have you treated a prospective fiancé as a rival for your child's affection and been unsympathetic and possibly unjust?

Have you abused your authority and exasperated your children by a gestapo régime? Have you made an unreasonable fuss when your children came in at night at a time generally considered reasonable for persons of their years?

Have you made your children deceitful by excessive inquisitiveness or meanness, by wanting to know everything they have done, everywhere they have been and every penny they have to spend?

Have you scandalized your children by gossiping in their presence?

Has the amount of money you spent on cigarettes made you neglect your children's comfort and welfare?

Have you put pleasure before duty? Have you allowed your children to go without meals or roam the streets, whilst you went off to the cinema?

In setting up your children in life, i.e., in your choice of a school, in your approval or disapproval of their friends or lovers, have you been guided by absolutely practical considerations, i.e., by merely materialistic ones?

Have you been jealous of the piety of your children and done your best to repress it, inspired partly by the fear that they might give themselves to God?

MARRIAGE

Have I made no attempt to discover God's point of view about the intimacies of married life? Have I refused to inform myself because an obstinate pride makes me unwilling to admit that my ideas on so important a subject have been wrong, or because I shirk the mental labour of recasting my ideas at my time of life?

Do I regard intercourse as a sacramental act arranged and blessed by God; or have I instead a nasty, resentful, heretical, Manichean idea of it, causing me to harbour a secret grudge against God and a latent contempt for my partner?

Have I habitually failed in my duty, by giving to intercourse only a reluctant and condescending acquiescence, and by my grudging attitude largely destroyed the value of such acquiescence?

Has my reluctance to give full sacramental and enthusiastic expression to my love loosened the bond of union (which it is designed to cement) and endangered the continence and marital fidelity of my partner?

Have I been selfish in the refusal or performance of intercourse? Consulted only my own mood and never attempted to accommodate myself to my partner's mood or done so only with the pose of a martyr to duty?

Intercourse is a duty whenever either party (1) seriously and (2) reasonably petitions for it. There is no obligation to accede to *unreasonable petition*; though—be it noted—a petition is not unreasonable merely because it finds you in an uncongenial mood.

For Men. In the preliminaries of intercourse, have I nauseated my wife by my complete failure to show a delicate and sensitive consideration for her feelings and desires? Have I ever tried to see intimate married life from her point of view? Refinement and unselfishness make intercourse attractive: crudity and selfishness make it repellant. Have I ever been mean enough to resort to moral compulsion and so sowed the seeds of hate?

Have I raised my mind to God during intercourse and humbly thanked Him for this pleasure, this sacramental expression of love, this complement of myself, and the privilege of co-operating with Him in the creation of a human being; or have I instead considered myself "outside the pale" and mentally skulked away from His presence and His love?

Have I been entirely sincere about my reactions to intercourse and not sometimes pretended that they were what I thought (wrongly) that they ought to be and were not? Has this insincerity been occasioned by a fear "to lose caste" in my own eyes?

Do I realize that whilst the biological purpose of intercourse is procreation, the psychological purpose is the expression and preserving of a unique love, and that in consequence this unique expression of love may, and should, continue even when the biological purpose can no longer be subserved?

Have I interfered with nature's course? If deliberate, this is always a serious sin, no matter how it is done.

Have I formed my own conscience on this question, in direct opposition to the Church's teaching, and so implicitly repudiated her infallible authority?—a fearfully serious sin, perilous to faith.

Have I deliberately—and on principle!—omitted to mention these sins in Confession; and followed sacrilegious Confessions by sacrilegious Communions?

Or have I confessed these sins when I had no genuine determination to amend my life and so nourished a false idea of magical absolution, deceiving myself that as long as I managed to extract absolution from the confessor my sins would be forgiven without amendment?

Have I induced others to follow my example in this, and so acted as the devil's lieutenant and the enemy of Christ?

IN CHURCH

Have I guarded my pew as if I owned and not merely rented it?

Was I rude to harrassed apparitors who requested me to allow others to use my pew? Did I even descend to rugby-scrum tactics to keep out trespassers?

Have I added to the scandal of disgusting selfishness by going immediately afterwards to Holy Communion before Mass, without having made any preparation?

Have I behaved in church as I should not be allowed to behave in a cinema or a bar?

Have I distracted others by endless whispering?

Have I been annoyed by Miss Modern's lip-stick, Mr. Goeasy's sprawling manner and Mrs. Gettingon's hat, forgetting that if I were minding my own business and saying my prayers I should not be likely to notice these things?

Have my genuflections suggested physical jerks or physical decrepitude rather than the worship of God?

Have I annoyed others by slipping into the confessional out of my turn?

Have I hurried over preparation for Confession, preoccupied all the time with the fear of being kept waiting or by the desire to get back home to do something infinitely less important, e.g., to read a thriller or spot a winner?

Have I been late for Mass through my own fault? To be late for Mass through one's own negligence is always a venial sin of irreverence towards the Blessed Sacrament and the Divine Victim; it is a mortal sin if one misses a principal part of a Mass of obligation, i.e., if one comes in after the Offertory.

"I accuse myself of having picked the sermon to bits in order to make fun of my parish priest."

"I accuse myself of having gone to hear the great preachers solely out of snobbery, because they were the rage . . . of having sought everything in such displays but the knowledge of God."[1]

GENERAL I

Have I been unpunctual through my own fault?

To be unpunctual deliberately for no sufficient reason is against charity and fidelity to one's word or contract, and may

[1] Jacques Debout, *My Sins of Omission* (Herder).

be a sign of ingrained selfishness which always puts the ego first.

Moreover, unpunctuality is an occasion of sin for others, because, taking human nature as it is, rash judgment, uncharitable thoughts, irritability, grumbling and bad temper, are practically certain to result from it.

On the other hand, the punctual who are kept waiting, must remember that they are not dispensed from the duty of exercising patience and charity. They must repress unkind thoughts and rash judgments and smother the leaping volcanic fires of fury, or they will be guilty of venial sin. Hard, I know, but who said the spiritual life was meant to be uniformly easy? On no account must they assume a sulky, testy, condemnatory manner before an explanation has been given, or demand an explanation in the menacing manner of a prosecuting attorney, and so make an explanation morally impossible and extremely unlikely. It is not wrong, of course, to remonstrate kindly and moderately, if a satisfactory explanation is not given or even attempted.

Have I "talked down" to anyone?

Have I talked too much and strummed perpetually on the "I" note? Has my talking been motivated by the vain desire to stay in the lime-light and convince my listeners what a wonderful, superior, admirable person I am? Have I talked principally and in fact almost exclusively about my own sayings and doings and ideas?

Do I talk with breathless haste so that others may not succeed in getting in a word edgeways?

Have I rudely interrupted conversation when it did not interest me or kept me in the background?

Have I been taciturn and talked too little? Have I adopted the pose of a sphinx, to convince others what pearls of wisdom I should proffer if only did I speak?

Have I developed an unduly ponderous personality and a one-track mind, as a result of despising small talk and not knowing how to relax?

Have I cultivated a sense of humour?

Have I been depressingly serious? The sour-faced are generally shallow and unbalanced and not serious, or are serious about the wrong things, like the Pharisees.

GENERAL II

"I accuse myself of never having accused myself of religious ignorance, of not even offering any excuse therefor, so normal does such an omission seem.

"I accuse myself of having taken no interest whatever in Christian doctrine, upon the pretext of respecting the more its mysteries and sacred character.

"I accuse myself of not having loved God with my mind, and of having unconsciously repudiated Him, because to affect no interest in His life and revelation is tantamount to genuine atheism.

"I accuse myself of a strong inclination to think, without precisely admitting it, that religious knowledge is very nearly as boring as it is useless, and that it is not intended for people in the world.

"I accuse myself of not having in my house either the Bible or the New Testament; of never having read . . . the Gospels through or any life of Our Lord.

"I accuse myself of having drifted into a wordly accomodation which enables the most repeated practices, in all sincerity, of a sensitive piety to be combined with an elegantly pagan state of mind and conception of life.

"I accuse myself of having laid up my talents in a napkin, like the servant in the parable, thinking them useless in regard to salvation, and dangerous to humility and discipline."[2]

"When we go to the cinema and see a picture about empty-headed people in luxurious surroundings, do we say, 'What drivel!,' or do we sit in a misty dream, wishing we could give up our daily work and marry into surroundings like that?"[3]

[2] Debout, *op. cit.* (This is a brilliant book, crowned by the French Academy, which all educated people should read—and possess.)

[3] Sayers, *op. cit.* (This is a searching and brilliant analysis of the fundamental evils of modern life.)

Have I tried to make my ideas and outlook Christian?

What attempt have I made to understand and assimilate my Faith—a necessary preliminary to practising it?

What have I done to reintroduce Christian ideas into the world? I may not be able to do much, but surely I could do something.

How often have I worshipped, praised and thanked God? These are *duties*, habitual neglect of which shows a stunted religious mind and probably involves some sin.

Have I allowed myself to be engrossed by human affairs?

Has my prayer almost entirely consisted of petitions for wordly favours, such as a better job or success in an examination; in other words, have I treated God as a useful business patron and nothing more?

Have I treated religion simply as a fire-insurance against hell fire; or served God simply because I feared I should have no luck otherwise?

Have I ever solicited for my soul light and love?

Have I ever made a really serious and sustained attempt to love God?

Have I "implored grace only as a means of salvation and not so as to be beautiful with the beauty of grace through living the life of grace"?

Have I "considered grace only as a lightning-conductor and not as a nuptial garment, as a guarantee and not a value"?

Have I "confused my spiritual life by a complicated ledger account of indulgenced prayers and practices," forgetting that "while formulas and practices are the symbol of indulgences, interior disposition is the cause"?

Have I treated prayer as an excellent substitute for personal effort, e.g., neglecting study and then staking all on a fervid novena before the examination and an attempt to bribe God by lighting lots of candles?

Has my devotion been an excellent labour-saving device, dispensing me, because of what I am, from the inconvenience and burden—and distraction!—of attending to my social, civic and national *duties*? Have I done more than my bit to make piety contemptible?

Has my prayer been a veiled dictation to God or an attempt to barter with Him on a *quid pro quo* basis, and not the humble suppliance of a universal debtor?

Has my prayer been: "Not Thy will but mine be done, because I've had the decency to ask Thee to do it"?

When my prayer has apparently not been answered, have I felt a grudge against God? Have I expected a slot-machine answer to prayer and refused to pray with perseverance?

Have I neglected prayers for the dead? Have I thus abandoned in their agony those I love best?

Have I failed to realize that a Catholic owes it to his God, to his Church, to his time and to himself, to be of some value intellectually? Have I realized that a man is truly human only if he uses his mind?

Have I made no attempt to develop my personality, prudently refrained from having any opinions of my own not culled from fashionable periodicals? Have I attempted to realize my personal dignity as a child of God and to cultivate appreciation of the beautiful in nature, literature, art or music?

Fear of doing wrong is no excuse for doing nothing, as the fate of the man who buried his talent proves. Yet have I not done precisely this; fearing to study my Faith, lest I should have doubts; fearing to use my mind, lest I should become proud; fearing reverent sex instruction, lest I should abuse it; fearing even my God-given ordinary duties, lest they should be a distraction?

GENERAL III

Has laziness in rising made me a nuisance to others? Have I made lying excuses to cloak my laziness? Has laziness led me into serious injustice, e.g., never doing a decent day's work?

Have I neglected house-work, nominally for devotion, really because it irks me?

Have I been slovenly in my dress, work, speech, et cetera?

Have I failed in duty to my husband and children, by

not making the home clean, germ-proof, moderately comfortable and attractive?

Am I always late with meals and behind with my work because I am too weak to wash my hands of gossipers who waste my time?

Have I weakly agreed to falsehood or connived at and even participated in bad talk, because I was afraid to be thought narrow, bigoted, not a sport?

Have I been guilty of jealousy resulting in unfriendly rivalry, strong aversions and a jaundiced attitude towards those who excel? Has jealousy caused me to impede and act as a brake on God's work—a very serious consideration?

Have I ever consistently tried to react in a Christian manner to insults, injuries and rash-judgment? Has my reaction been dictated by human respect, by fear to be thought weak or cowardly or wanting in spirit? Have I even prided myself and boasted about my non-Christian attitude?

Am I selfish? In my plans, is my own comfort and security always my first and principal consideration?

Have I annoyed others by appreciating highly what I do for them and little what they do for me?

When giving trifles or doing trifling services, have I conveyed to others the idea that I considered them under a serious obligation to me?

Embittered by ingratitude? To be hurt by ingratitude is natural and inevitable, but to be embittered reveals selfishness.

Am I too impressionable? Have I tried to control the imagination, thoughts, ups-and-downs of feeling, moods, whims, impulses? Am I volatile and unreliable?

Have I tried to rule my life by reason?

Have I been rash, head-strong and obstinate, rushing into action without taking counsel or thought and without having recourse to prayer; and then impiously blamed the Almighty because my affairs did not succeed?

Have I been a spend-thrift? Moderate thrift is a virtue, not a vice—whatever Big Business may say!

Have I chosen to forget that public money comes out of my neighbours' pockets and that no government can produce money by magic?

Have I been content with my lot? To strive to improve one's lot tranquilly and without greed is virtuous, to allow oneself to be devoured by senseless greed and envy is fatal to virtue and to happiness.

Under cover of raising my standard of living, have I allowed my life to be materialized and my spirit deadened, so that I spend more and more time on the body, and less and less time on the soul?

Why have I now so little time and inclination for religion?

Have I considered getting on in the world to be the chief object of life; in other words, is my *real* outlook on life pagan, not Christian?

Have I allowed a furious barrage of advertisement to flatter and frighten me out of a reasonable contentment into a greedy hankering after goods which will do me no good and which I do not really need?

Have I allowed advertisements, Big Business propaganda and party cat-calls to distort my ideas of life and make me a senseless pawn of commercialism?

Has my indignation against the rich been based solely on envy; in other words, am I as deficient in poverty of spirit and at heart as odious and selfish a snob as they?

Have I disguised mere covetousness as enterprise or go-getting?

Have my activity and zeal been inspired by *sloth*, by a desire to silence my own mind and avoid facing problems?

Whilst in theory decrying the materialism and mendacity of the press, have I, nevertheless, been content in practice to get most of my ideas from it?

Have I fallen a victim to the modern craze for speed? Do I, in consequence, get exasperated whenever I am delayed, even though the delay causes me no real inconvenience and despite the fact that I have no need to hurry? If I miss a bus or train, am I inclined to make frequent use of words beginning with "b" or "d"?

Have I grumbled at the arrangements of Divine Providence and expected, even demanded, to be shown the reason for everything?

Have I been discontented because of my limitations, poverty, ill-health?

Does someone "get on your nerves"? Then—

1. You have nerves.

2. Very probably you have the very faults which annoy you.

Is that person more popular, more talented, more esteemed than you or likely to keep you out of a position which you covet?

Have I got a suspicious mind?

Do I assume the function of a vigilance-committee over public morals and, in consequence, hardly ever mind my own business? Am I really the only person in the world with a sense of responsibility?

Our judgments reveal the nature of our own minds. As the tree, so the fruit. If habitually we suspect ulterior selfish motives in others, we are never disinterested ourselves; if we see impurity everywhere, something has gone wrong in our own lives.

Watch your judgments and you will learn to understand yourself.

Am I a smug hyper-critic?

Destructive criticism is the refuge of incompetency and a perverted technique of defence. By concentrating attention on the supposed or real faults and deficiencies of his neighbours, the critic hopes to distract attention from his own short-comings, of which he is painfully aware. By indulging in criticism, he tries to compensate himself for his feeling of inferiority.

To judge requires knowledge, prudence, experience and discretion. The critic implies that he has all these qualities, with the superiority they imply; and it is this self-assumed superiority which makes criticism so dear to him.

IX

Fuddle and Fif

It is an indisputable fact that of all fanatics the most difficult to deal with are religious fanatics. Religion tends to gather around it pious people who are supremely obstinate; scrupulous people who are morbid and unreasonable; and eccentric people who justify religiosity by saying that "their conscience is different" and by quoting intuition against—and even despising—commonsense. Religion, as history shows, often produces a crop of *illuminati*, irrationalists, and intolerant private pontiffs.

These are disturbing facts, well worth careful study. Many take it for granted that anti-social abnormalities are the natural outcome of religion; and on that account they despise and hate religion as the enemy of sanity and social progress. If we could rid religion of fanatics and eccentrics, we should have gone a long way towards converting the world.

Eccentricities, when they are not due to personality, are occasioned by misunderstanding of religion, especially by misunderstanding of the meaning of the word "conscience." Shakespeare has expressed a very common idea of conscience in the much-quoted lines of *Hamlet*:

> Thus conscience doth make cowards of us all;
> And thus the native hue of resolution
> Is sicklied o'er with the pale cast of thought:

And enterprises of great pith and moment,
With this regard, their currents turn awry,
And lose the name of action.[1]

Conscience is regarded as a sickly, emasculating thing, which causes morbid introversion, produces characters who shy at shadows, and destroys all strength of character. Nothing could be less true. Fidelity to conscience requires and produces the heroic courage of the saint. Disastrous misconceptions of conscience have arisen because it is so often confused with fuss, feeling, fuddle, funk and fif. Yes, these are the ingredients of which many consciences—or what unfortunately pass for consciences—are compounded.

Although "conscience" is a vital word very much in use, there are not many who could give a confident and accurate definition of it. Small wonder that people get fuddled about examination of conscience when they do not know what they are supposed to be examining. It is a pathetic fact that of those who examine their consciences regularly, the majority "know not what they do." Small wonder that their vain fears and irrational obsessions prove strangely difficult to dislodge. Experience teaches that many people entertain about conscience, not merely woolly notions, but even definitely wrong notions. In such a vital matter, haziness, not to mention error, is lamentable and disastrous. Fuddle about conscience leaves the door wide open to obstinacy, intuition, scruples, fanaticism and *fif*. (By fif is meant a tendency to substitute emotional intuition for reason.)

WHAT IS CONSCIENCE?

Conscience is not a special faculty.

Needless to say, conscience is in the soul. If you recall your catechism, you will remember that in the soul there are three powers—memory, understanding and will. No mention of a fourth power called conscience. In the soul there are two faculties, intellect and will. Neither philosophy nor

[1] Act III, Sc. 1.

theology mentions a third faculty of the soul called conscience.

Yet many people (one might safely say "most people"), if they reflected, would find that they cherish the notion of conscience as a special faculty, a kind of spiritual instinct, an inner voice whispering categorically of right and wrong, a mentor in the soul making instructive suggestions analogous to revelation, inspiration or immediate direction from God. Anyone with these ideas should pause to ask himself what and where his supposed special faculty is and how it operates. No such special faculty is known to theology.

Theology knows of two, and only two, faculties in the soul, intellect and will. Therefore, if conscience is in the soul, as obviously it is, it must be found in these two faculties.

In other words, conscience is not a separate reality, existing on its own. It is not a fixture, a permament thing. The mind and will are permanent, not conscience. Conscience is a *transient act* elicited by the mind in conjunction with the will. It is simply the mind and will in operation about a practical (as distinct from a speculative) moral issue, an *act,* not a habit.

There is the same difference between conscience and the soul as there is between a punch and a fist. The punch is an action of the fist, a thing the fist does. Similarly, conscience is an action of the soul, a thing the soul does. Precisely defined, conscience is the practical moral judgment of the intellect—the intellect being simply the soul itself, considered in its activity of knowing things.[2]

Conscience is defined in the text-books as a dictate of practical reason deciding that a particular action is right or wrong.

Whenever, in sermons, I have enunciated that definition, I have noticed animated question-marks on the faces of my listeners, registering doubt and the suspicion that this was a new-fangled and unorthodox definition of my own. No!

[2] F. J. Sheed, *A Map of Life,* pp. 90-91.

the definition is not copyright. It is the stock definition of the text-books.

Conscience is based on reason and is, in fact, almost the same thing as right reason in actual moral matters.

> Conscience, good my lord,
> Is but the pulse of reason.[3]

Here is an illustration of the working of conscience. On a very hot day in July, X. is out in the country, hiking. As he sits down to rest, weary and parched with thirst, he espies a tempting bottle of iced beer which is not for sale. Every moment the beer becomes more tempting, and something like this goes on in his mind. "Stealing is wrong," says the mind, enunciating a general principle of morality. "But," continues the mind, "if I took this bottle of beer, it would be stealing." "Therefore," concludes the mind, "if I took this bottle of beer, it would be wrong." Thereupon, the will, if it is rightly disposed, interjects: "Don't take it," which is a practical dictate of the mind.

If the will is not rightly disposed, something else may happen. If the will does not like the conclusion reached by the mind—and human nature being prone to evil, it often does not, as we all know from intimate experience—it will force the mind to reconsider the issue. Then something like this will happen.

"Stealing is wrong," says the mind. "Granted!" says the will, through the prompted mind, "as a general principle. But in these particular circumstances, isn't there reason for an exception? No decent person would refuse to give you the beer in these circumstances, so is it really stealing? Yes, all things considered, I think you may take it."

When the will is ill-disposed towards truth, the mind is often induced to indulge in wishful, or, better, in wilful thinking. When this occurs, we act against conscience. Conscience is always an affair of the mind, with the will butting in. Passions influence the will, the will influences the mind, and so "the wish is often father to the thought."

[3] Samuel Coleridge, *Zapolya,* I, 1.

> Men vehemently in love with their own new opinions, though never so absurd, and obstinately bent to maintain them, give those opinions also that reverenced name of conscience . . . and so pretend to know that they are true, when they know at most that they think so.[4]

The will has a powerful influence on practical moral judgments, i.e., on conscience; and that is why we must keep a vigilant watch on it, guarding it against impulse and self-will. Hence, too, the peace of God is promised, not to the "clear-minded," nor the "high-minded," but to "men of good-will." "Glory to God in the highest and on earth peace to men of good-will."

Possibly you are not conscious of any such process of reasoning in making your practical moral judgments. Probably not. In many moral matters, because you have thought out the issue before or been clearly instructed about it, the conclusion is immediately obvious and there is no need for a reasoning process. Conscience often gives its decision at once, without hesitation—in a flash. From this we get the idea of a voice. The dictate of conscience is, however, always the conclusion of a piece of reasoning, made now or in the past.

Ethics and moral theology supply the general speculative principles on which our actual moral decisions are based. Reason then applies general principles to our particular case and draws a practical conclusion, i.e., decides what must or must not be done here and now in *practice*.

Sheed explains the matter with his usual lucidity:

> . . . The intellect makes many judgments, and conscience only differs from the others by its special scope. If I answer the question: "Did Richard III 'murder the princes in the Tower?,' my answer is a judgment of my intellect; but it is purely a historical judgment, not a moral one; therefore, it is not my conscience. If the question is changed to: "Ought Richard III to have murdered the princes?"—my answer is again a judgment of my intellect, and this time it is a moral judgment, a judgment of right and wrong. But it is not my conscience, for it is not a *practical* moral judgment.

[4] Hobbes, *Leviathan*, Ch. 7.

that is to say, it is not concerned with what it would be right for me to do here and now. But if the question is again changed to: "Ought I to murder the man next door whose manners are so maddening?"—the answer is not only a judgment of my intellect and a moral one, but also a practical one.[5]

Conscience is, therefore, basically a matter of the mind, that is, of instruction, knowledge, clear thinking, mind-training.

Conscience is not an independent and self-sufficient guide. It is a judgment of the intellect, whose rectitude consists in its degree of conformity to objective truth. All men have the duty of conforming, as far as they can, to objective standards.

Conscience should depend not on what we think about things, but on what we *ought* to think about things. One of the greatest curses of religion is subjectivism. The subjective idea of conscience, the self-sufficient voice-theory, puts a premium on fanaticism, private interpretation, modernism, illuminism, and all those other fantastic pseudo-spiritual aberrations, which often have brought religion into contempt and diverted millions from it. Until the rational idea of conscience is made clear, there can be no cure for spiritual aberrations.

If a well-meaning yokel gets a fantastic pseudo-spiritual idea "into his head," nothing can be done about it, unless he can be brought to the bar of reason.

One youth "gets it into his head" that Christ was a pacifist; his conscience tells him so. His conscience is possibly a voice from the unconscious, originating in sheer funk. Psychology is very familiar with this kind of voice, e.g., a girl who died of starvation in a London hospital as a result of a self-immolation complex, told the house physician that "there was something at the back of her mind telling her it was wicked to eat."

One man "gets it into his head" that Christ was a prohibitionist, another that He was a nudist, another that He was a scientist, and so on, indefinitely; and even Catholics

[5] *Op. cit.*, p. 91.

shrug their shoulders fatalistically and say: "Well, after all, "it's his conscience. You must respect his conscience. You can't force a man to act against his conscience." And so Christ is made a mockery and His religion travestied, *in the name of conscience.*

Pathological symptoms must not be glorified with the name of conscience. Of course, you cannot force a man to act against his conscience, but you ought to be able to convince him that his conscience is wrong; and if he is not amenable to reason, he should be treated, not as a martyr for justice' sake, but as a spiritual invalid.

We must beware of muddling conscience with feeling and fif.

Conscience is not feeling. A guilty feeling is an indication, and establishes a probability, that we have acted wrongly; just as a feeling of satisfaction is an indication that we have acted virtuously. An indication and no more; because a guilty feeling is not necessarily induced by conscience and may be due to a phobia or an exsurgence from the unconscious mind of wrong ideas, due to a Jansenistic or Puritanical training. Certainly, a feeling of guilt should be firmly investigated and removed; by contrition and satisfaction, if it is found to be based on reason; by psychological means, if it is irrational.

Feelings must never be accepted as infallible guides in moral matters. If we pay too much attention to feelings, we shall become unstable characters, weather-cock personalities, "reeds shaken by every wind"; and we shall be in danger of imagining ourselves zealous or "pious, when we are only bilious." *De gustibus non est disputandum*—"argument is impossible about tastes." If conscience is made to depend on how we feel about things, the whole basis of the moral law is removed at one stroke; for then there can be no universal moral standards; in fact, no room for an infallible arbiter of morals, such as the Church.

The world would be a much saner place if all men could be prevented from confusing conscience with feelings and fif.

In his excellent book, *Now I See,* Arnold Lunn recounts

an amusing story which admirably illustrates the meaning of fif:

> "Oh, I think it's dreadful," I once heard a woman remark, "to deny that God exists. Of course, you can't prove He exists, but surely, surely, everybody must feel that there is a God."
>
> I happened to have been playing bridge that afternoon with the lady in question. She had a "feeling" that the blue cards would win. After the blue cards had lost, because she did not play the blue cards correctly, she had a "feeling" that the seat she was sitting in was unlucky. She changed seats, but she did not change her method of play, which was founded on emotion rather than on reason. After losing the second rubber, she had a "feeling" that it would help if she sat upon her handkerchief. Unfortunately, she never had a "feeling" that it would be wise to apply reason to her bids.
>
> I suggested to her that her intuition on the subject of God might not be much more trustworthy than her intuition on the subject of bridge.[6]

The same good lady probably had innumerable exasperating intuitions. It would not be surprising if, as a general rule, she "had a feeling" that it is wrong to play cards or the piano or the fool on Sundays. Or at least wrong for others to play cards on Sundays. If she were invited to have a game herself on that sacrosanct day, she would probably "have a feeling" that it was somehow right to play in the circumstances; and this—mind you—without deliberate insincerity and without the slightest advertence to her inconsistency. It is unnecessary to prolong the description. Haven't you met her? Could you not name her?

The Fifites are not insincere, but they certainly are tantalizing, and the harm they do to religion is incalculable. For all their tearful religious sentimentality, they are living on the level of "the ass and the ox which have no understanding."

A near neighbour of fif is bogus piety, sometimes called pietism, or "pietosity" (by those who think pietism too nice

[6] *Now I See* (Sheed and Ward), pp. 145-6. (See pp. 76-83 for an explanation of fif.)

a name). If piety is not carefully subordinated to reason, inevitably it degenerates into fif.

Sensible devotion is pleasant, and pleasant experiences we naturally desire to maintain or repeat. (By sensible devotion is meant, not commonsense devotion, but a feeling of satisfaction and relish in devotion.) Pleasure may easily be a snare and a delusion—even the pleasure called sensible devotion. After all, there must be some excuse for the puritans! Pleasure must be kept in its place, and its place is a secondary one. Pleasure is meant as a condiment of duty, mercifully given by God to make the fulfilment of duty easier. Sensible devotion, which is a form of pleasure, is no exception to this general rule.

Sensible devotion is of secondary importance and must not be sought for itself. We must not "seek the consolations of God, rather than the God of consolations," because, if we do, our quest is motivated by nothing nobler than self-love and refined sensuality.

Subtle self-seeking disguised as piety is one of the gravest and least suspected dangers of the spiritual life. Pietism originating in self-love leads to a systematizing of self-will, complete disregard of obedience and the will of God, and the glorifying, under false pretences, of self-indulgence.

The pietist has a false standard of values; he judges everything not by its conformity to or deformity from God's holy will, but by its capacity to occasion sensible consolation. Reading beautiful sugary prayers in church is more consoling than doing housework and makes one feel holier and more recollected, so house-work is neglected even though it is a duty, i. e., the clearly manifested will of God.

The pietist becomes unreasonable, head-strong, secretive and selfish. For the pietist the big world does not exist; its problems and perils mean nothing to him. He is detached; but with a detachment which is the last remove from the detachment of the saints. His detachment is founded on selfishness, laziness and sensuality. Provided he is left alone to continue his exercises of piety in peace, he is unconcerned if the rest of the world runs headlong into hell. Why should he concern himself about it? Is he his brother's keeper? Why should he go out into highways and hedges and compel them to come in?

The pietist has no sense of any obligation to inform himself and train himself to be an apostle of Christ, up and doing to win the world for God. If he is appointed to train the young, he concentrates almost exclusively on devotional exercises, and the impression is given that other things, such as study, deportment, culture and zeal are of very secondary importance. Is this a partial explanation of the ineffectiveness of Catholic countries and of some ecclesiastics and religious? The pietist cannot train strong, virile, broad-minded, energetic characters, because he is anaemic, sensual, spiritually flabby and purblind himself.

The pietists are affected with spiritual pride and patronize and look down on those who are not, in their esteem, pious. Newman and Ven. Dominic were crucified by complacent and supercilious pietists, not to mention the Master Himself, literally crucified at the instigation of the Pharisees.

Pietists are often given a false reverence and a very enervating tolerance. Despite selfishness, fatuity, lack of zeal, and other clear evidence of defective virtue, the pietist is treated as a bit of a saint "in his own way." His idiosyncracies and omissions are glossed over and palliated with the expression "after all you must admit that he is pious." Not at all —he is not pious. He is the worst of all the enemies of true piety and responsible for bringing the word "piety" into quasi-contempt. The pietist is warped, selfish and futile, and for his own sake, as well as for the sake of the nerves and souls of others, he should be made to realize it. Pietosity bears as close a relationship to true piety as lust bears to love.

The disastrous confusion of piety and pietism might be avoided if all understood the meaning of conscience and the implied supremacy of reason as the innate promulgator of the Will of God.

A right conscience depends on correct moral principles. Therefore, we must never cease to inform ourselves about the principles of morality and their application, nor allow our minds to get set and become closed.

We are never too old to learn, just as we are never too old to mend. We must always be prepared to revise our opinions and learn from experience. If we will not learn from experience, life is wasted on us. Whenever we suspect that our opinions are wrong or narrow, we must not shirk the mental labour of surveying honestly and, if necessary, re-laying our spiritual foundations.

The mind, instead of being a faithful mirror of objective truth, tends to be coloured and dulled by prejudice, fashion and environment. Beware of confusing conservatism with conscience, and manners with morals. Ideas are not necessarily correct because they are old-fashioned. We must keep the mind open to correction and to new ideas. Closed minds make moral and intellectual development impossible, and obstinacy and self-complacency inevitable.

"The fashions of this world pass away." We must not presume, therefore, that the fashions of our childhood were in every way correct and conformable to the best traditions of the Church. There seems to be a latent tendency in human nature to canonize the ideas and conventions that were fashionable in one's youth. Granny, for example, confident that she was correctly instructed in modesty, thinks that the modern bright-young-thing is a brazen wench; whilst Miss Modern, equally self-assured, thinks Granny a stuffy old fool. Neither has any doubt about the rectitude of her attitude, because, having been brought up in her own particular atmosphere, "she feels that way about it." Both have closed minds and are quite unprepared to modify their views. Neither will admit that something might be said for the other's point of view. Neither is entirely right, neither entirely wrong. They are both representatives of extremes; Granny of the Victorian extreme of hush-hush and unnatural reserve, Miss Modern of the opposite extreme of blasé rejection of reserve. Granny was hyper-modest and somewhat Manichean; Miss Modern is sub-modest and affected by naturalism.

If both parties had the humility to suspect the rectitude of their attitude, and bring the question to the bar of reason and faith, we might get somewhere and achieve sanity. But, instead of that, they continue complacently to sit in judgment and frown on each other, and display mutual irritation, with little or no regard for either charity or humility. Probably both experience difficulty in finding matter for confession!

Many of the disagreements of the old and the young, many of the recriminations of one generation against its predecessor, are traceable to a defective idea of conscience. Because all feel quite happy about their conduct, none see any reason why they should subject it to rational examination.

VOICE OF GOD

There is a consoling sense in which conscience can be called the voice of God, and it is this: God will always accept and approve our conclusions in matters of personal morals, whenever the conclusion is drawn in good faith—even if the conclusion is wrong.

Through no fault of our own, we may be misinformed; in which case, we shall start our reasoning from false premises and our conclusion will inevitably be wrong. God will not blame us for mistakes made in good faith.

Again, our logical powers may be undeveloped. We may start out with correct principles but by defective logic arrive, in good faith, at a wrong conclusion. God does not punish inculpable ignorance or incapacity, but only ill-will.

INDIFFERENCE

The study of conscience reveals the importance of what spiritual writers call indifference.

The will tends to exert undue influence on the mind and prejudice its judgments. To obviate this danger, the will must carefully be put in order before important moral judgments are made. The will must be reduced to indifference, i.e., to willingness to follow whatever course of action unprejudiced reason suggests. If, for example, we are undecided whether to go to the cinema or not, the will must be prepared to accept either decision, and await, not force, the decision. Beware of rationalization, i.e., of acting first, on impulse and without thought, and then thinking out reasons, or—better—excuses, for one's conduct afterwards. We must learn to look before we leap.

Practice should be adapted to principles; not vice-versa, principles adapted to practice, which human nature has a fatal tendency to do.

> In early days the Conscience has in most
> A quickness which in later life is lost.[7]

The reason for this fatal tendency deserves careful study. When the mind has drawn the same conclusion a sufficient number of times, it dispenses with the reasoning process and begins to take the conclusion for granted. The conclusion then becomes a premise for further reasoning. If the conclusion is a false one and is not quickly corrected, it is evident that a process of progressive distortion of spiritual vision has begun, which it will be difficult to arrest. False principles will lead to further false conclusions, and these in turn will lead to other false conclusions, and so on indefinitely.

The will adds to the danger of progressive moral deterioration, because it is a faculty very quickly influenced by habit. Acts of ill-will soon form habits of ill-will. When the mind and will conspire together against truth, the refinement and vitality of conscience must soon be destroyed. The mind may eventually cease to advert to its own mistakes and become "seared," to use St. Paul's expression; or "blinded," to use the still stronger expression of the Master.

We cannot guard the sensitiveness and delicacy of conscience too carefully. There must be no compromise with sin, no deliberate dulling, direct or indirect, of the sense of sin. Faults must be admitted as faults and amendment

[7] Cowper, *Tirocinium,* 109.

quickly made, or the consequences will be disastrous. We shall begin to live in a spiritual fog.

> This above all, to thine own self be true,
> And it must follow, as the night the day,
> Thou cans't not then be false to any man.[8]

There is great insight and wisdom in Shakespeare's words. But to be true to self is extremely difficult; in fact, the whole art of humility in compendium. If we are false to self, we shall be false to God. Human nature is so constituted that we must ultimately adapt our principles to our practice. That is why morals have such an important bearing on faith, why the practice of asceticism is more conducive to the knowledge of God than the study of theology, why those who count on a death-bed repentance are making such a perilous mistake, why Scripture says that "as a man lives, so shall he die."

"If thy eye be single thy whole body shall be lightsome. But if thy eye be evil thy whole body shall be darksome. If then the light that is in thee be darkness: the darkness itself how great shall it be?"[9]

Conscience is so important, and yet so mutable and malleable, that we must safeguard its integrity with most tender care.

HOW CAN WE SAFEGUARD CONSCIENCE?

First, by the practice of virtue.

Secondly, by training the faculties of the soul so that they may be prejudiced to act rightly in moral issues.

We must strive to keep the mind open, humble, unprejudiced and true. We must guard the will against precipitation, cowardice and passion. We can safeguard conscience effectively only by surrounding it with the armour of unexceptional virtue. One chink in our armour is enough to commence our undoing.

[8] *Hamlet,* Act. I.
[9] Mt. 6:22-93.

From what has been said, it should be evident that many of our expressions about conscience are inaccurate and misleading. Because of the complexity of conscience, strictly accurate terminology is difficult to find. "We say, for example, 'I have something on my conscience,' which is loose speaking. It would be more accurate to say: 'I have something on my soul.' "[10] We talk about "examining our conscience" and the impression is given of a permanent recording machine. It would be more accurate to talk about examining our *acts* of conscience.

Again, we are misled by the consecrated phrases of moral theology about an erroneous, a lax, and a scrupulous conscience. All these expressions seem to imply that conscience is at least a habit. Would it be more accurate to talk about a lax, erroneous or scrupulous moral *outlook*? No! that will not do either; because men who have a lax outlook where their own personal conduct is concerned, often (and, in fact, generally) have a very rigid outlook where others are concerned. In judging our own conduct, we are never disinterested nor entirely dispassionate, and a will prompted by passion and self-interest readily supplies excuses for loose conduct. When, however, we view the conduct of others, we are either disinterested and dispassionate, in which case we make no excuses; or we are passionate against them and moved by envy or dislike, and then we tend not even to allow for the excuses which could reasonably be made. There is liable to be a wide and unrecognized divergence between our outlook on other people's conduct and on our own. From the nature of the case, our judgment of personal conduct tends to be unduly lax, our judgment of other people's conduct unduly harsh. The die which is loaded in our favour is loaded against others.

The question of terminology is complicated by the inevitable intervention in actual moral decisions of passion and self-will.

The existing terminology will be passable enough if we know how to interpret it. When we examine our conscience,

[10] Sheed, *op. cit.*

let us be quite clear what we are supposed to be doing. We are not to examine our fears and the state of our feelings. Examining our conscience should mean a calm rational survey of our actions, contrasting them with the moral code to see how far they are conformable to it, and how far we recognized the conformity or deformity at the time of acting.

Beware of the voice, special-faculty theory of conscience. It is implicit heresy, and logically applied would dispense us from authority and lead to private judgment in the realm of morals. If we have an infallible guide within, we do not need an infallible guide without. The Church, however, is our infallible guide in morals as well as in dogma. By listening to her teaching, by absorbing it and making it our own, and not by cultivating subjectivism, can we form a right conscience.

Conscience depends on instruction and good-will. Let us, therefore, inform our minds and train our wills. We are not guaranteed personal infallibility, so we can never be certain of the objective rectitude of our decisions; but if we are humble and co-operate with grace, God will see to it that our judgments are always sincere, and therefore acceptable to Him Who "searches hearts and reins" and profitable for our eternal salvation.

What conscience dictates to be done,
Or warns me not to do,
This, teach me more than hell to shun,
That, more than heaven pursue.[11]

[11] Pope.

X

Feelings and Phobias

A SCRUPLE is often defined as "an uneasy and unfounded fear of having committed sin, based on feeling rather than on reason." Scrupulosity is an obsession of the moral conscience (technically called a phobia) causing a state of acute anxiety.

The scrupulous person lives in a spiritual fog which obscures all lines of demarcation between good and evil. Every moral issue which arises seems to present an insoluble problem. Whichever way the scrupulous look for a solution of their perplexities, their path seems beset with possibilities of serious sin. If reason says that a certain course of action is morally right, immediately a silly, nagging, interior voice pipes up that it is wrong, something at the back of their minds tells them so. Whatever the scrupulous want to do seems either wrong in itself or inspired by wrong motives. They are afraid to flout the nagging voice of the phobia, because they confuse it with conscience.

The scrupulous are sick and suffering souls who need to be handled with patience, reverence and tenderness. To tell them to pull themselves together is unkind and useless advice, because that is precisely what they want to do, but don't know how to do. To bait them as silly, obstinate or proud is uncharitable and may reveal either an insensitive or an unspiritual person. It is not very helpful either to tell the scrupulous that the funny-feeling inside is not conscience, because naturally enough they want to know what it is if it is not conscience.

The voice-theory of conscience confuses the issue. If conscience is a voice, and if in the souls of the scrupulous there are two contradictory voices claiming a hearing, how are they to decide which voice is the real voice of conscience? Must they follow the louder and more insistent voice? In that case, they must certainly follow the suggestion of the scruple, because it is the precise trouble of the scrupulous that the voice of reason is made scarcely audible by the megaphone clamour of the phobia.

The scrupulous cannot be cured until they are convinced that conscience is simply sound reason and that the phobia is merely the manifestation of a spiritual ailment. Once convinced of that, they can confidently turn a deaf ear to the nagging voice of the phobia. Ignoring the phobia will not cure it, but it will at least stunt its growth and, as it were, chop off the tops of the spiritual weeds as they appear. To remove the phobia completely, it will be necessary to find and remove its cause.

There are myriads of causes of scruples, ranging over the physical, psychological and spiritual planes, and to find the real cause in any given case is no easy matter and requires great patience, sympathy and skill. There is no panacea for scruples, no slick rule-of-thumb applicable in and sufficient for all cases.

SOURCES OF SCRUPLES

The cause of scruples may be and often is *physical.* People with indifferent health are an easy prey for worries, scruples and neuroses. Whenever we are unwell, we always tend to see the black side of things. People are often afflicted with scruples when they are suffering from shock, or from strain and nervous exhaustion caused by overwork, adolescence, change of life, et cetera.

It should be significant for these tortured souls that their attacks of scruples or, at least, their more violent attacks, are always contemporaneous with a severe nervous strain.

If the real cause of scruples is physical, the remedy must be sought on the physical plane and the person most competent to help is a doctor. The treatment will consist of drugs, tonics, rest, sleep, fresh air, nourishing food and such like. The confessor can help the doctor by assuring the patient that his trouble is really physical and that as his health improves, his anxieties and fears will vanish. Unless the physical nature of the trouble is realized, the patient will tire himself by endless self-analysis and a futile search for the non-existent spiritual causes of his worries. The patient must accept these interior trials as crosses permitted by God. He can help himself best by resignation, patience, refusal to follow up morbid thoughts suggested by his ailment, and by exercising the virtues of hope and charity. The more tranquil and cheerful he preserves his mind, the quicker will he recover both physically and mentally. A quiet mind has a very beneficial reaction on the body.

The idea of spiritual or mental trouble from nerves strikes some people as strange and materialistic. Obviously they have never reflected on the significance of Gethsemane. Our Saviour's physical agony in the Garden, severe as it was, was merely the redundance of the infinitely greater agony in His soul. In human nature there is a constant interaction of body and soul. A few examples from everyday experience should suffice to prove this. Melancholy, for example, easily produces digestive or heart troubles; temper and anxiety cause headaches; and so on, indefinitely.

The cause of scruples may be *psychological.* For example, an adult who has been brought up in ignorance of sex, will have scruples when he seeks to inform himself. However reverently he approaches the subject, however clearly he sees the need for instruction, he will not be able to prevent false ideas, the result of false upbringing, from surging up from the subconscious and unconscious mind.

A large percentage of the scruples of adults, especially of women, are traceable to failure to find the right attitude towards the fundamental instinct of race preservation. Many try to convince themselves that they are "above that sort of thing" and base their emotional life on a lie.

The scruples of adolescent girls are often due to an unconscious desire for attention, i.e., for love; especially if they are being starved of love, or the manifestation of love, at home.

Among adults, scruples often arise because, unconsciously, they are looking at things through the eyes of a timid parent or a prudish aunt. Unconsciously (note the word), they are asking at the back of their minds what So-and-So would say about this. Refusal to grow up and think for themselves accounts for the under-development, timidity and want of personality of some pious souls.

Other psychological causes of scruples are excessive emotionalism, a vivid and undisciplined imagination, a hyper-cautious spirit due to a too cautious upbringing "wrapped in cotton wool," and chronic lack of decision due to the fact that as a child the patient was never allowed to make up his own mind.

The causes of scruples may be *spiritual,* e.g., false ideas, bogey-ideas of God, defective knowledge of human nature, failure to distinguish between voluntary and involuntary actions, et cetera. All our conscious activity is conditioned by our ideas of God, and so it is almost impossible to exaggerate the importance of having correct ideas about Him. "This is eternal life, that you know the one true God, and Jesus Christ Whom He has sent."

False ideas of God often have a psychological origin; for example, a person who in childhood was so constantly found fault with and reprimanded by his parents that he got the impression that he could do nothing right and lost confidence in himself—such a one may unconsciously have transferred to God ideas of authority which derive from his parents' abuse of it. Hence he forms the idea of God as a fault-finder whom it is almost impossible to please.

The multiplicity and complexity of the causes of scruples should demonstrate the folly of doling out slick rules-of-thumb designed to cover all cases. There are no panaceas for spiritual ailments, any more than there are for physical ailments.

Scruples cannot be cured until the root cause of the disease is detected and removed. Every confessor is conscious of the fact that sometimes spiritual advice does not "register." The reason is because there is a hindrance to understanding on the physical or the psychological plane. A penitent, for example, who is addicted to vice is told to pray and go more frequently to the Sacraments and he seems almost to resent the advice. He does. In fact, he feels inclined to shriek: "I've tried all that, I've done all that, and somehow it doesn't work. Is there no other advice you can give me?" The penitent, who knows from sad experience that the advice is inadequate, not unnaturally feels resentful, and then probably gets a scruple that he has been critical and irreverent and disparaged the efficacy of grace and the Sacraments, with the result that his last state is worse than the first.

We must not expect God to work miracles to make up for our fatuity; and to expect a spiritual cure for a physical or psychological ailment is, in reality, to expect a miracle.

Scruples cannot be cured until it is recognized:

1. That phobias are not conscience; and
2. Whence the phobias originate.

The scrupulous naturally ask: "How am I to know what my reason does dictate? My reason is strangely silent."

A good plan is to ask what you would say to a junior sister or brother or friend if confronted with the same issue. Probably you would settle the question without hesitation. "Of course, it's not wrong. Don't be silly! Have you taken leave of your senses?" Apply the same decision to yourself, and don't say: "O! but my conscience is different." Your conscience has no right to be different. The moral law is the same for all, and, if rightly applied, leads to the same conclusions for all. Your conscience is not different; only your phobias, your nervous-system, your experiences are different.

Phobias must be combatted vigorously. The more ruthlessly they are trampled on, the better. Phobias are bullies; give in to them and they become paralysing tyrants; combat them and they soon slink off like miserable cowards. Scrupulous soul, prove yourself a disciple of Christ not Hitler. Beware of intuitions!

The scrupulous person should do everything in his power to cure himself of the dangerous malady of scruples. Here are a few suggestions to help in the work. The scrupulous person should:

1. Clarify his mind about the meaning of conscience.
2. Search for the root cause of his phobia.
3. Discipline his imagination, mind and will—the will, by forcing himself to make decisions.
4. Refuse to be side-tracked by every vain fear, and force himself to continue with his previous line of thought.
5. Develop his sense of humour.
6. Try to get a truer perspective of his own importance and realize that his ego is not a synonym for heaven and earth and the human race. There are at least a few other things worth thinking about! He could also profitably reflect on the following verse:

    Once in a fervent passion, I cried with
        desperate grief:
    "Oh Lord! my soul is black with guilt.
        Of sinners I'm the chief."
    Then came my Guardian Angel and whis-
        pered from behind,
    "Vanity, my little man. You're nothing of
        the kind."[1]

7. Try for a month to forget about himself and avoid any self-analysis. His problems can wait. If he will give his soul a "breather," he will be refreshed and in a better position to tackle his problems at the end of the month.
8. Think only of the goodness of God and pray for and develop hope and love of God.

[1] Anonymous.

9. Avoid all self-pity.
10. Ask his confessor to dispense him from integral confession and forbid him to examine his conscience before confession.
11. Throw off fear and act as though he were not afraid. Gradually there will be a beneficial reaction from the exterior to the interior.
12. Look after his health.
13. *Practice absolute obedience.* True, the confessor may not understand, but then neither does the penitent understand! Of the two, the confessor is by far the least likely to be mistaken.
    The penitent's spirit of caution should persuade him to obey, on the principle that of two evils (or dangers) it is always wise to choose the lesser.
14. Remember that no one was ever lost through obedience or saved by disobedience.

"Remember," says Quadrupani, "that according to the common opinion of the saints, the fear of sin is no longer salutary (and therefore cannot be from God) when it becomes excessive."[2]

In *The Screwtape Letters*, C. S. Lewis has revealed a shrewd insight into the tortuous subtlety of the devil. Screwtape owes much of his success to fuddle about conscience.

COUNTERFEITS

A bank which had no means of detecting true and false money, genuine or counterfeit cheques, would be liable to get into grave difficulties.

A spiritual soul who has no means of detecting counterfeit graces is at the mercy of the devil, whenever he chooses to appear as an angel of light. Without a clear understanding of conscience, it is impossible to have any true criterion for detecting bogus graces, with which the devil has broken many generous souls.

[2] *Op. cit.*, p. 61

Generous inexperienced souls often want to run before they have learnt to walk, and their impetuosity—which is due to the natural eagerness of youth and to secret pride—suits the devil very well. During times of great fervour, he insinuates the idea that God is asking for all sorts of "extras," and by so doing he throws the soul into a state of uncertainty and interior turmoil. The inspiration may or may not be from God, and the devout person is at a loss to decide. The inspiration may also be from the devil, who is anxious to overload and eventually break the soul with inevitable failure and discouragement. No possibility of a solution is offered by either the voice-theory of conscience or the special-faculty theory.

If the inspiration is rejected, the soul may be turning a deaf ear to God. If the inspiration is followed, the soul may be turning a too ready ear to the devil. If the inspiration is not followed, the soul may be minimizing and doing too little; if it is followed, the soul may over-reach itself by attempting too much. Whatever one decides, there is a possibility of mistake.

There is only one way of solving the problem securely, and that is by applying reason fearlessly, introducing the virtue without which there is no virtue—prudence.

Is the following of the suggestion beyond one's present development and grace, humbly considered? There is the crux of the matter. If it is, the inspiration is proved bogus, because to follow it would be unreasonable.

Lest this solution should sound too rationalistic, it is necessary to point out that there is no intention of insinuating that the conclusion reached by the conscience of the man of faith will always agree with the conclusion reached by mere reason. The man of faith starts out with different principles, and therefore his conclusions will frequently differ from those of the natural man. But, all the same, conclusions must always be drawn logically by the use of reason, even if the principles from which they are drawn are supernatural.

THE SAFE SIDE

In moral problems there is seldom an automatically safe side. Usually there is a juxtaposition of an obvious danger on one side and of a subtle and, therefore, graver danger on the other side.

The right side is always the reasonable side. And it is sometimes reasonable to take risks. "Playing safe" is not the same thing as prudence. In the parable of the talents, the Master castigates the man who "played safe," burying his talent to be on the safe side. He refused to trade, i.e., risk loss, and was condemned by his own servile principles. "Out of thy own mouth do I condemn thee. Thou knewest that I was an austere man, taking up what I laid not down, and reaping that which I did not sow. Why then didst thou not give my money into the bank, that at my coming I might have exacted it with usury."[3]

These words are being written in much-bombed London, where there are a few—very few—people who seldom leave their homes for fear that they may go into a district which will be bombed. It does not seem to strike them that their own district may be bombed in their absence and that instead of walking into danger they may be walking *out of it*. They are misled by a morbid, one-sided imagination, which concentrates on only one aspect of the question. As a result of their timidity and *false* myopic prudence, their lives are cramped and their normal activities considerably inhibited. How much cramping spirituality is due to a similar mistake!

The be-all and end-all of some selfish and stunted souls is personal security. "Safety first" is the dominating axiom of their spirituality. Their outlook starts and ends with self; and the main concern of their spirituality is about possible, and probably imaginary, perils to self. They must be on the safe side, they must save their skins at any cost; God's glory does not enter into their calculations. They treat God as a task-master and confuse servility and lop-sided sheer funk with prudence.

[3] Luke 19:22-3.

The moral virtues are always to be found in the middle between two extremes, *in medio stat virtus.* If we take sides at all, we take the wrong side. Timid souls, however, if they find themselves predisposed by nature towards one extreme, plunge right away into the opposite extreme in order to be, as they foolishly imagine, on the safe side. To avoid a possible mistake, they fling themselves headlong into making a certain mistake.

The man, for example, who finds himself strongly attracted towards women, becomes a "woman-hater" and commits innumerable sins of discourtesy and uncharity, becoming strangely unlike his Divine Master, Who was so courteous to women. Another person, naturally witty and jovial, adopts an attitude of taciturnity for fear of dissipation. In all this false prudence, of which examples could be multiplied, there is an admixture of laziness as well as of cowardice. These souls shirk the effort of self-control required to keep nature in its place, and strike the golden mean.

The remark was once made to a timid person: "If you had lived during the time of Jansenism, you would have been a Jansenist without a shadow of a doubt."

"Why?" he asked.

"Because," replied his friend, "whenever you are faced with a moral problem, instead of considering the matter calmly and rationally, you immediately get alarmed and plumb for the sterner side, which you mistakenly fancy is the safe side, and that attitude would infallibly have led you into Jansenism."

God has given us ten commandments only. If we make additions of our own, we imply that God's way is not safe, which is blasphemous nonsense and implicit, if unintended, lecturing of the Almighty. By all means let us do the harder thing, the supererogatory, provided our motive is love not fear; but let us not make commandments out of counsels.

To do the reasonable thing is never spiritually risky, whatever crabbed timidity may feel, because we can always count on the grace of God to assist us to do His will. In the name of conscience and prudence, the spiritually timid often throw grace and zeal and prudence to the winds. Mr. Funk, for example, is invited to become president of a secular society. If he accepted the invitation, the prestige of his office would greatly increase his power for good. He refuses, however, to accept the office for fear that his devotions might have to be curtailed or his humility be prejudicially affected. The office is accepted by a non-Catholic, possibly by an anti-Catholic bigot. Mr. Funk has no qualms or remorse, because he is too wrapped up in self to notice the opportunity lost or the implied insult to the grace of God. And all the time his real, though unconscious, motive was probably fear of not being a success and of the limelight revealing his limitations. What looked like humility was really pride. Funk, masquerading as prudence, is by no means rare.

To follow conscience faithfully in every circumstance of life is no mean nor easy achievement, and the man who genuinely attempts it soon becomes conscious of the inadequacy of human reason and of his need for the direction of the Holy Ghost. He is never sure that he has achieved objective rectitude in his actions, and so he is never self-satisfied nor impervious to advice nor critical of the actions of others. He is too much of a realist to have recourse to the stratagems of moral cowardice and seek refuge in safe-side tactics, misapplied, slick rules of thumb or in a self-righteous pose of consistency. He does not attempt "to be consistent but to be simply true." He is more anxious to be good than to appear good, even in his own eyes. Aware of human limitations, he expects to make mistakes, but he has sufficient trust in God to know that the Almighty will always be satisfied with an honest best and not blame him for mistakes made in good faith. And so, uncramped by fear, he has the courage of true humility. He lives and learns, because he is afraid neither to live nor to learn.

May the Holy Spirit grant us the liberty of spirit and the courage of true humility so that, like our Divine Master, we may grow in wisdom, age and grace before God and man, and reach the full stature of humanity and holiness planned for us by the Will of Good Pleasure of God!

No! Give to me, Great Lord, the constant soul,
Nor fooled by pleasure nor enslaved by care;
Each rebel passion (for Thou canst) control,
And make me know the tempter's every snare.[4]

[4] Newman.

XI

Bogeys

THERE is a good deal of truth in the saying that "the man you hate is the man you don't know." Not a few penitents are nervous about Confession, and if they do not exactly hate it, certainly dread it and suffer in varying degrees from an unreasoning dread of Confession—"the box."

One of the chief aims of these chapters is to show that this dread is due to misunderstanding and grossly exaggerated ideas of the requirements of Confession. The Confession you dread is the Confession you don't know. Many fear Confession not for what it is, but for what they think it is, most of their difficulties being home-made. Let us consider a few of the bogeys which often scare people as they approach the Sacrament of Penance.

DOUBTFUL SINS

Many penitents are tormented by doubtful sins. At the first onset of temptation, they become panic-stricken and confuse the sensing of the attraction of temptation with consent, so that every temptation becomes for them prospective matter for confession. About the past, too, they are always uncertain; uncertain if they confessed the sin at all, uncertain if they confessed it sufficiently, uncertain if they made the sin black enough, uncertain if the priest understood, uncertain if they were really sorry, uncertain until they are driven to distraction—if not to drink. Here is a specimen worry.

Remember that night some years ago when you were going home from a party. The sky seemed crammed with dancing stars as merry as yourself. The lamp-posts were obviously up to tricks and never seemed to be there when you tried to lean against them. Somehow you don't remember much more about it except that you woke up next morning with a bad head and got a terrible scolding from your wife. Unfortunately, there is no doubt about the incident, but you are not sure whether you realized at the time what was happening or was likely to happen, nor whether you have already confessed what did happen. Two problems worry you:

1. Was your lapse deliberate or indeliberate?
2. Have you ever confessed the incident; and if not, must you confess it now?

There is no obligation to confess doubtful sins. The catechism for the Diocese of Rome, approved by Pope Pius X, has this question: "If a person is not sure of having committed a sin, must he confess it?"

And the answer is: "If a person is not sure of having committed a sin, he is not obliged to confess it; but if he wishes to, he must add that he is not sure of having committed it."

The Council of Trent tells us that we are bound to confess all mortal sins of which we are conscious. In this case you are conscious, not of sin, but of a doubt about sin; and you cannot simultaneously be conscious of doubt about sin and of sin, any more than you can be conscious simultaneously of certainty and uncertainty in the same matter.

Common sense tells us that a doubt cannot create a certain obligation, any more than uncertainty can, of itself, produce certainty. If there were an obligation to confess every sin of which we are not quite certain, Confession would become a bugbear, especially to people with a bad memory. Doubts are, therefore, matter for solution rather than absolution, and are to be solved not absolved.

Many people will be inclined to object to this: "Yes, that's all very well in theory, but in practice, is it not far better to tell doubtful sins? In fact, would it not be unwise to omit them?"

It all depends. If very occasionally you remember such sins and do not make a habit of it, nor "get in a state" about it, then it is better to confess them just as they are, and have done with them. But if, on the other hand, you do make a habit of it and are constantly afraid of having omitted sins, then it is far better not to confess.

Experience ought to have taught you that you will not remedy things by repeating confessions. Be honest with yourself—has the repetition of confessions brought you any nearer to *lasting* peace of mind? If you are obsessed by doubts about past sins, you will not rid yourself of the obsession until you find and remove its cause. You are definitely in the scrupulous class and should employ the technique suggested in Chapters IX and X; and above all, you should contemplate assiduously the infinite mercy of God.

In all probability you are much more concerned about the damage and danger to yourself than about the injury done to God, so your scruples have no kinship with true contrition. Moreover, you are making the mistake, elsewhere indicated, of trying to make yourself secure by your own devices. You will never obtain the mathematical certainty which you desire, not even if you go on repeating confessions until Doomsday; so the sooner you give up trying and trust the mercy of God, the better for yourself. Behind all this worry there is probably a subtle worship of the "Great-I-Am." You are so surprised and indignant that the "Great-I-Am" should have failed so badly that you can't get over it, and turn in fierce indignation against yourself. The remedy for this fierce vindictiveness is humility.

MORE BOGEYS

A scrupulous person will still feel inclined to object: "But suppose I did omit a serious sin! You must admit that I *may* have left something out!" Granted. It is possible, though unlikely, that you may have omitted a serious sin in confession; *but even if you did,* provided the omission was not deliberate nor due to gross negligence, the sin was covered by the absolution. The sin is forgiven, you have satisfied the law of confession as far as you can; therefore, no further obligation can arise unless a *certain unconfessed mortal sin comes spontaneously to mind.*

The next move is with the Lord. If there is still a serious outstanding sin which He wishes you to confess, it is up to Him to bring it to your mind; and if He does not trouble to do so, it is safe to conclude that He wishes bygones to be bygones. If He does not recall the sin to your mind, He has no one to blame but Himself. Of one thing we can be certain and it is this: He will not half-do anything; whatever He does, He will do thoroughly and well. If He chooses to recall a sin to your mind, He will recall it with clarity and certainty, and not in a vague, foggy, disturbing way. His inspirations *never* destroy our peace of mind.

It should be easy to see that the Lot's wife obsession is a grievous temptation of the devil, who hopes by it to destroy your concentration on the present. Your concentration on the present, and the *graces* of the present, must suffer if you are always thinking of the past. Walking backwards, like walking blindfold, may be great fun in household games, but it is grave folly elsewhere. You cannot be always thinking of the past without being spiritually blear-eyed. If you would give as much time to finding and correcting your predominant fault as you give to worrying about the past, you would soon become a saint.

Before there can be any obligation to go back on the past, three things must be certain:

1. That what you did was a mortal sin in itself.
2. That it was a mortal sin to you.
3. That you have not already confessed it.

Consider the conditions carefully:

A Mortal Sin in Itself—Doubts about the objective seriousness of the sin can be solved easily and quickly by inquiry or study.

A Mortal Sin to You—In your childhood or youth you may have done something gravely sinful, without realizing the sinfulness then. God will judge you according to the knowledge you had *then,* not according to the knowledge you have *now.* "No afterthought or view of a past sin can make it a sin if, through ignorance, it were not such when committed, nor can any afterthought or subsequent knowledge make a sin greater than it actually was when it was committed."[1]

Many people in their youth practise self-abuse without knowing the seriousness of it. It would be a *lie* to confess such things as serious sins, because the knowledge required for serious sin was lacking. Mortal sin always presumes full knowledge of the gravity of the offence and full consent.

Not Already Confessed—If you have reason to believe that you did confess a sin, even if you have also reason to believe that you did not confess it, there is no obligation to go back. In practice this means that those who have always done their best at each confession, at least since their conversion, need never go back, because it is *morally impossible* that they could have omitted anything really serious. Therefore, they have *no real doubt* at all; or, at any rate, no doubt which cannot be solved quite easily by the application of a little calm commonsense.

A FALSE ASSUMPTION

Behind the worries of the Lot's wife devotees there often lurks a false assumption. Many people imagine that what they say in the confessional must correspond exactly, and to the letter, with what they did. If such accuracy were necessary, Christ might just as well not have instituted the Sacrament of Penance at all, because it would be practically no use to us. Probably we never, or hardly ever, tell our sins exactly as they are before God. In many cases it is *morally impos-*

[1] Walshe, *op. cit.*, p. 8.

sible, without special illumination from God, that we should achieve literally exact statement of what we have done. Take the case, not by any means unheard of, of a man who has been forty or sixty years away from the Sacrament. If he has to tell his sins with absolute accuracy, he might as well give up his soul as lost.

Had Christ required that in every circumstance, confession of past sin should be materially complete, allowing nothing for possible lapses of memory, He would have subordinated His gift, in practice, to the retentiveness of memory of the persons concerned; and as a man's sins accumulated in the course of his life and the necessity of receiving the Sacrament became the greater, the less capable would he have been of making the necessary dispositions, since to him, this integral confession would then be morally impossible. It was imperative, therefore, that however material this integrity must be in principle, it should be reduced in practice to such an integrity as circumstances of time and persons should permit.[2]

Absolute integrity in our confessions is generally unattainable and, therefore, not required: no one is bound to the impossible. *What is necessary* is that we *do our best* (not necessarily our bestest-best) to make what we say correspond with what we did, and having done that, we have done all that Our Lord expects or demands. He has not guaranteed us infallibility in Confession and therefore He neither expects nor commands it. Let us beware of insulting Jesus by presuming that He demands more than we can possibly give.

SPIRITUAL HYPOCHONDRIA

Another worry of penitents is sometimes occasioned by the foolish conduct of those who have an unhealthy craze for making general confessions. The example of this bogus thoroughness creates in sensitive souls a suspicion and fear that, because they never go back on the past, they may be too lax and easy-going. The devil seizes the opportunity and suggests that they are too lazy and cowardly, and too con-

[2] Galtier, *op. cit.,* p. 170.

cerned about their confessor's good opinion to do anything of the kind themselves.

The craze for making general confessions is a symptom of spiritual hypochondria and is distinctly unhealthy and morbid. We should think a man morbid if he wanted a regular X-ray of his internal organs just to reassure himself that they were in good condition. This is an almost exact parallel of what the spiritual hypochondriacs want to do, and one line of conduct is as wise as the other.

General confessions should be used sparingly, like castor oil; otherwise, the remedy will cause far more damage than the disease. A general confession is useful, if one has not been made already, when we are taking some very important step, for example, joining a religious order, or getting married. "It should be made once and well, and once for all."

Towards the close of life, or annually at retreats, it is profitable to make a simple review since the last general confession. An occasional overhaul is useful, but frequent overhauls are as useful for the soul as they are for a car.

Beware of spiritual hypochondria—it is a disease.

WANT OF FAITH

Worries about the past are generally the outcome of want of faith. "I should be so happy," says the doubting Thomas, "if only I knew that my past sins are forgiven!"

These unbelievers want experimental knowledge and *visible* proof of forgiveness, they desire to *see* their souls pure after Confession, just as they see their hands clean after washing. What they *need* is more virile faith. The desire for proof amounts to a refusal to live by faith. "Blessed are they that have not seen and have believed," and blessed are they who are content to take Our Lord at His word. He will not gratify the desire for the evidence of the senses, because He is too kind to deprive us of the merit of faith and trust.

Instead of following up their worries, the scrupulous would be far better employed making acts of faith, "I believe, Lord, help Thou my unbelief!" Instead of cherishing a secret notion of their own hyper-prudence, let them regard themselves instead as sadly deficient in faith and humility. In all their worries there is not a particle of piety but only a considerable amount of pride, cowardice and unbelief.

THE QUESTION OF CONSENT

It would not be surprising if the reader has already sighed with disappointment and said: "O! He's missed the very point I thought and hoped he was going to discuss. My main difficulty is not the distant past but the immediate past. What worries me most is the question of consent to sins of the mind, to sins of thought, especially in the matter of purity."

This is a big question, which cannot be adequately treated here. It is hoped, however, that the few principles which follow will be sufficient to solve the majority of cases of doubt about consent.

Let us consider the question of impure thoughts. It is morally impossible for a person who is habitually careful about purity to give full consent to impure thoughts without being fairly certain of it. When the will is habitually set against impurity, full consent to impure thoughts implies a somersault of the will, a *volte-face,* a turning round from North to South Pole. It is impossible for such a complete change to take place in the will without the mind being pretty certain about it. Uncertainty is, therefore, a clear sign that there was no full consent. In this matter we should go by what the theologians call "the law of presumptions." If a person regularly gives way to sins of impurity, in case of doubt it is probable that there was sin. If a person never or hardly ever gives way to sins of impurity, in case of doubt it is morally impossible that there was serious sin, for the reason just given.

In the latter case, there is *no real doubt,* and so no question of taking the benefit of the doubt, if we ignore the worry and, after making a short act of contrition for any partial consent there may have been, go blithely on our way.

Unless we do this, we shall fall easy victims to the devil of scrupulosity.

NOT BLACK ENOUGH!

People often worry about the confession of sins of impurity because they imagine that they did not make them *black enough.*

When confessing sins of impurity, it is neither necessary nor wise to go into details unless the circumstances change the nature of the sin. All that is required is to tell the kind of sin and the number of times it was committed. "Immodest touches once" would include any number of such touches at the *one session.* In this matter quite a lot is taken for granted; if, for example, intercourse is confessed, it is taken for granted that there were accompaniments; and so it is unnecessary to mention the fact. The time element need not, as a rule, be mentioned; because it makes no essential difference whether the sinful acts endured for five minutes or five hours.

In confessing sins of impurity, the rule is "No unnecessary circumstances, please!" In other words, there is no need to make them black—which statement can be taken in two ways with equal truth.

CONFESSION OF DOUBTFUL SINS

Do not confess doubtful sins as certain, to be on the safe side; because if you do, there won't be any doubt about your lie. It is a lie to confess as certain what you know to be uncertain; and such a surrender to unreasoning fear and timidity weakens both character and spirituality. Tell the truth and be simple and terse about it. If you think it more likely that you consented to sin, say so; if you think it less likely, say so—and don't waste a lot of time about it.

If you are doubtful about a sin, do not spend much time trying to solve the doubt, because the longer you analyse yourself, the more confused you will become, and you may even renew the temptation.

A SLIP OF THE TONGUE

Not infrequently one finds penitents who are distressed because they imagine that they have told a lie to the Holy Ghost and received absolution sacrilegiously. The genesis of the worry is generally something like this.

The penitent has neglected to tell the number of times he has committed a certain sin, probably a venial sin. The confessor asks: "About how many times have you committed this sin?" The penitent is confused, his mind suddenly goes blank and he blurts out an answer, which is, of course, nothing more than an honest guess. On reflection, he realizes that his guess was very wide of the mark and, possibly, a considerable understatement. He is paralysed by fear that he has committed a sacrilege.

Sacrileges are not so easily committed. An indeliberate mis-statement or error is not a lie. An honest guess is not a lie. The priest knew that a considered answer was impossible and, therefore, to safeguard the penitent, asked for an approximate number, *"about* how many times?" An approximate number was all that could be given in the circumstances and all that was asked.

What is the penitent to do when he discovers his mistake?

1. Learn wisdom. If sins are worth confessing, they are worth confessing accurately.
2. If there was a question of mortal sins, the penitent must confess the surplus at his next confession, which he need not anticipate.
3. If there was question of venial sins, he need do no more about it except learn wisdom.

You may ask: "If there was question only of venial sins, why did the priest ask about the number of times?" Probably to teach you to be more workmanlike and less slipshod in your accusations. More probably because he wanted to find out if the fault was inveterate or just a casual one. This knowledge might make a considerable difference to the advice he would give you. Dismiss your worry but learn from your experience.

THE OLD, OLD STORY

In the chorus of an old popular song, the words occur: "telling the old, old story, over and over again." Perhaps these words strike you as an uncomfortably accurate description of your ordinary confessions. For many people the sameness of their confessions is a real worry. "Father," they say ruefully, "I've always got the same old story. My weekly budget hardly ever varies. I have always the same list of sins." Well, cheer up—you always will have.

This worry reminds one of some of the old stories of the comedians: for example, of the story of the Scot and the Jew who went to see a play called *The Miracle*. The Scot went ahead to the box office and paid for both of them, whereupon the Jew turned on his heel and walked away. The commissionaire, seeing the Jew walk away, said to him:

"Aren't you coming in to see *The Miracle*?"

"No," said the Jew, "I 'as seen ze miracle."

The point of such stories is the shock or absurdity of a man suddenly doing something so utterly contrary to his disposition. Any such moral miracle would be so unexpected as to seem incongruous and make us laugh. Now, we all inherit a certain disposition which inevitably determines the tendencies of our personality. Both our virtues and our vices will follow in the wake of our disposition. If we began to act habitually in a way contrary to our known dispositions, our neighbours would decide that we were acting a part. If they saw that the change was genuine, besides having a fit, they would recognize a miraculous transformation and become either scared or amused.

If you are naturally inclined to be dour and humourless, you will not have to confess levity, nor excessive hilarity, and you will tend to be rather hard on those who have to confess them. Liverish, wet-blankety types won't be liable to fits of the giggles; it is a pity, but a fact! The naturally generous may have to confess prodigality, but never parsimony. Prodigality will not be included in the budget of the mean; though it might be a blessing if it were, because such a swing of the pendulum to the opposite extreme might tend to restore the balance.

Your nature remains the same, your temptations remain the same, the circumstances of your life remain the same, so it is hardly surprising that your faults remain the same. You can take it for granted that they will remain in the same grooves unless the circumstances of your life are radically changed.

If you were born with a short temper or a long tongue, you will always be troubled by your pet foible; but don't settle down to it in a fatalistic way as though nothing could be done about it. You cannot eradicate natural tendencies, but you can learn to control them, and the maintenance of steady self-control is the making of character and holiness.

It has often puzzled me how comparatively little even good people have to show for their many confessions, how they settle down into a sort of fatalism, as if they never could be or hope to be markedly better than when they started. There is no need to worry, then, because you have always the same list of faults; but there is real need to worry if you are doing nothing about it and taking the situation for granted, as though you could never reasonably hope to diminish the number of your failures and achieve gradually almost perfect self-control. It is a wise plan deliberately to persevere with the same list of sins, until you get sick of it and are driven in desperation to strong effort. You simply cannot, week after week or fortnight after fortnight, see yourself as you are, steadily fix your eye on a glaring fault, be heartily sorry for it and thoroughly ashamed of it, and yet do nothing to amend. Remorse, self-reproach, will after a time become so intolerable that they will goad you into action.[3]

Do not quote your disposition as excuse for your faults. One often hears people say: "O! it was my nerves!" "Nerves" are no excuse for getting on everybody else's nerves. We should be careful about our habitual faults, which harm our spiritual life and embroil our social relations more perhaps

[3] Considine, *op. cit.*, p. 108.

than we care to realize. We are aware what harm may be caused in the body by a slight derangement of one small bodily organ, for example, a bad tooth, a sore throat, or a spot on the lung. In the spiritual order, probably half or three-quarters of our troubles of mind and soul are due to similar spots, and if we removed them, life would be happier both for us and for others.[4]

Our faulty tendencies, like the poor, we shall have always with us, the occasion of myriads of graces and incalculable strengthening of character and enriching of personality, if we fight; the occasion of innumerable sins and of steady deterioration of character, if we shirk the fight.

THE SAME AGAIN

Another worry which bothers many people is often expressed like this: "Father, I am sure I shall do the same thing again, so my contrition cannot be genuine."

This very real worry is worth careful analysis. It originates in this way. First of all, the mind reviews the spiritual situation and surveys the past, the present and the future. Looking back, it sees many falls and considerable evidence of weakness of will. Looking to the future, it sees difficulties ahead, the same stale irritating difficulties; it takes into account the weakness of human nature, the difficulty of sustained effort, the monotony of routine, the effect of bad example, and so on. Having considered all this, the mind turns very cynically to the will and says: "It's all right for you to make your fine resolutions now. At the moment you are all keyed up, but tomorrow you will slacken off and then down you will go again."

The point is: Are you keyed up now? If you are, that is enough. All God asks is a firm resolution here and now; He does not demand a guarantee that your resolution will remain firm until the crack of doom. No one could give such a guarantee. "If anyone thinketh himself to stand, let him beware lest he fall." If here and now you are determined to try not

[4] Cf. *Ibid.*

to fall again, it is waste of time to speculate about the future. If you want contrition, you have it.

It is never wise nor humble to be cocksure of our resolution. Cocksureness is as disastrous and odious in the spiritual life as in ordinary life, and its root is pride, not strength. There are some who, after a good confession and after working themselves up to sensible sorrow, seem to imagine that they are quite changed beings, who will never be in danger of falling again. As a result of this delusion, they confide in their own imaginary strength. Their cry is very like that of St. Peter: "Lord, though all should deny Thee, I will never deny Thee!," and very unlike that of St. Philip Neri: "Lord, beware of this Philip or he will betray Thee! Lay Thy Hand upon my head, for without Thee there is not a sin I may not commit this day!"

When the presumptuous fall into sin again, they are surprised and indignant and become almost bitter and spiteful with God, as though He had let them down. It does not seem to strike them that they hardly deigned to ask God's help, and that since, in their hard-headed presumption, they tackled the task single-handed, they have no one to blame for their failure but themselves.

One strong resolution is not going to make us saints. The coalition of Satan, the "old Adam," the world and the flesh, is not so easily broken. It is neither wise nor humble to persuade ourselves that we shall never sin again. "He that thinketh himself to stand, let him beware lest he fall. . . . We carry our treasure in frail vessels." "We must reckon with possibilities of sin and even probabilities, if there is question either of venial sins or of mortal sins by which we have long been enslaved."[5]

Moral re-integration requires an uphill and tedious struggle and is hard to achieve, "the kingdom of heaven suffereth violence, and the violent bear it away." The wise man says: "I shall most likely fall again, but I am going to do my very best not to fall." The proud man says: "I shall never sin again."

[5] Scharsch, *op. cit.*

As you are making your purpose of amendment, the devil may insinuate into your mind something like this: "Don't flatter yourself! Do you fancy that *you* are going to avoid all sin? Why! you are still the same person, the same old two-and-sixpence, and always will be." The way to answer him is: "Yes, I know that I am the same person, the same old two-and-sixpence, and always will be. I know that I shall never be strong enough to vanquish you by myself. Of myself I can do nothing, but I can do all things in Him Who strengtheneth me." "Power is made perfect in infirmity." Spiritual strength comes from the recognition of our weakness and impotence, the strength of Divine Omnipotence.

Most worries about Confession would cease if all cultivated a spirit of trust in our Divine Saviour. Father Dignam, S.J., was once accused of treating a penitent with too much kindness. He replied, as a look of indescribable sweetness suffused his face: "Ah, you don't understand what a priest's heart is." Those who approach Confession with unending misgivings and torturing scruples do not understand the Heart of the Great High Priest, Our Lord Jesus Christ.

In the confessional, the priest feels an enormous compassion and a boundless desire to help. Add together the compassion of all priests who have ever been or ever will be and you have garnered nothing comparable to the Infinite Compassion Incarnate which broods over you whenever you present yourself at the confessional.

His compassion is more than maternal. If you were confessing a fault to your mother, you would be quite certain that she would make allowances for your confusion and shame and defective memory. The compassion of Christ is infinitely greater than the combined compassion of all mothers of all time. If you believe that, you must not treat Our Lord as if He were a proud, stony-hearted tyrant. We are missing the whole point of the Sacrament of Penance unless we approach it in a spirit of deep trust.

XII

Crocodile Tears

UNQUESTIONABLY the most important act of the penitent is contrition. The catechism tells us that when we have examined our conscience, "we must take time and care to make a good act of contrition." Note the words "time and care."

The Council of Trent defined contrition as "sorrow and detestation of sins committed, combined with the intention of sinning no more." The sorrow required must, of course, be based on supernatural motives.

Any misunderstanding of the meaning of contrition would entail misdirection of the penitent's effort and lead to innumerable worries and scruples. Contrition must on no account be confused with emotional sorrow.

BEWARE OF SOB-STUFF

It would be wrong to disparage the emotions and tenderness in devotion. The Missal has a prayer for the gift of tears; the saints often wept copiously, and the Master Himself did not disdain to weep. Tears and tenderness are useful when they are an overflow from the soul and not mere sentimental sob-stuff. God thinks as much as we do of worked-up emotions, and emotion which is an empty show and has nothing behind it, annoys us beyond endurance. Tears of contrition which are directly and deliberately induced, will inevitably be crocodile tears. If we weep at all, we must be able to say:

> I have that within that passeth show;
> These but the trappings and the suites of woe.

True contrition has no essential connection with tears and sighs because it is in the will, not in the feelings. It is possible, as a great theologian has said, to shed bitter tears over the death of a pet dog, and then make a good confession of mortal sins without shedding a single tear. At first sight it does seem absurd that we should feel so insensible about sin and be apparently more upset by the loss of a pet dog than by the loss of grace. Many find it difficult, in fact almost impossible, to believe that such insensible contrition can be really genuine.

A lady once told a saintly confessor that she had made a bad confession, because she had not had true contrition for her sins. "When my mother died," she said, "I wept greatly over my loss; but when I went to Confession, I did not weep over my sins."

The priest asked: "Would you commit a mortal sin, if you knew that thereby you could get your mother back with you?"

"Oh, no!" replied the pious lady quickly.

"That is enough," said the priest, "your sorrow for sin is greater than for the loss of your mother."[1]

Similar questions might be put to penitents who worry about the reality of unemotional contrition. If they were asked:

"Which would you prefer to lose, your pet dog or the grace of God . . . your best friend or the grace of God?," they would probably consider the question impertinent and answer indignantly:

"Why, of course, there is no comparison. It would be infinitely worse to lose the grace of God."

[1] Crock, *Grace and the Sacraments* (Wagner), p. 164.

"Quite so! But which would you *feel* most?" Would they not be forced to reverse their answer?

It is as impossible for the will to feel as it is for the eyes to smell or the nose to hear. A glance at the constitution of our faculties will make the reason for this clear and remove several misunderstandings. The reader is asked not to take fright and imagine that what follows is going to be difficult to understand. No ideas nor words will be introduced which a child could not understand with a little application.

In the body we have five senses, each with its own proper and exclusive function, namely, the senses of sight, taste, touch, smell and hearing. The senses are concerned with *material* things which we can see, taste, touch, smell or hear. In the course of life the senses come into contact with material things, by some of which they are attracted and by others repelled. As a result of the attractions and repulsions of the senses, the feelings (emotions, passions) come into operation. If an object is pleasing to the senses, the senses desire it and we have the passion of desire or physical love; if the object is displeasing to the senses, we have the passions of fear, hatred, et cetera. It is important to remember that the feelings respond to *material* objects and are normally affected only by material objects.

Now, in religion, we are not primarily concerned about material objects. Religion is concerned about God and the things of the spirit, with which the senses can have no direct contact at all. Truth is the object of the mind, not of the senses. The mind, therefore, has its own proper object and function, and we have as much right to expect the mind to get emotionally excited about the contemplation of truth as we have to expect the nose to start thinking deeply or the ears to prove themselves masters of logic.

The mind does not and cannot feel; it *evaluates*. An object may appeal to all the senses, and yet, although all the senses may clamour for it, the mind may decide that it is valueless or harmful or that to take it would be dishonest.

The senses and emotions respond to what is on the surface of things (the accidents); the mind tells us what things really are and their true value (the substance). The savage is deceived by gaudy trinkets and exchanges diamonds for them, because he is still an intellectual child who has not yet learnt to think, i.e., evaluate things. To safeguard a child against its own intellectual immaturity, we often warn it that "all that glitters is not gold," and that "appearances are deceitful." Emotional devotion stops at the surface of the things of religion and, because it contents itself with the titillation of the feelings and the arousing of the emotions (emotional sorrow, for example), never acquires a true sense of real spiritual values. This accounts for the intellectual immaturity which is unfortunately such a marked characteristic of pietists. Undue concern about emotional contrition betokens a person who has still to grow up intellectually and spiritually, or at least a person whose intellect has never been exercised in the sphere of religion.

The *will* is a spiritual faculty which follows the mind in its operations and is, therefore, no more capable of emotional excitement than the mind itself. The *will* is the faculty of *spiritual desire,* which loves with the love of *appreciation* and is as incapable of sensible love as the nose is of seeing, or the ears of smelling. Love of appreciation is exemplified when, for instance, we *appreciate* and love a person who has no superficial attractions, a "rough diamond."

Most of the worries about contrition arise because of ignorance of the respective functions of our various faculties. Penitents are distressed because the mind and will do not do something which they were never intended to do, that is, feel. The senses respond to *material* things; the mind and will respond to immaterial or *spiritual* things.

Now, when we consider the motives for contrition, for example the goodness of God, we are concerned with *spiritual truth,* which has no direct appeal to the senses. Even when we consider the mysteries of the Incarnation and Passion, we are not considering objects actually before us. The imagination, which is a sense-faculty, may try to conjure up sense-pictures of these events; or to help the senses we may make use of actual pictures; but it is obvious that these fantasies cannot affect the senses as powerfully as the living reality. The conclusion, therefore, is inescapable that we cannot normally expect contrition, even intense contrition, to produce outstanding physical and emotional effects. It is, of course, true that in human nature there is a constant mutual interaction of body and soul, and sometimes an intense attraction or repulsion of the will may react on the body and the feelings; as, for example, in the Garden of Gethsemane when Our Lord's mental passion produced the sweat of blood. This reaction, however, is by no means certain, even when the operations of the soul are most intense. Sometimes, as in ecstasy, the powers of nature are so completely used up in the soul, that the body is left in an almost dead condition. Sometimes intense sorrow petrifies the feelings. Real sorrow is often too deep for tears, and a person whose spiritual distress is so intense as to threaten life may seem calm and utterly unemotional. This is a common theme of the poets.

She must weep or she will die.[2]

Give sorrow words: the grief that does not speak
Whispers the o'er fraught heart and bids it break.[3]

The reaction from soul to body may also be inhibited because the body is in a particularly irresponsive condition, e.g., exhausted, nervously prostrated or emotionally aroused in a contrary direction.

It is a mistake and a temptation to set too much value on emotional contrition. If emotional contrition is an *unforced* overflow from the soul, it is a great grace and a sign and effect of the intensity of genuine contrition. If it is merely worked-up, it is worse than useless and is calculated only to induce hysteria. If emotional excitement were necessary for true contrition, sentimental and tearful penitents would have an unfair advantage; and the sentimental lady "who sends flowers to murderers and stinging letters to governors and gets guilt all mixed up with mother's silver hair and

[2] Tennyson.
[3] *Macbeth,* Act. IV, Sc. 3.

baby's tiny shoes" would positively wallow in contrition and get a delightful thrill out of it.

In striving to obtain contrition, it is a complete mistake to start with the emotions and try to make oneself "*feel sorry.*" As our supply of energy is limited, to use up more energy than is necessary in the emotions, actually impedes contrition. We shall obtain contrition by considering quietly the spiritual motives for contrition and by striving to stir up the will to a firm determination to avoid sin and its occasion. Strong characters are seldom highly emotional. "Though He slay me, yet will I trust in Him"—that is the spirit of true contrition. Though I find it hard to trust, though my senses still crave for sinful pleasures, though I am still spiritually insensible and emotionally cold, I will steel myself to do His holy Will, come what may. Steel myself—that is what we should aim at; steel myself to stand up to and overcome the difficulties involved in removing the occasions of sin.

If God gives us a passing, unforced grace of tears, it is a help which we should receive graciously and gratefully without cultivated hardness of heart. God is then the giver. If, however, we are cold and dry and have to struggle and do violence to ourselves to fulfil our obligations, then, in a sense, we are givers to God and "it is a more blessed thing to give than to receive."

Contrition consists in bracing the will to action. To feel sorry and to be sorry are not by any means the same thing. True contrition is essentially effective not affective; it may also be affective but it is not essential that it should be. Sorrow that is merely affective, sorrow that contents itself with sighs and tears is merely the sloppy sentimentality of those who "have only succeeded in softening the heart by previously softening the head."

A TEMPTATION

When it does not arise from ignorance and confusion of thought, there is self-love in the craving to *feel* sorry. We want to satisfy ourselves as well as God, and enjoy the *con-*

solation of feeling that we are forgiven. The desire for tangible reassuring proof of forgiveness reveals a character too immortified and weak to live by faith and reason. Let us beware that we do not pander to self under false pretences and secretly aim at satisfying ourselves when we flatter ourselves that we are aiming at satisfying God. It is well to remind ourselves from time to time that we should not go to Confession to enjoy pleasant things but to atone for the evil we have done.

A FURTHER QUERY

If the state of the feelings is never a reliable indication of true contrition, the reader may not unnaturally ask how he is to know that his contrition is genuine.

Do you wish to have contrition? "Of course!" "Then," replies St. Francis of Sales, "you have contrition by the simple fact that you wish to have it." "See," says St. Teresa, "if you have a sincere purpose not to commit sins which you confess; if you have, doubt not that you have also true sorrow."

Just as the proof of the pudding is in the eating, so the proof of contrition is in amendment of life. If you have amended your sinful life, there can be no possible doubt about your contrition. If you are really striving to amend, even though you are not entirely successful, you certainly have contrition.

Sometimes penitents who are striving to break away from an illicit attachment say: "My whole being seems to go out to X, and only my mind and will are on God's side," and on that account they doubt their own sincerity and contrition. Obviously, they have *great contrition,* since they are so anxious to centre the whole being on God. Great contrition can exist side by side with great weakness. Strength can be acquired only gradually. One intense act of contrition may rectify the will but it cannot make the will strong. The will is strengthened by habit, and a habit cannot be formed by one act or in one day.

Once again we are back at the old question of feeling

and willing. Scruples about contrition inevitably arise when the feelings are still violently attracted or repelled by the object of sin.

Many penitents scruple to go to Confession when they still feel angry or "hurt." Hurt feelings, like wounded bodies, can be cured only by time and nature's own healing forces. You can no more stop a wounded spirit from hurting than you can stop a flesh-wound from smarting.

"I said I couldn't help hating Dewsbury," said Freddy Carr. "He asked me if I really wanted not to hate him, and if I would try to be decent to him next time I met him. When I told him that I would, he said that would do, and the feelings part didn't matter, because you couldn't help your feelings."[4]

RELAPSE INTO SIN

Doubt about the sincerity and sufficiency of contrition is naturally occasioned by relapse into sin.

I am not suggesting that relapse into sin, whether mortal or venial, or going again into the occasion of it, proves want of amendment. On the contrary, avoidance of sin for a few weeks or a month or two, is evidence of true amendment, even if there is another fall. Even a fall soon after confession, in some peculiarly strong temptation or in dangerous and unforeseen circumstances, is no evidence against the goodness of previous confessions.

But, relapsing again and again, going into dangerous occasions again and again and making only weak efforts or only for a few days, are circumstances which cause very grave doubts as to the goodness of our confessions.[5]

A stock distinction of theology, the distinction between sins of malice and sins of weakness, will help us to judge the reality of our contrition:

Sins of malice are those committed in cold blood, with forethought and deliberation. Such sins imply a perverse will and should not be tolerated.

[4] Richard P. Garrold, *Freddy Carr and His Friends* (Benziger).
[5] Walshe, *op. cit.*, p. 12.

Sins of weakness are those which proceed from inadvertence, nerves, surprise and the infirmity and frailty of our nature, e.g., impatience, sudden spasms of temptation against purity not due to carelessness and toying with temptation, or perverse inclinations left by former bad habits of which we have repented.

St. Francis of Sales says that we shall do well if we get free of sins of weakness a quarter of an hour before our death. "We are obliged," he says, "not only to bear with the failings of our neighbour, but likewise with our own and to be patient at the sight of our imperfections. We must try to correct ourselves, but we should do it tranquilly and without anxiety. We cannot become angels before the proper time."

We must beware of bitter and anxious contrition, because it is counterfeit. The devil exploits the temptation of bogus contrition with great success.

True contrition, although it may rive the soul, never disheartens nor discourages nor demoralizes. "By their fruits you shall know them." True contrition renews our confidence, because it is founded on the certainty of pardon and help, and is inspired by the Holy Ghost, Whose office is "to fill us with ever-increasing confidence in God, by which we cry: Abba, Father." Our Lord would gain nothing by discouraging us, and to discourage is not His way.

Excitement and want of moderation in sorrow are alone sufficient to render it suspicious. "The sorrow of the saints, despite its strength, was always calm: there was about it nothing confused and anxious, nothing depressing and discouraging, no trace of anger and indignation."[6]

Depressing contrition, if it is not the outcome of temptation, is merely an ebullition of wounded self-love. Distress is caused because we have humiliated the Great-I-Am, not because we have offended God. We don't expect much from a dolt, and we are neither surprised nor disappointed if he acts foolishly. If, therefore, we are surprised and depressed when we act foolishly, it is evident that we cannot have realized before what spiritual dolts we are. We must have

[6] Scharsch, *op. cit.*, p. 124.

had a "big idea of ourselves" or we could not be so shocked and surprised.

Too much spiritual success would not be good for us. Our task is not so much to conquer as to fight and persevere and plod on patiently. We can command neither success nor sensible devotion. All we can do is offer God our feeble co-operation and leave the rest to Him, confident that "He Who has begun the good work will perfect it unto the day of Christ Jesus."

XIII

Remorse and Repentance

SORROW for sin has two aspects, two slants as it were, one backwards and one forward. Looking back, the penitent regrets and detests sin; looking forward, he determines to avoid it.

Determination to avoid both sin and its occasions, in other words, firm purpose of amendment, is the crucial test of the reality of contrition. He who is determined to do his best to avoid sin, undoubtedly has true repentance, even though he feels spiritually dry as a desert and indevout as an iceberg.

The proof of contrition is in the effective *will* to reform. It is all-important that there should be no misunderstanding about the true meaning of contrition; remorse must on no account be confused with repentance.

Judas said: *"Peccavi"*—"I have sinned"; David said the same. Judas had remorse; David had repentance. David was contrite, Judas was not. Both were sad about sin, both regretted it, both did not have repentance. Judas made a public confession of sin: "I have sinned in betraying innocent blood"; yet, despite his remorse and confession and restitution of his foully-gotten gains, he did not have effective repentance.

Remorse is a product of wishful-thinking and implies the *wish* to avoid sin; repentance implies the determined *will* to avoid it. Remorse is conditional; repentance is absolute.

The remorseful would like to avoid sin *if* doing so did not entail so much effort and sacrifice, and if he had enough faith, hope and charity. Contrition admits neither "ifs" nor "buts," and does not recognize the sacrosanctity of ruts. The remorseful would like to undo his sin, but he has not the requisite determination to remove the occasions of sin and surmount the obstacles to reform.

On this death-bed de Medici was filled with remorse and confessed to Savonarola. He would not, however, remove certain voluntary and unnecessary occasions of sin, so Savonarola rightly refused him absolution. His sorrow was selfish and sentimental, not effective.

A well-known principle of scholasticism: "*qui vult finem, vult media*"—"he who wills the end, wills the means," suggests the only true practical test of contrition, which is—willingness to use all the *necessary means* to avoid sin.

If we truly hate sin, we shall do all in our power to avoid it. If, however, we are unwilling to use the means, we deceive ourselves if we fancy that we *will* the end. Pilate *wished* to release our Divine Saviour; had he *willed* it, he could have released Him at once.

We must be careful not to confuse velleity and volition. A firm purpose of amendment implies more than a wish or desire; it implies determination.

The firm purpose of amendment is the most difficult act of the penitent. It is easy enough to have remorse for sin; in fact, unless our conscience has become completely atrophied, remorse is inevitable. It is not so easy to have effective repentance. St. Alphonsus says that most bad confessions are bad through lack of practical amendment; and authorities and citations to confirm his opinion could be multiplied.

Owing to the subtleties of self-deceit, it is fatally easy to mistake remorse for repentance. A penitent says, for example: "I am sorry for my sin, but do not ask me to break off abruptly and completely from the occasion of sin. I could not bear to appear unkind to one who has been so good to me. I do not want to hurt his feelings." Such a soul, like Pilate, is trying to serve two masters and have it both ways, and that is certainly not effective repentance.

Sometimes a penitent confesses theft. "When are you going to pay back the money?" asks the priest. "What are you going to do to get the money together?" The penitent has not thought of that; he has a vague intention of paying back at some uncertain date when he can do so without the slightest inconvenience, but the idea of doing anything practical here and now has not entered his head. That is not effective repentance either; in fact, such a confession is probably only a sop to conscience.

The story is told of an old woman on her deathbed, who was asked to renounce the devil. "Father," she replied, "is there any need to make enemies unnecessarily?" We may easily laugh at her *naïveté* without having even a suspicion how often we do the same sort of thing ourselves. Often we neglect our Divine Master through human respect, i.e., because we don't want to make enemies unnecessarily; we don't want to offend Caesar nor Jones. Effective reform of human respect is very difficult, and in this matter we are extremely prone to mistake remorse for repentance.

It is to be feared that the confessions of pious people are often deficient in true contrition. St. Francis of Sales complains: "Many confess their venial sins superficially and from sheer habit, without giving any thought to amending their lives."[1] They get "into the habit of thoughtlessly rattling off a list of habitual sins, which they have never seriously resolved to correct." These habitual sins they commit without remorse and confess without repentance.

I am not suggesting (and please note and remember this well) that the confessions of the pious are frequently bad. Not at all. Their confessions are saved from invalidity because they are habitually sorry for their more serious past sins, and probably for *some* of the less serious sins which they confess. Not infrequently, however, they are not sorry for *all* the sins they confess; and St. Francis of Sales says: "It is an abuse to confess small or great sins, if we do not intend to

[1] *Introduction to a Devout Life,* Bk. II, Ch. 19.

avoid them." Although we are not obliged to confess venial sins, we are obliged to be sorry for them *if* we do confess them; otherwise our confession is insincere, irreverent and pointless.

It is easy to imagine the following dialogue taking place in the confessional. After the usual preliminaries, the penitent begins to rattle off his customary list. The priest interposes:

"Now, look here, you have often confessed this sin before, haven't you?"

"Yes, Father."

"Any improvement?"

"No, Father."

"Well, what have you decided to do about it? What practical steps have you decided on to combat the sin?" Silence; and then the penitent blurts out:

"I have resolved not to commit the sin again."

"Very well! He who wills the end, wills the means. What means have you chosen to help you to avoid the sin?" The penitent has not thought of this and has contented himself with a vague resolution to avoid all sin. Vagueness in resolution creates suspicion of the reality of repentance. Whoever is very keen about a project, instinctively begins to consider ways and means of promoting it.

A woman, for example, who wants a new coat or another pair of stockings, and has used all her coupons, instinctively begins to look around for a likely donor of coupons; and the zeal of her search reveals the measure of her desire. During the war a man who was due for Home Guard duty on a particular night when he wanted to go to the theatre would naturally try to get a substitute or an exemption from duty. If he was very keen on going to the theatre, he would go to great trouble to make it possible; if he was moderately keen, to middling trouble; and if he was merely wishful, to no trouble. It is hard to conceive a keen desire that does not automatically lead to accurate planning and a careful survey of ways and means of achieving its purpose.

This reasoning makes our vague and general resolutions

seem very unreal and suggests wishful thinking rather than contrition. The way to Purgatory is paved with good intentions born of wishful thinking.

These considerations emphasize once more the folly and *danger* of dedicating the major part of preparation for confession to examination of conscience. If we are not sorry for sins, to confess them is humbugging irreverence; and if we have not decided to do anything practical to avoid the sins which we confess, there is serious reason to suspect that we are not really sorry for them. If we confess a big list of sins, it is hard to see how we can possibly have decided to do anything really practical about every single item on our list, and this for many reasons:

1. There isn't the time. The evolution of such a scheme of resolutions would require hours. Then,
2. We should require pencil and paper and many notes or an unusual photographic memory to enable us even to remember, let alone practise, our resolutions.
3. We should require very strong determination and unusually intense sorrow to be able to conduct a wise attack on such a broad front; and it is difficult to see how we could be roused to such resolve by a preparation for confession which leaves time for only a casual attention to contrition and amendment.
4. Vague resolutions leave a large loophole for subconscious self-deception; for example, a vague resolution to be kind to *everyone* may easily overlook the one person about whom it should principally revolve, i.e. that person at home or in the office who is really difficult and gets on everybody's nerves.

   Quite a number of people go regularly to Confession and yet never make the slightest effort to be less surly at home or more kind to someone at the office whom they dislike or of whom they are jealous. They go straight home from Confession and without any remorse are as cold and forbidding as ever. If they were taxed with this, they would immediately attempt to justify themselves by saying: "Why should I make all the advances?" Not only do they make no positive attempts to overcome their fault, but they don't even see why they should make any attempt; and yet they fancy that they mean what they say when they make a vague resolution to be kind to *everybody*!

People often sigh and look round for opportunities of proving their love of God and neglect the opportunities on their doorstep. Providential crosses are hard to bear, and we readily make excuses for dodging them.

Philanthropists are legion who will organize collections and raise funds (and take their expenses!) for destitute people in distant lands, and yet remain quite unconcerned about the destitute at home whom they shun with a shudder, fearing contamination for their hyper-hygienic selves. Philanthropy is an excellent exercise of charity because it enables one to feel self-satisfied, altruistic and important and does not disturb one's comfort, and it is quite compatible with emotional religion and fine resolutions.

There are plenty, too, of ranting sociologists who prate incessantly about social justice and *Rerum Novarum* wages and pay their own maid a mere pittance and their workmen the lowest wage they can "get away with."

"Humanitarians," says G. K. Chesterton, "go to look for humanity in remote places and in huge statistics. . . . But humanitarians of the highest type . . . do not go to look for humanity at all. For them . . . the nearest drawing-room is full of humanity, and even their own families are human."[2]

Theoretical virtue is one of the scourges and scandals of humanity. If we content ourselves with fine ideas and grand, untried resolutions, we shall practise fairyland spirituality and fail to see that in cold fact our virtue is all "in the air." It is comforting to feel how wonderful we are, even if it is only in the land of

[2] *Robert Browning*, "English Men of Letters" (Macmillan).

dreams; our fantastic eminence is a soothing compensation for our paltry achievement in the land of reality. Beware of fine-sounding, sweeping and vague resolutions!

5. Unnecessary compiling and reciting of a big list of sins may be subconscious escapism, a subtle evasion of the difficult task of really tackling them; in colloquial language, a "get-out."

   When we have made a big fuss and worked up considerable remorse and sentimental sorrow, it is easy to deceive ourselves that we are really contrite. Punctiliousness about peccadilloes makes us feel how careful and conscientious we are, and so restores our damaged self-respect. We are not so bad after all, and if you are sceptical enough to want proof, you have it abundantly in our fussiness and distress of soul.

   Sensible sorrow may be a snare and a delusion, because a penitent who rests content in it may not trouble to get down to brass tacks.

Confession without repentance involves self-deception and does us positive harm. The Sacrament of Penance does not operate like a charm, and absolution touches only those sins for which we are truly sorry.

It is possible to have a genuine general purpose of amendment against any and every sin, without an explicit purpose against each sin; but it is never wise to rely on such a general resolution, because, besides being in all probability ineffective, it does not enable us to discriminate surely between remorse and repentance. We should test our repentance by testing our resolution. "Am I willing to employ all the necessary means to avoid this sin, no matter what the cost?"—that is the crucial test of repentance. If we are determined to avoid a certain sin, we shall inevitably, and as a natural consequence of our determination, consider *how* we are going to avoid it.

Father Walshe, S.J., says very wisely: "Prayer, examination, confession, the act of contrition, all taken together, are easier, require less grace and far less mortification than conquering the dominant sin which I naturally like and that dangerous occasion which I naturally love."

The purpose of amendment is the most difficult act of the penitent, and therefore we should dedicate to securing it the major portion of our time and energy. At least a third of our preparation should be given to consideration of the motives for contrition; at least a third to formulating our purpose of amendment and preparing our plan of campaign; and never more than one third to examination of conscience, and sometimes not even that. Put first things and essential things first. Remember it is on contrition and amendment (which are really different aspects of the same thing and are not usually separated in the decrees of the Council of Trent) that the reality of our repentance and the value of the Sacrament depend.

It is not easy to detect our most real and insidious faults, and one of the chief reasons for our blindness is failure really to tackle the faults we do know. Perhaps the best way to discover the faults we don't know is to fight the ones we do know. In battle the weaknesses of an army become painfully evident, whereas in reviews and military exercises they may easily be overlooked. If we engage in real spiritual warfare and attack our enemies wherever we find them, our real deficiencies will soon become painfully evident.

It is not wise to spend almost all our time of preparation trying to find out faults, because we shall be better employed facing the faults that find us out and doing something practical about them. If we fight bravely and skilfully, our faults will find us out.

To sum up the whole matter in one sentence: Do less fault-finding and more fault-facing.

XIV

Tempered Optimism

IN PRECEDING chapters it has been pointed out that pious penitents are inclined to drift into a habit of rattling off a long list of sins, for many of which they have no effective repentance; and that remorse and repentance are not synonymous terms.

A sermon on these lines is generally considered very discouraging, and somewhat aggrieved listeners are liable to comment: "It made me feel that I have never made a proper confession in my life." To which remark, perhaps the best answer is: "Well, have you?"

Of course, all depends on what is meant by a "proper confession." What is your standard? What are your terms of comparison?

There are two possible terms of comparison:

1. *Validity*—i.e., a good confession as opposed to a bad confession.
2. *The Ideal*—i.e., a good confession as compared to a perfect one.

Between a good and an ideal confession, there is room for a vast difference of degree and intensity.

If the preceding chapter has made you feel, dear reader, that you have been making invalid confessions, then you have probably misunderstood it. If it has made you realize that your confessions have been far from ideal, it has done you great service. Complacency is a curse and the child of delusion. Blessed Claude de la Colombière said: "I think there are no souls with whom God is less pleased than those who are most pleased with themselves."

To avoid any danger of misunderstanding, it may be well to insist once more how easy it is to make a *valid* confession. (Cf. Chapter II.)

If a penitent goes to Confession sincerely desirous to avoid all mortal sin, it is morally impossible that he should not have the minimum of contrition required for the validity of the Sacrament. If he is not deliberately insincere, the mere fact of going to Confession proves contrition, or why would he go? The *onus probandi* is on the devil, not the penitent. No need for the penitent to prove that he has contrition; this can safely be presumed until the contrary is proved.

To secure validity, it is enough to be sorry for:

1. Past mortal sins, or for
2. One venial sin confessed; or
3. If the venial sins confessed are old favourites, hardy habituals, it is enough to confess with the intention of *reducing the number of faults*. This is a very important and consoling point.

It is neither wise nor humble to persuade ourselves that we shall never sin again. In the supreme and most sacred hours of life we must reckon with the possibility that we shall sin again. For this possibility always exists. It exists for all men in regard to venial sins; it exists also in regard to mortal sins for those who have long been the slaves of some vice. If such persons, when making a good resolution, honestly and sincerely admit: "I shall most likely fall again," they act more prudently than those who, by a sort of self-deception, persuade themselves that they will never sin again. It is a mistake to shut one's eyes to the realities of life. Therefore, when we have firmly resolved to sin no more, let us boldly say to ourselves (I speak here of venial sins only): "I shall sin again."[1]

[1] Scharsch, *op. cit.*, p. 189 (to whom I am much indebted in this chapter).

A humble realist will not promise or expect greater success. That does not mean, of course, that we can reserve a number of sins which we intend to commit in the future; we intend to try in every case, but we don't promise to succeed in every case.

It would not be surprising if this doctrine shocks some people and strikes them as dangerously lax. A reader who is inclined to be shocked by it could profitably answer these questions before God:

Have you not been confessing practically the same sins for the last year . . . ten years . . . twenty years? Have you even diminished the number of your "regulars"? Could you not almost confine your confession to saying: "Same again, father"? Are you not morally certain that you will have the same sins to tell next week?

In that case, if the above doctrine is lax, what becomes of the sincerity of your confessions? Do you mean to tell me that you expect to do more than diminish the number of your habituals before next week?

If this doctrine is lax, what of your conduct which falls below these lax standards? Harsh theory is usually a sign of lax practice. Rules seem easy on paper, but they are not always so easy when we come to try them out.

We could learn wisdom from an Italian boy, Livio Galeota, who died at the age of five. When he was preparing for his first Holy Communion, he wrote down the following resolutions:

"I will be a little better than before.
I will hardly ever get angry.
I will do my English a little better.
I will hardly ever do underhand things.
I will hardly ever be rude.
I will hardly ever do mean things to my brothers.
I will hardly ever do spiteful things to my brothers and sisters.
I will almost always do my English lesson well."

Of course, the wise little boy meant to try always to avoid these faults, but he did not expect to succeed, and with the genuine transparent honesty of a child, would not promise more than he felt able to fulfill. Would that we had some of the wisdom of that child!

St. Thomas has recorded the same childlike wisdom. "To repent of *venial* sins," he says, "it is necessary that the penitent purposes to avoid each particular sin, but *not all, because this would exceed our ability in this life.* He must, however, resolve to make an effort to reduce his sins; else he will run the risk of sliding backwards, because he gives up the desire to go forward."[2]

"It is not possible," says St. Francis of Sales, "to acquire dominion over your soul by your first effort. Be content with gaining a small advantage over your passions from time to time. We must learn to bear not only with our fellowmen, but also with ourselves, and have patience with our imperfections."

In the will, there must always be determination and hope to succeed in every case.

In the mind, however, there should be a wise recognition of the fact that we shall not succeed in every case, despite our best endeavours.

The mind, however, must not be allowed to depress the will. If our best efforts are hardly sufficient, indifferent efforts would doom us to disaster.

"He who has ceased to move towards God," says St. Leo the Great, "has ceased to approach near unto Him," and one might add, has begun to drift far from Him. The inevitability of failures should act as a spur and a warning against the folly of relaxing our efforts.

To say to oneself, therefore, "I shall most probably sin again," is a wise and humble facing of facts and a great safeguard against surprise and demoralization in failure. When sinful habits are combated, failures are to be expected. Without an exceptional grace, a habit is never broken at once, and a long struggle and many failures are inevitable before self-mastery can be established. Forewarned is forearmed.

[2] III, Q. 87, a. 1, ad. 1.

When a priest talks like this to ordinary penitents, his remarks are often received with surprise and suspicion. Obviously he is taking a low view of things and minimizing the power of grace; morever, he obviously does not know the strength of their resolution! Now that *they* have started in earnest, he will see!

Such thoughts are strongly reminiscent of St. Peter's words on the eve of the Passion. When warned of his impending fall, Peter by implication as much as told the Master that He did not know what He was talking about. Peter knew better than the Master. He found out his mistake to his cost. Beware of self-confidence based on ignorance and presumption and the notion that you know better than the confessor and the Church.

If you imagine that you will henceforth avoid all sins, even venial, besides being very unrealistic, you are getting dangerously near to heresy. Attentive study of the following words of the Council of Trent might chasten and correct your ideas:

"If anyone says that a person, in a state of grace, can avoid all sin, even venial, throughout his whole life, without a special privilege from God, let him be anathema" (i.e., he is a heretic).

Note well that the definition refers:

1. To a person in a state of grace, and
2. To a privilege, i.e., an exemption from the common lot, and
3. To a *special* privilege.

It would hardly be in accordance with Christian humility for any of us to presume that we are specially privileged.

BEWARE OF OVER-CONFIDENCE

Father Faber gives this wise warning:

> Resolutions must be founded on solid motives, and have been often meditated, not rash, or off-hand, or above our courage when we cool down out of prayer.

If anything, they should be below what we might reasonably hope to do and very humble. For things seem easy in meditation, so that we do not distrust ourselves sufficiently and God rarely strengthens an over-confident soul, and so we fail.

How many of the downcast tales which people tell about their not advancing, should go to the account of reckless resolutions made in the half-natural, half-supernatural heat of prayer?

Resolution must be tempered by prudence and humility. "He who thinketh himself to stand, let him beware lest he fall." "Power is made perfect in infirmity."

A sick man who had just emerged from hospital would not expect to walk at once with his accustomed stride. One who has been weakened by sin or who is still a novice in the spiritual life must not expect miraculous progress.

Over-confidence is a sign of ignorance or the self-deception of pride. No one would expect to get a consistent sixty-mile-an-hour from a Baby-Austin. And if you are still given to sin—occasional mortal sin or frequent venial sin—you are still only a spiritual Baby-Austin.

Over-confidence implies that we are too proud to admit our weakness or too ignorant to recognize it. The spiritually immature do not know what they are up against, i.e., the strength of the opposition; nor with what they are up against it, i.e., the weakness and treachery of the forces of human nature. They fail to appreciate the difficulty, not to say moral impossibility, of achieving complete sinlessness in fickle human nature prone to evil from childhood.

The sinner knows practically nothing of temptation, sin, and human weakness; ordinary souls know little; the saints know much. C. S. Lewis has made this point clear:

> No one knows how bad he is till he has tried very hard to be good. There is a silly idea about, that good people don't know what temptation means. This is an obvious lie. Only those who try to resist know how strong it is.
>
> After all, you find out the strength of the German army by fighting against it, not by giving in. You find out the strength of a wind by trying to walk against it, not by lying down.

A man who gives in to temptation after five minutes simply doesn't know what it would have been like an hour later. That is why bad people, in one sense, know very little about badness. They've lived a sheltered life by always giving in.[3]

The better you are, the more you will realize how bad you are. The more your strength increases, the more conscious will you be of weakness. The sinful and tepid follow their impulses without a second thought and give way to self in blissful ignorance. Fervour, however, excludes one from this fool's paradise, and intimate experience soon convinces the fervent of the cunning of self-love and the difficulty of self-control.

Those who expect to weed the garden of the soul easily and quickly are still wearing blinkers and betray ignorance of the extent of the overgrowth and the tenacity of the weeds. If they had started to weed, they would not nurse such great expectations, nor be so ready with stern rules.

"To expect to keep any resolution," says Father W. Doyle, "till repeated acts have made it solid in the soul, is like expecting to learn skating without ever falling . . . the more falls, the better, i.e., if you don't mind bumps."

So do not doubt the reality and strength of your resolution because you find the fight harder than ever, and do not expect swift or complete victory. Untempered optimism leads to inevitable and shattering discouragement and sometimes even to spite and bitterness against God. The self-confident, who never really relied on God, tend to feel that He has "let them down."

We shall save ourselves from disillusionment, if we strive to appreciate *what we are up against*—and what entire freedom from sin would imply.

We have, first of all, to contend against three powerful enemies—the devil, the world, and the flesh.

Then, it is presumed that we are struggling against a habit of sin. A habit implies that acts in accordance with it are easy and almost second-nature; acts against it, difficult. A

[3] *Christian Behavior* (Macmillan), pp. 57-8.

habit of sin implies that sinful acts are easy; acts of virtue difficult. When, therefore, we are combating sinful habits or a natural perverse inclination which is equivalent to a habit and called a quasi-habit, *the odds are against us.* Fighting against odds, we cannot reasonably expect an unbroken succession of victories. We cannot expect to win all the time.

WITH WHAT WE ARE UP AGAINST IT

"We carry our treasure," says St. Paul, "in frail vessels." Human nature is a damaged and second-hand instrument of war. God gave it to Adam intact and in perfect working order, but Adam did not pass it on to us in the same condition. Poor fickle human nature!

> . . . Sometimes joyful, at other times sad; now at peace, again troubled; at one time devout, at another indevout; sometimes fervent, at other times sluggish; one day heavy, another elated. . . .
>
> As long as we carry about this frail body, we cannot be free from sin, nor live without weariness or sorrow. . . . Oh, how great is human frailty, which is ever prone to vice! Today thou confessest thy sin, and tomorrow thou again committest what thou didst confess. Now thou purposest to be upon thy guard, and an hour after thou art acting as if thou hadst made no resolution.[4]

We are liable to an endless variety of evil inclinations; inclinations to unkindness, obstinacy, defiance, impatience, quarrelsomeness, annoyance, touchiness, desire for revenge, pride, overbearing vanity, ambition, selfishness, contempt of others, egoism, hypocritical piety, lying, cowardice, human respect, disloyalty, self-deception, deceit, carping criticism, rash judgment, idle gossip, tale-bearing, temper, sloth, waste of time, laziness, effeminacy, neglect of duty, immoderate worry about worldy affairs, sensuality, impurity, lust, injustice, intemperance, gluttony, et cetera. What a list one could compile!

Promptly and decisively to oppose these natural tendencies towards sin, i.e., as soon as we become aware of them and

[4] *Imitation of Christ,* Bk. III, Ch. 33; Bk. I, Ch. 22.

without hesitation and dilly-dallying, would require a persevering vigilance, a supremely alert and firm will and tremendous spiritual energy such as only the saints had: and even they not without failure.

Not to oppose these tendencies at once means semi-deliberate venial sin. If this doctrine seems discouraging, think again, and on second thought you will find it pregnant with encouragement. In any case, discouraging or not, it is true. Face facts, but please take careful note of the facts.

Note well what is asserted and what is not asserted. It is *not asserted*:

1. That these tendencies are in themselves sinful; or
2. That failure to oppose them at once, i.e., semi-deliberate consent, is ever a mortal sin; or
3. That these failures may not easily be corrected and are not generally repaired. Father Faber was fond of quoting the saying of St. Francis of Sales that as we often fall almost without advertence, so we often rise almost without advertence.

In other words, what is asserted is simply this, and no more, that to oppose, invariably and without delay, the evil tendencies to which human nature is prone, is extremely difficult; in fact, without a very close union with God and an outstanding development of the gifts of the Holy Spirit, morally impossible.

Without a doubt, the grace of God confers on us power to vanquish all our spiritual enemies, "I can do all things in Him Who strengtheneth me." "My grace is sufficient for thee." Invariable victory, however, implies invariable and instant recourse to God; and, for the moment, we are speaking of those who, because they do not realize the strength of the opposition or the frailty of human nature, rely on themselves and therefore do *not* call upon God.

"Power is made perfect in infirmity . . . When I am weak, then am I strong." Until self-reliance is shattered to bits, until we despair of ourselves, until we are stunned by the magnitude of the task before us, we shall go on *unconsciously* trusting in ourselves, subtly flattering ourselves that we are something "in ourselves, as of ourselves," and, in consequence, we shall not employ, or only half-heartedly employ, the power of God. "Power is made perfect in infirmity" and only in infirmity, fully admitted and firmly embraced.

Our impotence need not scare us; in fact, we should love and hug it. "Gladly therefore will I glory in my infirmity, *that the power of Christ may be made manifest in me.*"

If our spiritual incapacity does scare us, we have still an inadequate comprehension of it. Our failures are due, not to our weakness, but to our refusal—or, better, our neglect—to employ God's strength.

The remedy for failures is to be found neither in bemoaning our weakness nor in trying to bolster it up by practising spiritual gymnastics recommended by psychologists, but in striving for closer union with God and in turning with renewed confidence to His power and omnipotence. If we clung to God without fail, we should advance without failure. The weapon of spiritual victory is always at hand—God's omnipotence; and failure means that we have neglected to use that weapon. The remedy is obvious—use it now. The power of Christ will not be made manifest in us until we give it full scope and full credit.

We must not expect self-conquest to be easy. There would not be much point in it, if it were. An athlete would not derive much satisfaction from beating a rabbit. A victory is hardly worth winning unless our opponent is a match for us. Now, if you wrestled with an opponent who was a match for you, you would not hope to win easily and quickly and to have things all your own way. You would be up one moment and down the next; the contest would sway backwards and forwards. The strength and agility which you showed in the contest would not be so important as the spirit. An actual defeat might be a moral victory.

Suppose John and Tom are contesting the high jump. The pole is at five feet. John clears it easily at the first attempt. Tom has to make four attempts before he succeeds. Which of the two requires and shows the greater determination and spirit?

To refuse to be daunted by failure shows a brave and determined spirit. V.C.'s are not always given to those who succeeded at the first attempt. The steadfast refusal to be stopped by failure reveals a strong purpose of amendment, not lack of it.

When it is asserted, therefore, that the proof of contrition is in effective reform, it is not implied that if you are truly penitent you must be winning non-stop and convincing victories, with never a stumble nor a check. Do not decide, therefore, that your purpose of amendment is dubious because you have not yet managed to crush habitual faults. If you are determined to go on trying, all is well. "He to whom God has given a firm will to serve Him," says Blessed Claude de la Colombière, "should be discouraged by nothing." "Strive manfully, and let thy heart take courage."

We cannot command victory. Our task is to sow the seed, but it is God Who gives the increase. "We must, therefore," says the *Imitation*, "have patience, and wait God's mercy, 'till this iniquity pass away, and mortality be swallowed up in life.' "[5]

To persevere without faltering we shall need great *patience with ourselves*. Patience, like charity, begins at home, for we need far more patience with ourselves than with others. The idea is very prevalent that impatience with self is commendable and a sign of earnestness, whereas it is almost certainly a sign of ignorance or pride.

Reflect well on the admirable advice of St. Francis of Sales:[6]

Believe me, Philothea, as the mild and affectionate reproofs of a father have far greater power to reclaim his child than rage and passion; so when we have committed any fault, if we reprehend our heart with mild and calm remonstrances, having more compassion for it than passion against it, sweetly encouraging it to amendment, the repentance it shall conceive by this means will sink much deeper, and penetrate it

[5] 2 Cor. 5:4.
[6] *Op. cit.*, III, Ch. IX.

more effectually, than a fretful, injurious, and stormy repentance. . . .

Raise up your heart, then, again whenever it falls, but fairly and softly; humbling yourself before God, through the knowledge of your own misery, but without being surprised at your fall, for it is no wonder that weakness should be weak, or misery wretched: detest, nevertheless, with all your power, the offence God has received from you, and return to your way of virtue, which you had forsaken, with great courage and confidence in his mercy.

The whole chapter could be read with great profit. Elsewhere the same wise director says:

Whenever we commit a fault, let us at once examine our heart and ask whether it does not still entertain an ardent and definite wish to serve God. I hope it will answer "Yes" and will rather suffer death a thousand times than be false to this resolution.

Let us then ask: "Why did you stumble now? Why are you such a coward?"

It will answer: "I was taken by surprise, I know not how; I feel so dull at present."

Ah, our heart must be forgiven; it failed not because it was perfidious. We must correct it meekly and calmly, but not grow angry at it and thereby add to its confusion. We should say to it: "Dear heart, take courage in the name of God! Let us rise and go ahead; let us be on our guard and soar up to God, our Saviour." Our soul deserves to be treated kindly as long as she does not deliberately fall into sin.[7]

In the spiritual life, real success and apparent success may be poles apart. Real success is proportioned to our effort not our victories. It is possible to be making a greater effort than ever before and yet not be as successful as we were.

This apparent retrogression may be due to a variety of causes, amongst others, to the fact that the strength of the opposition has been increased.

For example, suppose your major habitual difficulty is impatience due to temperament. If you have become a confirmed invalid, your nervous system will be adversely affected and your tendency to impatience increased. The opposition

[7] Quoted by Scharsch, pp. 190-191.

will be, let us say, twice as strong as before, and victories may be halved, no matter how hard you try.

Or you may have been transferred to a more trying environment, and, instead of being surrounded by agreeable people, be thrown in with disagreeable and uncongenial ones. Obviously, results will tend to vary. Examples could be multiplied.

Novices in the spiritual life usually make rapid initial progress, and faults are quickly eliminated and narrowed down to a few. Then progress seems to stop or become negligible. The tenacity of faults increases as their number decreases. The remaining faults we shall never completely vanquish and drive from the field—not even if we become saints. "We shall be lucky," says St. Francis of Sales, "if we get rid of some faults half an hour before our death." And elsewhere: "Self-love dies with our natural death . . ."—and not a second before!

This truth should neither discourage nor dismay us. It is *God's plan.* Our weakness is permitted, to drive us like frightened children into the arms of our heavenly Father, to prevent us from acquiring that independence which was the undoing of Adam and the fallen angels, and to present us with innumerable opportunities of self-conquest and increase in grace.

"If strength were always our share," says Bossuet, "we should soon grow proud and overbearing; therefore, God has found a middle way: He gives us strength, that we may not perish in our infirmity; but lest we become overbearing in our strength, He wills that it be perfected by infirmity."

St. Francis of Sales puts the truth still more forcibly:

> Solomon says that the bond-woman who is raised to the rank of mistress is an unbearable cad. A soul that has been the slave of evil passions for a long time, would be in great danger of becoming proud and vain if she suddenly became sole mistress over them. This dominion must be acquired gradually, step by step, as the lives of many holy men and women, who spent years in attaining it, bear evidence.
>
> We must have patience with the whole world, and most of all with ourselves. As soon as you begin to exercise your-

self a little in patience, everything will move along splendidly; for the meek and loving Redeemer, who has inspired us with an ardent desire to serve Him, will furnish us with opportunities to do so.

He undoubtedly delays the hour of fulfilment, in order that it may be more beneficial for you; for behold, His loving heart calculates all events of this world and disposes them to the advantage of those who wish to submit without reserve to His divine love. The happy hour for which you long will come on the day which Divine Providence in the sweet councils of His mercy has set aside for it.

"I do not say to you," writes St. Teresa, "that no imperfections must creep into your life; but I do say that, when something of this nature occurs, we should take notice of the fault and realize that we have failed." Apparently she thought honesty and sincerity with self more important than victory. One of the major difficulties of the spiritual life is to learn to face our faults without bluff, presumption or discouragement.

The weakness of human nature should not scare us, but it should chasten us and make us chary of rash promises. Those who, at each Confession, glibly promise to sin no more and say without qualms or hesitation: "I will not commit any more venial sins," obviously do not realize the full import of their words and reveal rash self-confidence or superficiality and spiritual immaturity.

It is laudable to wish not to sin again, but to wish is not to will. Let us beware of emotional bluff and wishful thinking. When we make our resolutions, our dispositions should resemble those of a man throwing at cocoanuts. There is nothing to stop him from knocking a cocoanut over at every throw, but, in his heart of hearts, he does not really expect to do so, and he is not discouraged, but even made more determined, by failures. Each time, when he is about to throw, he is certain that he is going to succeed this time and puts all his energies into his effort. "Every time a cocoanut," cries the stall-owner, and we smile and don't believe him. "Every time a cocoanut," whispers our wishful-thinking, presumptuous self-love, and without a smile we do believe, to our own detriment and discouragement.

Let us learn wisdom from experience and not go on forever making the same elementary and childish mistakes. We must not allow the blinking of our weakness to produce false optimism and presumption, nor must we permit the recognition of our weakness to produce discouragement and despair. "Our help is in the name of the Lord."

"Man's perfection does not consist in being perfect, but in constantly striving to be perfect," says St. Bernard.

Virtue results from perfect co-ordination of distrust of self and trust in God. The secret of perseverance and spiritual success is to be found in a careful assimilation of two texts of sacred Scripture: *"Without Me, you can do nothing,"* and *"I can do all things in Him Who strengtheneth me."*

XV

I Will Repay

THE Sacrament of Penance! It is significant that this designation of the Sacrament of Forgiveness is seldom used nowadays except in books. The word "penance" is unpopular and falters on modern lips.

Penance, a relic of cruder and less enlightened times, is outdated. Our approach to God is now more spiritual and attaches less importance to the merely corporeal. We prefer to mortify the spirit—the mind, the will.

It is to be feared that if we do not mortify the whole of our nature, we do not really mortify any of our nature. Human nature is made up of body and soul, and spirituality which tries to divorce what God has joined together cannot be sound. Penance which does not crucify soul and body can be neither adequate nor effective.

In the early Church, the Sacrament of Forgiveness was indeed a Sacrament of *penance*. Severe, and sometimes prolonged, penances were invariably given for serious sins. The primitive custom was to defer absolution until penance had been performed, and to this rule no exceptions were made apart from a case of urgency or danger of death.

In later times, there has been a marked mitigation in the administration of penance, and today corporal austerities such as fasting, abstinence, denial of comforts, etc., are practically never imposed. It does not fall within my scope to discuss the reasons for this change of policy.

A survey of the discipline of the early Church would almost inevitably lead one to wonder if our modern sacramental penances are adequate. It is not hard to imagine an early Christian denying most emphatically that they are adequate. In fact, when one comes to think of it, it is not easy to see how they can be adequate. Does it not seem absurd to imagine that an easy devotional exercise, such as the Rosary, can make adequate satisfaction for mortal sin? How can a sin which merited hell be so easily atoned?

We must not overlook the fact that sacramental satisfaction gains its efficacy principally from the infinite satisfactions of Jesus, our Saviour. "We are bought with a great price. By His bruises are we healed. We were not redeemed with corruptible things, as gold and silver . . . but with the precious blood of Christ, as of a lamb unspotted and undefiled." "Who His own self bore our sins in His body upon the tree; that we being dead to sins, should live to justice."[1]

In the Sacrament of Penance it is not so much we who satisfy, as Christ Who satisfies in us. The making of sacramental satisfaction is a corporate effort; the penance which is performed in union with Christ is Christ's penance and, therefore, it is impossible to fix any limits to the potentialities of sacramental penance except those fixed by defective co-operation.

Co-operation presumes and postulates operation. The early Christians stressed the necessity of the maximum operation of free-will and did their best to secure it. Modern practice stresses the aspect of Divine co-operation and would have us use Christ's satisfactions to the full.

It is possible that the early Christians somewhat overlooked the vicarious efficacy of sacramental penance. The tendency today seems to be to lay insufficient stress on the necessity of personal penance. Possibly the early Christians did not leave enough to Christ, and it may be that we, forgetful of the axiom that "God helps those who help themselves," tend to leave too much to Christ.

Each practice of the Church has its reason and its lesson.

[1] Peter 2:24.

It is absurd to suppose that a Rosary said anyhow, with little devotion or love, can make adequate reparation for mortal sin; and if we think it can, we reveal a *very* imperfect appreciation of the heinousness of sin. Tepidity leaves very little scope for Divine co-operation. We must beware of a slipshod perfunctory performance of penance, motivated and occasioned by a presumptuous and quasi-Protestant reliance on Christ's satisfactions.

One is inclined to wonder how our modern light penances can ever be adequate for the perfect obliteration of mortal sin. Perhaps the truth of the matter could be stated this way: comparatively light devotional penances may be adequate satisfaction for mortal sin, if they seem to us inadequate; whereas, they are almost certainly inadequate, if they seem to us adequate.

Perfect contrition obliterates all sin. "Many sins are forgiven her, because she has loved much." Perfect contrition obtains complete forgiveness from God; but the perfectly contrite cannot forgive himself.

Some years ago a priest had difficulty in convincing a convert of the legitimacy and utility of re-confessing past sins which were presumably already forgiven. "After all," he said, "the sin is forgiven, so why drag it up again? Does not God say that 'He will cast all our sins into the bottom of the sea'?[2] 'As far as the east is from the west, so far hath He removed our iniquities from us.'[3] It seems to me, Father, that all this raking up of the past is morbid and dangerous and savours of distrust and false prudence."

The priest knew that his friend was happily married and still very much in love with his wife, so he said to him: "Look here! if you have hurt your wife by doing something thoughtless or selfish, do you apologise once?" "No, I don't, father," was the reply, and further argument was unnecessary; in fact, the convert became quite enthusiastic about this doctrine of renewed apologies.

The true penitent has no doubt about his forgiveness,

[2] Matt. 7:19.
[3] Ps. 102:12.

but the very certainty of pardon only makes his sin seem all the more unpardonable. God's love has withstood the most crucial test, He has refused to be embittered by our snubs and insults and neglect; His patience and long-suffering have given us an intimate and touching revelation of the strength and immutability of His personal love; and the more we realize His love, the more we realize and regret what we have done.

The older we grow together, the more I understand His delicate sympathy of heart, the more I realise what it is that I have done. It is a lasting shame to me, a lasting agony, which only increases with time. He has forgiven; all the more it is impossible for me to forgive myself. He has forgotten, at least so far as not to let it come between us; all the more can I not forget, but must be drawn the more to Him on its account.

Though all is past and done with, yet the sorrow abides; though love has increased, yet the pain is always there; though friendship has restored me to equality, yet the craving is greater now than ever it was before to make atonement and to show Him that I am true.

I know now of what I am capable; I know now how much His friendship can be trusted; and the fact that we both love each other the more because of what has happened, does but make me remember without ceasing the injury that I once did Him.[4]

Peter had no doubt about his forgiveness, it was the very manner and ease and certainty of his forgiveness that afflicted him most—the refusal of Jesus to upbraid or demand an apology, the pathetic piercing look of sorrow not anger, the utter lovableness and gentlemanliness of the Master, was just what made the thought of having denied Him so utterly intolerable. Peter never forgave himself and we are told that the tears of his repentance wore furrows in his cheeks.

"My sin is always before me," said David. This is the authentic cry of the true penitent. The really contrite can never apologise enough. The more he thinks of his fault,

[4] Archbishop Goodier, *The Meaning of Life* (Benziger), pp. 25-6 (slightly adapted).

the more does he want to make reparation. The true lover of the Master is not content to give as much pleasure as he has previously given pain, he wants to give more and more and more.

There is nothing morbid about true contrition, no gloom nor discouragement nor despair. Counterfeit contrition is morbid, but true contrition is consistent with great joy of heart.

Contrition is bogus and morbid if the desire to go back on the past is based on a determination to "make assurance doubly sure." Bogus contrition implies defective faith and hope, and manifests excessive self-love not fervent love of God. Bogus contrition bewails the hurt to self not the hurt to God.

Abiding sorrow for sin, based on faith, hope and charity, is one of the greatest graces we could ever receive, softening the heart, fostering humility, patience and charity, and safeguarding us impregnably against pride and presumption.

Abiding sorrow for sin will tend to make us dissatisfied with the light penances given in the confessional. Contrite love is ingenious in finding means of making reparation; feeble love baulks at the very idea of reparation and sees no necessity for it.

If we are content to say our penance casually and then think no more of our sin, it is morally certain that our penance is not adequate. The less we need penance, because of the intensity of our contrition, the more we shall desire to do penance; and the less we desire penance, the more we shall need it.

The efficacy of sacramental satisfaction is determined by our dispositions, for grace can effect nothing without the co-operation of free-will. The doctrine of free-will is the key to the understanding of the necessity for penance and satisfaction. God respects our free-will and will do nothing without our free co-operation. If the will turns out of the straight, nothing can turn it back into the straight except itself.

Every sin is an abuse of free-will and implies two things; first, a turning from God; and, second, an inordinate turning to the creature. Rectification of the will after sin requires an equation between the turning from and the turning to God. Otherwise, the will still remains somewhat out of the straight. To repair the damage caused to the will by sin, we must mortify ourselves to the same extent that we have previously indulged ourselves unlawfully. Contrition may be sufficient to restore us to the friendship of God, and insufficient for the perfect rectification of the will; and when that is the case, sacramental satisfaction will have to be supplemented by private penances.

Note well that when any necessity for private penance still exists, the obligation arises from the nature of the case and not as the result of implacable Divine vindictiveness.

The effect of sin on the soul may be compared to the effect on the leg of a loose cartilege in the knee. A loose cartilege, besides impeding and damaging the knee, causes a sympathetic nervous shrinking and weakening of all the muscles of the leg. When the offending cartilege is removed by surgical operation, the damage done to the muscles of the leg is not automatically repaired. To restore the leg to its former strength and agility, massage and vigorous exercise are required. Similarly, when the guilt of sin is removed by sacramental Confession, the effects of sin, such as the weakening of the will, the furrows of habit, the increased sensibility and accentuated proneness to sin, etc., are not necessarily completely removed *ipso facto*.

In many cases, too, sin reveals to our spiritual enemies the breaches in the ramparts of our souls. Renewed and vigorous attacks are to be expected at our weakest points, and to meet them we shall need increased and not diminished strength. The enemy gains renewed strength and confidence when he discovers where we are vulnerable.

Moreover, many of our sins besides offending God and damaging us, also damage the soul of our neighbour. This damage, too, must as far as is possible be repaired. If you had set your neighbour's house on fire, and the fire was still raging, you would not consider that a casual apology absolved you from all further responsibility and left you free to go your own way in peace, leaving others to put out the flames. "So the tongue also is indeed a little member, and ... behold how small a fire what a great wood it kindleth."[5]

Uncharity, anger, jealousy, pride, frivolous behaviour are the occasions of many sins. If we have injured our neighbour by scandal, justice requires that we should make reparation and, by prayer and penance, obtain for our neighbour at least as much grace as we have previously caused scandal.

From the obligation of making satisfaction for the harm done to others, God could not dispense us without being unjust to our neighbour. From the necessity of making satisfaction for the harm done to ourselves, God could not dispense us without being unkind to us. God would not be truly kind if He seconded our laziness and allowed us to remain the shrunken, desiccated relics of our former selves that sin has made us. The exaction of the last farthing of satisfaction is evidence of God's anxiety to bring us up to the ideal which He had in His Divine Mind when He created us.

The exacting of satisfaction is also intended as a deterrent against sin. If we "got away" with sin too easily, we should inevitably conclude that sin was a matter of little moment.

God's wisdom and mercy alone would demand that He bring home to men the evil of sin; otherwise, the very ease with which forgiveness is obtained would be an incentive almost to further sin, since, with no evil consequences to bear, they would see in it little to fear and would thus give way to it without resistance.[6]

Sin cannot be repaired without trouble, i.e., without sorrow, mortification and penance. This is not a pleasant truth, but it is the truth, and nothing is to be gained by bluffing ourselves that the way to Paradise is through a fool's paradise.

The temporal expiation outstanding for sin may be very considerable, and this many do not realize. Especially where

[5] James 3:5.
[6] Galtier, *op. cit.*, p. 191.

sin has accumulated through the whole course of a person's life, where little or no attempt at reparation has been made, where perhaps the prospect of complete forgiveness at the last has even led on to further sin, we cannot wonder that the debt should also be increased, for the discharge of which many works of satisfaction will be required.[7]

Our Lady alone was Immaculate and sinless; therefore Our Lady alone had no need of personal penance. The majority of us are far from sinless, and therefore emphatically do need penance, and perhaps a considerable amount of penance. Are we doing penance? Have we the spirit of penance?

The spirit of penance is a reliable test of the reality of our love of God. The true lover can never forgive himself for having hurt the Master, and his sorrow expresses itself not merely "in word" but "in deed and in truth." Abiding sorrow for sin is an outcome and sign of intense love of God. The holier we are, the more penitent we shall be. The spirit of penance of innocent saints is one of the most striking paradoxes of hagiography.

If we have not done penance for sin, we need wonder no more why the spiritual life remains difficult and our success negligible. There are too many obstacles in the way of the operation of Divine Grace.

Legitimate self-love, therefore, as well as love of God, should impel us to be instant in making satisfaction for sin. That fine old English prayer, the Jesus Psalter, has an invocation: "Jesus, send me here my purgatory!" The attitude of mind implied by that prayer has much to recommend it, because:

1. Satisfactions made in this life are meritorious and win for us new degrees of grace and glory.

   Satisfactions made in Purgatory are not meritorious and merely satisfy.

2. Satisfactions made here on earth are more efficacious than those made in Purgatory.

   If we utilize the satisfactions of Christ (which we can

[7] *Ibid.*, p. 193.

> do only on earth) He will, as it were, pay nine-tenths of our debt; whereas, if we leave off payment till Purgatory, we shall have to solve the whole debt ourselves.

It is, therefore, incomparably easier to make satisfaction here on earth than in Purgatory. These truths, which have been briefly stated, are worth careful pondering.

Let us beware that we do not allow the present mild practice of the Church in the matter of penance to mislead us into thinking that it is an easy matter to make adequate satisfaction for sin. "Unless you do penance, you shall all likewise perish . . . do penance for the kingdom of God is at hand." These words have not been, nor ever will be, revoked. "Heaven and earth shall pass away, but My word shall not pass away."

Beware of a careless attitude towards sin and a slipshod approach to the Sacrament of Penance. To approach the Sacrament of Penance without a spirit of penance is ridiculous; and such an approach reveals a spiritual dullard.

Is there any voluntary penance in your life? When did you perform your last act of penance? Is your sin always before you?

Thanks to the influence Christ exercised over our souls, there is nothing in our lives that cannot be used to make compensation for our offences against God. In order to lead an upright life, even to pray well, we must needs put ourselves to inconvenience and to trouble. The material element of satisfaction, then, is to be found in every work that we do, and we are constantly meeting opportunities of suffering in our path. It only remains for us to animate our conduct with the intention of making satisfaction; then, even those vexations and trials from which there is no escape, even sickness and death, can be made a real reparation for sin, provided that we accept them according to God's intention, as the chastisement for sin.[8]

In a spirit of penance let us try to sanctify the trials of life. It might also be wise for us to suggest bigger penances, such as we can conveniently perform, to our confessor, e.g., the

[8] Galtier, *op. cit.*, pp. 189-90.

Rosary every day for a week. If we usually say the Rosary daily, why not give our recital sacramental efficacy as well? The confessor is often restrained from giving an adequate penance by the fear of scaring us from the Sacrament or of imposing an obligation which, if not satisfactorily discharged, may be an occasion of further sin.

"Ego retribuam"—"I will repay." That should be our motto with regard to sin, and we should not be afraid to make our motto known to our confessor.

XVI

The Centre of Gravity

A TANTALIZING question for spiritual writers is why Confession produces such apparently insignificant results. One confession, perfectly made, could transform a life-long criminal into a saint; in fact, a priest once saw a sinner, who died after Confession, go straight to Heaven. This fact suggests some disconcerting considerations, for we who have been to Confession hundreds or even thousands of times cannot help contrasting what our confessions might have done with what they have actually done. The contrast is disappointing and suggests something wrong in our method. However, notwithstanding their partial failure, it is probable that our confessions have done very much more for us than we realize. Indubitably they have saved us from innumerable falls and may have prevented complete moral collapse. Rowing against a swift stream, it is no mean feat to have maintained our position.

Confession has done much for us, yet there is no doubt that it has been partially ineffective and might have done much more. Several reasons for our failure have already been suggested. If we desire to get the maximum benefit from Confession, we must

1. *Know what we want,* and
2. *Want what is best.*

The man who knows exactly what he wants, usually gets it; whereas the one who does not know what he wants, merely flounders about. If we know what we want, we can choose our means wisely; but if we do not know where to go, we cannot decide which way to go.

Father Faber attributes the comparative failure of our confessions to *want of purity of intention;* and undoubtedly he has hit on one of the major causes of our failure.

It is to be feared that penitents often go to Confession without any very definite aim; they would be at a loss to give a prompt answer if they were asked suddenly what exactly they hoped to achieve thereby.

Some penitents approach the Sacrament of Penance simply because they are in low spirits and want comfort and consolation; or because they desire spiritual direction; or just because it is Confession day; or because they meet a friend going to Confession, who asks them to go with him. Other penitents go to Confession solely because they want to prepare well for Holy Communion, or because they desire to be able to gain plenary indulgences and shorten Purgatory, or because they fear punishment for their sins.

Now, no one can quarrel with these as partial motives, because unquestionably they are good motives, but all the same they must *not* be the *principal, dominant* ones.

FOG OF SELF

Read through the list again, and you will see that all these motives are actuated by self-love, legitimate self-love, but self-love all the same.

Motives which terminate with self do not go far enough, because our aim should be Divine Satisfaction, not self-satisfaction. Our major motives should always be Deo-centric, not ego-centric.

The danger is that we may go to Confession mainly because we want to restore or safeguard our peace of mind, or because we "feel better for it." The accent in that case is very obviously on self. Refined self-interest is not a satisfactory principal motive for Confession.

We should approach Confession because we desire to love God more and serve Him better, so that He may look upon us with greater pleasure and satisfaction; in other words, "that we may know Him more clearly, love Him more dearly and follow Him more nearly."

Let us beware of spiritual myopia.

SPIRITUAL MYOPIA

It is true that Penance is a sacrament specially designed to remove obstacles to God's love and service, but we must not lose sight of the end which it serves. Removing stains, deleting sin and restoring peace are not the final ends of Confession.

Today people are asking how we can prevent world war happening again. To rest content with military victory would be fatal. We shall have laboured in vain if, now that peace has come, we simply sigh with relief and settle down to selfish self-content. We won the last war and lost the peace, and by so doing threw away the fruits of victory. War is always unavailing unless its lessons are assimilated and applied.

Every good confession is a real victory over spiritual enemies, and the result is peace, the peace of God which surpasses understanding, peace so sweet as to put us in danger of clinging to it inordinately and with self-complacency.

Our peace must be temporary, however, unless we learn the lessons of war and prepare for war. We have a right to rejoice in victory, but we must not stop there. Our outlook must be broad and comprehensive and take in its survey past, present and future—the past, that we may recognise and remedy our mistakes; the present, that we may stifle any renascent self-reliance; the future, that we may prepare our plan of campaign. We ought to be more concerned about God than self.

God will not treat us like robots, so the spirit in which we approach Confession is all-important.

Our first task is to *purify our intention* and *clarify our minds*, so that we shall know exactly what we want and want what is best.

Then we must approach the sacrament in a *spirit of confidence*. We shall acquire confidence easily if, first, we pray for grace to make a good confession. We may spend as much or as little time in this as we choose, but we must never omit it.

CONTRITION

It is especially important that our attempts to excite contrition should be God-centred. This is where many fail.

Contrition will be proportioned to our love of God; therefore, we should study the lovableness of God more than sin.

Sorrow always depends on love. Love is the quicksilver which makes the barometer of interest go up or down. If, for example, you do not love Mr. Pugsnap-Browne, you are not much concerned what happens to him. If you loved him, you would follow his fortunes with intense concern. A young man in love with his fiancée is tormented by the least offence against her, because no offence is trivial to intense and sincere love.

Whoever loves God intensely cannot be indifferent to sin. Seek, therefore, for contrition in the study of the lovableness of God; it is a disastrous mistake to seek it amongst the tangles of sin. The remedy for all our failures is to love God more.

Father William Doyle quotes his Tertianship Master, Father Petit, as saying: "The reason why we find life so hard, mortification so difficult, and why we are inclined to avoid all that we dislike, is because we have no real love for Jesus."[1] That remark is obviously true. Do not, therefore, attempt to excite contrition by studying:

1. Self—how imperfect, how ungenerous, you are. The best product of such analysis will be wounded self-love; the worst, hopeless discouragement.
2. Sin in itself, trying to hate it in itself. This is sometimes

[1] William J. Doyle, S. J., *A Year's Thoughts* (Longmans), p. 87.

impossible and often dangerous. Philosophical contemplation will produce only philosophical sorrow, compounded mainly of remorse because we have betrayed the Great-I-Am. Do not study the *action* of sin, but its *reaction* on the Sacred Heart; always concentrate on the Offended rather than on the offence.

As little time as we choose. The grace to make a good confession does not need to be wrung from God, who is literally "dying to give it." Grace will infallibly be given to us, if we ask for it properly, because it is there for the taking, having been won for us by the Precious Blood. Our Lord has promised to give us whatever is good for us if we ask in His Name: there can be no doubt that the grace to make a good confession is good for us, and, therefore, the answer to our prayer is infallible, if only we take the trouble to ask humbly and fervently.

As long as we choose. The longer our prayer, the more certain shall we feel of our Lord's assistance, and with His assistance it is a foregone conclusion that we shall make a good confession. He is infinitely more anxious than we are that we should make a good confession.

After prayer, we can approach Confession with confidence, knowing that Our Lord's assistance is guaranteed. We should steep ourselves in confidence and expel any misgivings about Our Divine Saviour's loving-kindness and welcome. Do not allow yourself to remain downcast or uneasy or suspicious of Our Lord. The devil will suggest that there is a wall between you, that things can never be the same again, and that the Friendship of Christ has been lost for ever, to be replaced by a cynical tolerance. The devil will see to it that such ideas tend to cling. Do not go on with your preparation until you have utterly routed them, or they will put a brake on your entire effort.

You would not expect a doctor to be angry with you, because you were sick when you approached him for treatment. Why then should the Divine Physician be angry because you are sick? "There is joy before the angels of God upon one sinner that doth penance, more than upon the ninety-nine just who need not penance."

Before you go on with your preparation, convince yourself that no matter what your failings and sins may have been, the Sacred Heart is bounding with joy because you have come back to Him. "A contrite and humble heart He will never despise."

Throughout our confession, our attitude of mind should be God-centred. We should be intimately conscious of Our Lord's presence, assistance, sympathy, forgiveness and love.

Because of their love of God, the saints had greater contrition for semi-deliberate venial sins than sinners have for grave mortal sins. The love of God is the key to contrition. Never go to Confession without spending some time considering the goodness and lovableness of God.

Study of the Sacred Passion is, of course, an admirable means of obtaining true repentance and practical hatred of sin. If, for instance, you have committed sins against purity, contemplate the Scourging. His Sacred Body was torn and hacked to pieces to atone for sins of impurity, so your sins were a partial cause! If you had never sinned, the Scourging might have been less severe and terrible. Your sins were the scourge! You had a very definite part in that mystery. Such cruelty was not intended and was due to want of thought; "with desolation is the whole land made desolate, because there is none that considereth in his heart." The remedy is to give more time to thought, so that you may stamp a sense of the realities of sin on your mind.

SATISFACTION

Throughout this book the truth has been emphasized that our outlook in Confession must be God-centred. In one part of the Sacrament, however, we are inclined to be too God-centred, and leave all the penance and the task of making satisfaction almost entirely to Christ.

Some heretics maintain that since the satisfactions of Christ are of infinite value, satisfaction on our part is entirely unnecessary. Our paltry satisfactions, they say, could add nothing to His, and the very idea of any such satisfactions being necessary, seems to imply doubt about the sufficiency of His.

For these reasons, Protestants claim that we can and should leave all the satisfaction to Christ; and it is to be feared that, on this point at least, many of us are Catholics in theory and quasi-Protestants in practice, for, relying on His pains, we tend to let ourselves off very lightly.

Christ's infinite merits and satisfactions are enough and yet not enough, because God will not treat us as robots or automatons. Protestants often accuse us of attributing magical effects to the Sacraments. We retort that they are the culprits, who attribute magic to Redemption, whereas we assert that there is magic neither in the Sacraments nor in Redemption. God respects our free-will, and without the co-operation of our free-will will do nothing. His operation is dependent on our co-operation, just as the electric current is dependent on the lamp for the production of light. Confession has the innate power to remove all traces of sin, but, before it can do so, there must be perfect co-operation, i.e., perfect rectification of the will. Free-will is the core of the difficulty.

An illustration may help to clarify the issue. Suppose two men had a quarrel, and one of them got into an uncontrollable rage and struck his companion so hard that he damaged his own hand and wrist. Afterwards the aggressor apologized and his apology was accepted. Would you call that the end of the incident? "No," you would say, "what about the hand?" Acceptance of the apology would not heal the hand.

So it is with us. By sin we damage our will; and the damage is not necessarily repaired by God's decree of pardon. Sometimes when we sin we turn to the creature with great intensity. Completely to rectify our will, we must turn back to God with equal intensity; that we frequently fail to do, with the result that our will remains scarred and out-of-the-straight. The will must be rectified before we can be fit for heaven.

If we turn back to God with an intensity equal to or greater than our intensity in sin, Confession takes away both the guilt of sin and the temporal punishment due to sin.

If we turn to God with less, though with sufficient intensity, the will still remains damaged, and other good works will be required to complete its rectification.

Here we have the explanation of the heavy penances imposed in the early Church. The early Christians did not doubt the efficacy of the Sacrament of Penance, but the adequacy of their own repentance. This is the explanation, too, of Christ's own insistence on penance.

One of the most crushing indictments of Protestantism is that it has rejected the idea of the necessity of penance, and by so doing has out-dated and made meaningless large sections of the Bible. Probably no virtue is more insisted on in the Bible than the virtue of penance. "Unless you shall do penance, you shall all likewise perish." His Cross does not dispense us from the obligation of taking up our cross: "Unless a man take up his cross and follow Me, he cannot be My disciple." If Christ's sacrifice made further sacrifice unnecessary, the continuance of pain in the world presents more than a problem, in fact a contradiction.

Let us convince ourselves of the complete adequacy and efficacy of the Sacrament of Penance, but at the same time let us never lose sight of the fact that we are not robots. Flattering ourselves that God will treat us as robots is an implicit denial of free-will and the sin of presumption.

Do not be misled, therefore, by the light penances in vogue today, and draw the false and fatal but natural conclusion that adequate reparation of sin is easy. Adequate reparation for sin requires the expenditure of the same amount of energy and enthusiasm that we dissipated on sin.

It is evident that a perfunctory examination of conscience, a slick and mechanical confession of sins, and a careless, scatter-brained and gabbled recital of one's penance are insufficient to effect complete rectification of will. "Unless you do penance, you shall all likewise perish."

Only the penance given by the confessor has sacramental

efficacy, because the priest alone has instrumental control of the electricity of Redemption. Should you forget your penance, it is useless, except to show good-will, to substitute another of your own choice. Let the fussy and the scrupulous take careful note of this. When the confessor gives a penance of three Our Fathers, presumably he means three Our Fathers, not nine, i.e., the penance three times over to make sure of saying it properly. The extras are *not* your penance, but private devotions dictated by obstinate self-will and ignorance.

If you did not hear the penance, or are uncertain about it or have definitely forgotten it, then if you are still in the confessional ask for a penance again; if you have left the confessional, go back if it is convenient or wait till your next confession. This will be unnecessary, if your confessor always gives you the same penance.

Incidentally, if occasionally you have to ask for your penance again, be kind in your judgment of the priest if he seems to snap out the answer. Far too many penitents make a habit of forgetting their penance, and the forgetfulness, which is not really genuine, is a morbid psychological symptom of "safism." They have not really forgotten, but only want to make assurance doubly sure. If they were asked: "What do you think it is?," they could give the right answer every time. Some penitents come into the confessional so afraid or so convinced that they will either not hear their penance or forget it, that they won't believe their own ears and are afraid they have not heard the penance when they have.

For the saying of the penance there is no time limit, unless:

1. The confessor expressly imposes one; or
2. The nature of the penance demands it, e.g., restitution required at once to save a creditor from bankruptcy.

Obviously, the sane practice is to fulfill your obligations at once and so prevent uncertainty and worry and needless repetitions. The obligation of saying the penance never ceases from lapse of time. It is sinful to keep putting off saying the penance until there is danger of forgetting it altogether.

EMOTIONAL INFANCY

Devotion should always be characterized by reasonableness and common sense, and not be, as unfortunately it sometimes is, a manifestation of emotional infancy. There are some who go to Confession only when they "feel like it" and because they "feel like it"; they imagine that it would be irreverent to go unless they feel in the mood. One must not go against one's will: it would be a poor compliment to Our Lord to approach Confession with reluctance and without enthusiasm.

These emotional infants should learn to differentiate between the emotions and the will, and regulate their spiritual lives by reason, not feeling.

Spasms are never an indication of health. We do not regulate our ordinary lives by feeling, at least not unless we are spoiled children or adherents of the sect of impossible people. If you opened your shop or went to work only when you "felt like it," only when you were in the mood, you would soon find yourself in the bankruptcy court. Confession is more, not less, valuable when it involves the discipline of feelings, i.e., when it requires self-conquest. The greater the effort, the greater the grace, "the kingdom of heaven suffereth violence, and the violent bear it away." Be done with fastidious and delicate attention to moods and feelings and rule your spiritual life by consistent reason.

REGULARITY

It is an excellent plan to decide on a regular time for Confession. Has not experience taught you what happens unless you adopt a regular programme? This week you will not go to Confession because you are not in the mood; next week, you are tired, but you will definitely go the following week; the following week, Mrs. Gossipworth-Smythe comes to tea and you are loathe to leave her; and so it goes on, until you are embarrassed at the thought of having to survey such a long period and admit such a long absence. Add to this the lethargy created by drifting and loss of grace. *Laissez-faire* devotion inevitably causes demoralization, spiritual paralysis and loss of peace. Regularity, on the contrary, safeguards and creates lightness of heart and spiritual vigour.

This disinclination to confess which we may sometimes feel may be created by the devil or generated by spiritual sloth.

ROUTINE

It is true, of course, that regularity is exposed to the danger of inoculation with the germ of routinism; but this danger can be obviated and must be obviated if steady progress is ever to be made. Without regularity nothing worth-while is ever done in any walk of life. The axiom that "Practice makes perfect" is as true of Confession as it is of everything else.

MIRAGE OF ROUTINISM

Sensitive souls are sometimes scared by a mirage of routinism; they are troubled because Confession appears to make less impression on them than it did when they approached it infrequently. They seem to make less effort than formerly and are not so affected in imagination and feeling. The conclusion they draw—and one must admit that at first sight it seems reasonable—is that they are suffering from routinism, and that it would be better if they went to Confession less frequently.

This is a subtle temptation which the devil exploits with great success. Even comparatively pious souls often use this line of reasoning with great conviction, as an argument against frequent confession. This temptation, which is specious and apparently inspired by true zeal, deserves careful refutation.

A survey of the development of the technique and reactions of a skilled pianist, in the various stages of his training, may illustrate the fallacy underlying this subtle temptation.

Once the pianist becomes proficient, his playing does not require nearly as much conscious effort as it did in the beginning, yet he plays far better and is more sensitive to good music. It is doubtful, however, if he ever gets quite such superficial thrills as he did in the beginning. His initial thrills were created by the joy of conquest and the sense of developing mastery of his art; in other words, by satisfaction with self rather than by appreciation of music. As his appreciation of music develops and the ideal becomes clearer, he becomes increasingly less self-satisfied. That is why true artists are always humble, never self-satisfied and habitually inclined to discouragement. The less an artist need concern himself about technique, the more he can concentrate on the unattainable ideal, and then what he has achieved is overshadowed by what he has failed to achieve.

This is a fairly apt analogy. Those who go infrequently to Confession need to make a considerable effort, and therefore, quite naturally, are more conscious of effort, and because their vision of the ideal is still obscured, they are not conscious of the amateur nature of their efforts and tend to be self-satisfied. Habit always gives ease of movement, and easy movement seems effortless; consequently, those who have acquired the habit of confession are not conscious of effort.

But they are more conscious of God and more sensitive to sin, the conscience is more refined and delicate, and the mind and will more God-centred.

And it is this very sensitiveness to God that makes them so inclined to discouragement and so suspicious of themselves. The very fact of being afraid of infection by routinism is a fairly certain indication of immunity. Let the self-satisfied take warning and the diffident take courage.

The devil makes frantic efforts to avert us from regular confession and by so doing testifies eloquently to its value. It is not unusual for souls to find that their preparation is disturbed by swarms of temptations, sometimes by horrible, gross and unusual temptations. On top of all this, they are often haunted by a feeling of hypocrisy. They are afraid that people will think them very holy because they go to Confession so often, and they feel that it is not honest to mislead them into such a false belief. The devil suggests that they are actuated by merely human motives, by the desire to make a good impression on the confessor, or by pig-headed self-righteousness which is too proud to break its own resolution.

The best way to deal with these suggestions of the devil is not to make a fuss about them and fight and rebut them, but simply to ignore them, renew one's intention and go calmly on. The intention you want to have is the intention you really do have.

The more we progress in the spiritual life, the more our centre of gravity will shift from self to God. The person who is approaching sanctity will seldom be guilty of fully deliberate sin, but his eyes will be fixed on the ideal of holiness and he will be so well aware of his own shortcomings as to be tempted to despondency rather than to self-complacency. He will spend his preparation time not so much in searching out sin as in contemplating God's infinite goodness and regretting the fact that he has ever betrayed it. He will implore God to strengthen him so that he may not fall again; he will protest his desire to be "all for Jesus." The saint approaches Confession "to be washed yet more from his iniquity and cleansed from his sin," and to be safeguarded against future temptations. Anyone who is self-reliant about the future and has ceased to "work out his salvation in fear and trembling," has already committed the sin of presumption. The saint is more intimately conscious than the sinner of his complete dependence on God and so can never have too much of grace and the sacraments.

Penitents who genuinely cannot find present matter for confession may renew their sorrow for past sins, and then spend their time repeating or ruminating over such words as: "My God and my All." These words will serve as a useful examen, for they will begin to stick in the throat if the soul has been guilty of deliberate infidelity.

When we approach Confession, let us do our best to have

the correct centre of gravity, putting the accent of thought and effort on God not self, and seeking the Divine satisfaction not self-satisfaction and personal profit.

If Confession has not done us as much good as it might have done, the reason probably is because we have been wanting in purity of intention. The spirit in which we approach the Sacrament of Penance is of supreme importance.

Let us be clear what we want and want what is best: let us be resolute, regular and reasonable, and then we may hope to obtain the maximum benefit from Confession.

XVII

Inside the Sacred Tribunal

DEVOTION should never be divorced from reason and commonsense. In matters of faith we must use our brains. Some Catholics dispense themselves from this obligation by saying that they prefer to "take things on faith," i.e., without thought or a serious attempt to understand, which is like continually swallowing food without attempting to chew or masticate it. No wonder such Catholics remain "woolly" about the Faith all the days of their lives. This is credulity, not faith, and credulity is defenceless against superstition and counterfeit devotion. Reason-shy devotion brings true piety into contempt and gives non-Catholics the impression (and how much harm this does!) that we are not allowed to think.

Would that all Catholics heeded St. Teresa's advice and added to their litany: "From silly devotions and sour-faced saints, good Lord, deliver us!" Yes, from silly devotions and from silly devotion. It is regrettable, but true, that pious people are sometimes ridiculous. Unreasoning devotion is a compound of sentimentality and sensuality, "near neighbours and ill-bred." Give the sensually pious a sermon that titillates their feelings and excites sensible devotion, and they are thrilled: make them think—or be foolish enough to try—and they are positively resentful. Ill fares the priest who disturbs their lazy complacency; he cannot be a prayerful or devout priest.

Silly devotion is nowhere more evidenced nor more irritating than in the confessional. "Pi-pi" penitents are often shocked by the business-like, matter-of-fact behaviour of the confessor. Would that they had the humility to suspect that perhaps he is right! Penitents should keep their wits about them. There is absolutely no need for fussiness, frenzy, anxiety or strain. Quiet workmanlike, practical commonsense is what is wanted.

We shall he helped considerably to acquire a sane attitude towards Confession if we learn to discriminate between essentials and non-essentials. The Church has surrounded the essential formalities of Confession with other devotional accretions, which are not strictly necessary. We should have no doubt as to which formalities are strictly necessary and which are devotional additions. We must be careful not to seem to disparage the devotional non-essential accretions to Confession—it is eminently fitting that the Church should add splendour and ceremony and safeguards to this wonderful Sacrament, for we always protect and pad and embellish a precious thing—but, at the same time, we must keep our sense of proportion and avoid confusion of thought. We must not confuse essentials and non-essentials, nor magnify the sancrosanctity of accidentals until they seem as important and necessary as essentials; nor should we cling to non-essentials to the detriment of charity, reasonableness or commonsense.

It will help us to get a sense of proportion if we consider to what the formalities of Confession may be reduced in cases of necessity.

For the valid administration of the Sacrament of Penance, it is necessary and sufficient for the penitent:

1. To be sorry.
2. To confess as far as is possible in the circumstances.
3. To be absolved.
4. To accept the penance.

Sometimes, in actual life, the administration of the Sacrament of Penance is reduced to the absolute essentials:

1. On the battle-field, for example, before an action, general absolution is sometimes given. The soldiers confess their sins in a general way, make an act of contrition, receive a penance and are given absolution *en masse*. All the non-essential formalities are omitted.
2. In hospitals, where two beds are often almost contiguous, so that it is impossible for a penitent to make a full confession without being overheard by his neighbour, it is enough for him to make a generic confession ("I have sinned"), after which he receives absolution and a penance.
3. Those who are travelling abroad and have difficulty with the language, may receive absolution after they have confessed and displayed sorrow by signs and gestures.

It is hardly necessary to remark that, in all these cases, penitents who had been guilty of mortal sins would have the obligation of confessing them at the next confession made in ordinary circumstances.

With the distinction between essentials and non-essentials clear in mind, we are now in a position to survey the formalities of Confession.

THE BLESSING
(non-essential)

Penitents are instructed to begin by asking for the priest's blessing. "Please (pray), father, give me your blessing, for I have sinned." The reason for this petition is two-fold:

1. It requests a sacramental of considerable value. Many of the saints had a great devotion to a priest's blessing.
2. It "apprizes the priest of the fact that there is someone behind the grille. (He may be reading or—asleep!)"[1]

If the priest gave you the blessing as you were coming into the confessional (no! he was not just muttering to himself

[1] Fr. H. Day, S. J.

nor talking in his sleep!), do not ask for it or you may get more than you asked for, though hardly more than you deserve. Keep your wits about you and do not troll out the request like a gramophone record incapable of adapting itself to circumstances. Imagine the feelings of the confessor when he is asked, for the *n*th time, for a blessing which he has already given.

THE CONFITEOR
(non-essential)

The confiteor is a devotional general confession, for which the Church has always shown a special fondness in her liturgy. The ritual directs that it should be said as a preface to confession, at least in the abridged form of "I confess to Almighty God and to you, Father. . . ."[2] It need hardly be said that this devotional exercise has nothing to do with the validity of the sacrament. The obligation to say it is a light one arising from our duty to obey the Church's liturgical rules with childlike simplicity.

Nowadays, most priests prefer that the *Confiteor* should not be said in the confessional, because as a rule it could not be said without detriment to charity and commonsense. The question of the *Confiteor* should not be divorced from considerations of time, commonsense and charity. It is mainly a question of time. If sixty people are waiting for Confession and each penitent says the *Confiteor*, taking roughly half a minute per penitent (and some who spell and drawl it out take even more!), then the unfortunate one who chanced to come last is kept waiting half an hour "whilst the devout indulge in a pious luxury which they could have enjoyed just as well outside."

Granted there will seldom be sixty people waiting at once, but do not forget the confessor, cooped up inside, who does have to wait an extra half-hour whether the penitents are there at once or not. Often it is difficult for a priest to find time and energy to hear all the penitents who come to him,

[2] See article "The Confiteor," *Catholic Encyclopedia.*

and every minute saved is a consideration. It is not very pleasant, either, for the confessor, who is pressed for time, to have to listen at one session to fifty or a hundred or more unnecessary repetitions of the *Confiteor.*

Lest it should be thought that we are pandering to modern impetuosity and restlessness, it may be well to remind readers that the concourse of people to the confessional is a recent development occasioned by the reintroduction of frequent Communion. In olden days, it was unusual to have crowds thronging the confessionals except at the time of missions.

It would be a pity, however, if the present practice led to the *Confiteor* not being said at all, and it would be a bad sign if we thought ourselves too spiritually developed to need such simple exercises of piety. The danger of omitting the *Confiteor* could be removed for school-children by their saying it aloud together before they begin to go into the confessional. With grown-ups the risk could be minimized by an occasional reminder from the pulpit and a few words on the beauty and aptitude of the prayer. The prayer can have little value if it is said merely because the priest insists on it.

Perhaps the best solution of the problem would be to adopt the ritual's own suggested abridgement and say simply: "I confess to Almighty God and to you, father," or the plan could be adopted of saying the *Confiteor* inside the confessional whenever you are the only penitent or one of a few; outside, whenever there are a number of penitents waiting. In using our commonsense about the ritual, we must be careful not to lose our sensitive regard for it and become careless.

HOW LONG SINCE LAST CONFESSION?

(non-essential)

Stating how long it is since your last confession is a useful non-essential introduced to help and not to embarrass you, and if you omitted it altogether your confession would not be invalidated. If you are anxious about it and spend a considerable amount of mental and nervous energy striving to fix the exact time since your last confession, you defeat your own purpose. An approximate estimate is enough, e.g., "about a month" would cover three to five weeks. No need to worry if you discover after confession that your estimate was a good deal out.

Why should you introduce the time-factor at all? (I wish Catholics were more reverently "querious" about faith.) There are several reasons:

1. The estimate of time enables the confessor to diagnose better your spiritual condition. The priest is there in the capacity of spiritual doctor and the more accurately he diagnoses your spiritual ailments, the more effectively will he be able to help you.

   It obviously makes a difference whether you got into a rage five times in five days or five times in five months. In the first case, anger would be indicated as your predominant fault; in the second, as one of your faults.

   Sometimes penitents confess one sin against purity in a month. This gives the confessor a clue that they are probably referring to nocturnal pollution, which is no sin at all. It is not usual for people to commit one such sin in a fairly long period.
2. The time-statement also saves many questions; so be careful about it, but please don't "worrit." Keep a sense of proportion.

Incidentally, it is not necessary to add: "I received absolution, said my penance, and went to Holy Communion." That you received absolution and said your penance is taken for granted: that you went to Holy Communion is matter for the recording angel, not for the confessor.

Neither is it necessary to give a lengthy and very apologetic explanation why you did not go to Holy Communion. If there has been any sin or grave imperfection in these omissions, the proper time to mention them is when you are making your confession.

CONFESSION

A rule proposed to after-dinner speakers is: "Be bright, be brief, be gone!" One can hardly expect a penitent to be bright; so perhaps we might amend this rule for penitents and say that they should "be blunt, be brief, be gone."

"Be Blunt"—This does not mean "be crude." All the same, "there is nothing against true modesty in calling a spade a spade." It is unkind to constrain the priest to ask questions that should be unnecessary. It is irritating to find penitents obstinately fastidious about formalities and negligent about essentials; penitents, for example, who will insist on saying the *Confiteor*, even when asked to refrain (either because they are too obstinate to heed or too fussy to hear) and then follow with the most inaccurate confession, saying, for example, "I committed sins against purity," without giving even a hint of number or kind.

Here are a few typical examples of inaccurate statement:

1. *"I was rude."* They mean "impure," not impolite. Why not say what you mean? Rude does not mean impure.
2. *"I was impure."* Why not mention number and kind? There are various kinds of sins against purity.
3. *"I told lies."* "White" lies? Lies involving calumny, serious uncharity or injustice? If lies are worth telling they are worth counting. Were they real lies, or legitimate mental reservations? In case of doubt, ask. You have no right to confess lies at all, if you feel that you were justified in what you did and mean to do exactly the same next time the occasion arises. Thrash the matter out. Perhaps you were justified, not, of course, in telling lies, but in using legitimate mental reservation. Do not add this item to your list without reflection or resolve, simply because you got into the habit at school.
4. *"I was late for Mass."* How late? Did you miss an essential part of the Mass? through your own fault?
5. *"I missed Mass."* With reason or without reason? Was

attendance impossible or very difficult? You are not bound to Mass in face of serious and solid difficulties.

6. *"I had bad thoughts."* What do you mean? Uncharitable thoughts are bad thoughts. Did you consent? Was your consent fully deliberate? If you dallied or were sluggish in repelling impure thoughts, your sin was venial; if you deliberately entertained them, your sin was mortal.

   What is an impure thought? If you are not clear about that, you may be worrying unnecessarily. A temptation is not a sin. A temptation conquered is grace gained. If you confess mere temptations as sins, you mislead the priest.

7. *"I missed my grace before and after meals."* An imperfection, not a sin. You are not obliged, but recommended, to say the grace before and after meals.

2. *"I stole."* What? One is reminded of the woman who confessed stealing a rope and forgot to mention that a pig was at the end of it.

A complete list of common inaccuracies would involve a survey of the commandments and require a book for itself. When a penitent rapidly trolls out a long list of such inaccuracies and refuses to be interrupted, the priest's task is made very difficult. Accusations should enable him to judge whether you are confessing mortal or venial sin or no sin at all.

A confession that conveys nothing is hardly a confession at all, and suggests a suspicion of culpable ignorance, fatuity or insincerity.

So don't be *vague.* Tell the exact kind and number of sins. If they are mortal, this is necessary; if venial, this is useful. If it is impossible to state the exact number of times, give a round number, "about twenty times," or say how many times per week or per month, for how long.

Don't waste time looking for the nicest way of putting things, i.e., the way least offensive to your pride and self-love. If you have calumniated someone, do not say: "I did not speak as kindly as I ought to have done," or, "I was not as exact in the matter of truthfulness as I ought to be."

In Confession, there is hardly ever need to use the word "perhaps," though some people use it frequently. "Perhaps I was uncharitable . . . perhaps I told lies." Did you or didn't you?—that is the question. You should settle the "perhapses" before you come into the confessional. "Let your speech be, Yea, yea, and nay, nay."

There is seldom need to explain a sin. "Explanations are usually nothing more than thinly disguised excuses."

If we make a clean breast of things, we shall get the fullest measure of relief of mind. If we often "feel as if we had not been," probably our fastidiousness of speech is responsible. If we only half get our sins off our mind, we cannot expect full relief.

Let us manfully embrace our shame. It is absurd to be squeamish about the statement of sin, when we were so careless about sin itself. Let us remember the shame we caused our Saviour in the Garden of Gethsemane, and not spare ourselves salutary and just humiliation. Let us drain the chalice of our shame to the dregs, in order to make amends to the Sacred Heart.

"Be Brief"—The priest wants to hear about your sins and imperfections—nothing else. *Don't make excuses* and blame circumstances, or in-laws, or your husband or wife for your sin; like the wife who so exasperated the priest by her insistence on her husband's foibles that she received as penance three Hail Mary's for her own sins and three rosaries for her husband's.

Tell what you *have done* and not what you have *not done.* Occasionally a penitent insists on going through the commandments. "Against the first commandment, no, I don't think I have done anything against that, father." "Against the second commandment, no, nothing against that either," and so on through the decalogue until he finds something that he has done.

Other time-wasting penitents say: "I had a temptation to anger, or impurity, but I don't think I consented." You are telling your virtues not your sins. Quite unintentionally you are boasting. If you didn't consent, why mention the matter at all? Perhaps you say: "To make assurance doubly sure." You have no right to do that, for you are misleading the priest.

If you have any doubt about consent to temptation, you should mention the doubt, because in that case, it is not honest to say: "I don't think I consented." The most you can say is: "It is probable, or more probable, that I did not consent."

If you have no genuine doubt about consent, to mention the matter at all is a surrender to scrupulosity. We must crush ruthlessly and bravely all *unreasoning* fear, and rule ourselves by reason not feeling. This is an exercise of the virtue of hope. If you confess as doubtful what is not really doubtful, you tell a lie in the interests of self-love, prompted by a selfish desire to *feel safe,* not being content to *know* that you *are* safe. Mere self-satisfaction is not a good end to have in view and a lie is not a very good means to obtain it.

In confessing your sins, confine yourself to what is strictly relevant. When circumstances do not alter the nature or the gravity of sins, the confessional is not the place for them. Would that the prolix and the meanderers could take note of this! " 'Twere a consummation devoutly to be wished!"

Father Zulueta gives an amusing story of classical irrelevance:

Sara Tick, residing at 4A, Paradise Alley, has had a passionate quarrel with a fellow-lodger, and used insulting and profane words, and broken her neighbour's wrist with a poker. She tells the priest:

"I occasionally has words with Mrs. Scrooge. She's the lady in the back-parlour. A good woman, according to her light, your reverence, but, like all on us, has her faults. She *has* a temper, father! Well, she called me out of my name. It was this way, to put it short-like. It was last Sunday fortnight come tomorrow—no, asking your pardon, it was Saturday, I mind me, because our Susan Victoria had just come in from Noggins', at the public, with a pint of porter for my husband. Not that Tick's a drunkard, you know. Bless you there's not a soberer, cleaner-living man in the alley. Well,

Mrs. Scrooge, to be short, came in all of a bounce-like into my parlour, and says to me: Mrs. Tick, she says, where's my best teacup gone to—the one with a handle?

"Well, to think as I would have took it, your reverence! Well, God forgive me! I used words and did things as I oughtn't, and me a respectable married woman, too, with six childer, and me eldest boy in the Post Office . . . and I often has words like that, your reverence."

Now it will be seen that this good woman has told the priest everything he did not need to know, except that there was a wordy quarrel, and omitted just what was wanted. As to what *kind* of words she used in her wrath, or what kind of unlawful acts she was guilty of, she gives no inkling, nor any indication of the number of occasions. And she mentions names, and tells Mrs. Scrooge's weaknesses as well as her own.[3]

Such types *are* met in the confessional, though not often, thank God. If they were always as amusing as Mrs. Tick, they would not be unwelcome; but even unconscious humour is rare among them, and sometimes the priest feels that they are a direct answer to prayer, the prayer of the Jesus Psalter: "Jesus, send me here my Purgatory."

On a Saturday night, when scores of penitents are kept waiting, loquacious irrelevance is an offence against charity as well as a fertile occasion of scandal.

Manners—Before entering the confessional, penitents usually deposit handbags, umbrellas and suchlike outside (or did before the stealing epidemic began!): there is no need to leave one's manners to keep guard. Good manners are as necessary and appropriate in the confessional as anywhere else.

Some penitents will not let the confessor get a word in edge-ways. No sooner has he managed to interject a few syllables than off they go again. Others are so very anxious to convince the confessor how much they need advice that they won't even pause for breath lest he should have the opportunity of giving it. After having talked and talked and talked, they go out unadvised and apparently without noticing it, so full are they of themselves.

[3] *Op. cit.*, II, 294-5.

Bad Manners—It is bad manners not to listen to the priest. It is exasperating for the confessor, when he is rapidly working up to the climax of his masterly *fervorino,* to hear the penitent query: "What did you say my penance was, father?"

Sometimes, when the confessor finishes giving advice, the penitent takes up her story just where she left off—fairly conclusive evidence that she has not been listening at all, but merely waiting for him to finish. Occasionally, when advice is being given, the penitent leaves the confessional in the middle of it; sometimes an irrelevant remark reveals that the penitent has been wool-gathering, not listening; on other occasions, the mention of the word "sickness" calls forth a homily on the penitent's lumbago or indigestion.

Granted these cases are not frequent, but is there any need for them at all? Nerves, anxiety, loquacity, egoism, may explain them, but they do not justify them.

A Hint—When you are confessing your sins, it is a good plan to put the big things first. If you have difficulty in telling a certain sin, get it off your mind at once; if you don't, you will run the risk of omitting it altogether, because the devil will have time and opportunity to play on your imagination and magnify the sin out of all proportion. Besides, to put first things first is the commonsense thing to do. If you went to a dentist for a tooth extraction, you would not start the proceedings by calling his attention to a slightly discoloured tooth. Some preface their confessions with a long list of peccadillos and things they haven't done, and the implication of their remarks seems to be: "I'm not so bad, in spite of what is coming . . ."

As regards the confession of venial sins, the following are a few suggestions made by Father Scharsch:[4]

1. "Accuse yourself preferably of those faults which you need most to amend."
2. "Accuse yourself of that sin for which you are particularly sorry."
3. "*Ceteris paribus,* accuse yourself of your more important faults rather than of those that are less important."

[4] *Op. cit.,* pp. 165, ff.

To do otherwise would create a suspicion of insincerity or imperfect compunction or "playing-up." Be honest with the confessor, don't try to make a good impression on him.

4. "The penitential spirit should urge us to confess preferably the faults which humiliate us most deeply."

A Worry—Some people worry because they are afraid that the confessor does not understand them, which is, as one author justly remarks, "paying an unmerited compliment to themselves and making very little of the confessor."[5]

To such a one the confessor might reasonably say: "My dear penitent, you are not nearly such a unique specimen as you imagine!"

"No, it's not that, father. I don't explain myself properly."

1. Of course not. Do we *ever* explain ourselves properly? How often do you ever say exactly what you want to say? God instituted Confession not for geniuses with an unusual gift of expression, but for ordinary folk like you.
2. In any case, *it is not necessary to express yourself very accurately*. When you go to the doctor with measles, you may and probably do explain your symptoms badly, but unless the doctor is very fifth-rate, he soon realizes what you mean, because he has heard all that so often before. Therefore, it is not unfair to say that if you imagine you are so difficult to understand, you either make too much of yourself or too little of your confessor.

If the priest does not understand, it is up to him to ask more questions, and if he neglects to do that when he should, it is his responsibility, his funeral, not yours: though of that you are most certainly not the judge. It is presumption and uncharity for you to decide that the priest is failing in his duty. Even if he is, provided you have done your duty, his omissions need not trouble you.

[5] Walshe, *op. cit.*, p. 9.

Jesus absolves, not Father So-and so. It would be a poor compliment to our Divine Master to presume that He would allow Himself to be baulked by human carelessness. What the worrying type need is more faith in the realities of Confession and a prolonged meditation on the words: "Whatsoever you shall loose, *shall be loosed*."

If the priest is satisfied with you, then you ought to be satisfied, for remember that he is the judge, not you. Don't usurp the confessor's position and imply that Confession is worth next to nothing! Confession would be valueless if a quasi-infallible confessor were essential for its successful administration.

"But the priest may be mistaken!" Of course, he may. But remember this:

1. *If the priest is fallible,* he is certainly no more fallible than you. This desire to revise his judgments amounts to an unconscious usurping of his position. It is judging God's appointed judge, and that is pride and want of faith and has no kinship whatever with zeal or tenderness of conscience. It is the self-opinionated attitude of private judgment.
2. *Fallible or not, the priest is reductively infallible,* because his judgment will be respected in heaven. "Whose sins you shall forgive, they are forgiven them. Whatsover you shall loose upon earth, shall be loosed also in heaven." Your judgment isn't guaranteed anything, so you will be wise to relinquish it and leave judgment to the priest.

Remember St. Philip Neri's wise saying: "No penitent was ever lost by obedience, nor saved by disobedience." God instituted Confession for human beings, who are incapable of mathematical accuracy in moral matters, and therefore He neither expects nor demands mathematical accuracy.

One sometimes meets a strange perversity in penitents. They make the priest infallible when he isn't and fallible when he is reductively infallible. They should remember that:

1. If the penitent has done his best, ***absolution is infallible.***
2. If the priest gives advice, his ***advice is not infallible.*** Its value depends on his learning and on his natural and supernatural prudence.

Yet the worrying type, if they have been disturbed by harsh, scrupulous or imprudent advice, insist on repeating: "But Father So-and-so said so-and-so." They will not say what Father So-and-so *did*, i.e., that he gave absolution. Absolution needs no revision, whereas advice may need it; but it is the absolution they insist on revising, not the advice.

ROUNDING OFF THE TALE OF WOE

The catechism suggests: "When you have told all your sins, say: 'For these, and all my other sins which I cannot recollect, I most humbly ask pardon of God, and penance and absolution of you, my ghostly father.' " Better, "of you, father." To the modern mind "ghostly" suggests "ghosts" and nothing else. Also "humbly" seems preferable to "most humbly." Be most humble but don't broadcast the fact.

It is a good plan to memorize these concluding words; otherwise, like many preachers, you many not be able to finish, or there may be a pause before the priest realizes that you have finished, or your concluding words may be very inappropriate. Without being stiff or artificial or stilted, we should study decorum in God's tribunal.

The following boy's confession, while probably very earnest and sincere, is hardly commendable for form: "Stole. Swore. Finish." "That's all," "Nothing else," "I have finished" are not commendable either.

To secure the validity of the Sacrament, it is suggested that when you have only venial sins to confess you should mention a sin of your past life for which you are certainly sorry, e.g., "for these, and all the sins of my past life, especially for sins of impurity . . . of Mass-missing . . . of serious injustice . . . of child-murder . . . I am heartily sorry and humbly ask pardon of God, et cetera." It is advisable to mention the most humiliating sins in order to frustrate any danger of vanity because of present achievement.

This suggestion is made because in ordinary devotional Confessions we may have insufficient matter or defective contrition and so expose the Sacrament to invalidity. This danger is obviated by confessing a sin which is certainly sufficient and for which we are certainly sorry. A detailed confession is not necessary, and it is sufficient to say: "In my past life I have broken the fourth, fifth or sixth commandment."

MORE ABOUT MANNERS

Perhaps a few words about the regulation of the traffic outside the confessional would not be inopportune. There should be no need of a traffic-policeman. The order of precedence should be punctiliously observed. Even in public houses, unless the company is getting maudlin, the rule is: "First come, first served." This much elementary charity and mutual consideration, we should be able to take for granted among those who are preparing to receive a great Sacrament. A preparation for Confession which consists mainly in eyeing the door, spying for an opportunity of slipping in out of one's turn, can hardly be called edifying, and must cause irritation and scandal. An act of selfishness and uncharity is a bad preparation for Confession. It is absurd to be committing sin as we cross the threshold of the confessional, presumably for the purpose of ridding our souls of sin. At the same time, those who are foiled of their turn, should exercise patience, though they are not forbidden to make a calm and dignified protest. It is not edifying to hear people haranguing each other in heated language immediately outside the Sacred Tribunal.

Those who are waiting for Confession should keep their wits about them. It is annoying to the priest when there are unnecessary intervals between confessions because penitents are too much *in excelsis* to watch the exits from the confessional. An ecstasy would excuse this, but ordinary devotion does not.

Sometimes penitents ring the confessional bell or send for the priest before they have made their preparation, with the result that the priest is kept waiting, possibly ten minutes, whilst they indulge their devotion and complete their preparation. The idea seems to be: "If anybody is kept waiting, it must not be me." This is hardly charity.

"Where there are several priests hearing confessions, it is a distinct advantage if the penitents can be distributed fairly equally. The preference for going to the 'box' nearest the door should not be indulged in unduly." Well said!

If you find a certain priest really helpful, no one objects to you adding yourself to a numerous queue outside his confessional. What is objectionable is that many flock like sheep to the confessional where a crowd is kneeling and not because of deliberate choice, but simply as a result of herd-instinct and because they are too sheepish to look around and see if any other priest is "hearing."

Do not choose a confessor merely because he gets you out of the confessional in the minimum possible time. Such conduct on your part suggests a want of earnestness which must be reprobated. If penitents do not want advice, it is to be feared that they have little or no sincere desire to reform and that Confession has become a routine formality, to be got through as quickly as possible. One is inclined to wonder why such people bother to go to Confession at all, if they think so little of it.

THE ACT OF CONTRITION

Confession over, "the priest," says the catechism, "will give you a penance, which you must take care to perform in due time and in a penitential spirit. He will then pronounce over you the words of absolution, during which you will say the Act of Contrition."

The words that the priest uses are very thought-provoking and deserve careful attention. Here they are:

P. *Misereatur tui omnipotens Deus et dimissis peccatis tuis, perducat te ad vitam aeternam.*

R. *Amen.*

P. *Indulgentiam, absolutionem, et remissionem peccatorum tuorum, tribuat tibi omnipotens et misericors Dominus.*

R. *Amen.*

Dominus noster Jesus Christus te absolvat; et ego auctoritate ipsius te absolvo ab omni vinculo excommunicationis et interdicti in quantum possum et tu indiges. Deinde ego te absolvo a peccatis tuis in nomine Patris et Filii et Spiritus Sancti. Amen.

Passio Domini Nostri Jesu Christi, merita beatae Mariae Virginis et omnium Sanctorum quidquid boni feceris et mali sustinueris, sint tibi in remissionem peccatorum, augmentum gratiae, et praemium vitae aeternae. Amen.

P. May Almighty God be merciful unto you, and, forgiving you your sins, bring you to life everlasting.

R. Amen.

P. May the Almighty and merciful Lord grant you pardon, absolution, and remission of your sins.

R. Amen.

May our Lord Jesus Christ absolve you, and I by His authority absolve you from every bond of excommunication and of interdict in as far as I can and you require it. I absolve you from your sins in the name of the Father and of the Son and of the Holy Ghost. Amen.

May the Passion of Our Lord Jesus Christ, the merits of the Blessed Virgin Mary and of all the Saints, whatever good you may have done, whatever evil you may have suffered, be to you unto the remission of your sins, the increase of grace, and the prize of life everlasting. Amen.

A memorized set form is not necessary for the act of contrition, though it is obviously useful and commendable. The act of contrition adopted should be short and simple. The confessional is not the place for private devotions and privately composed acts of contrition, however beautiful they may be, are not recommended. Prolix devotional effusions are to be reprobated, as also are dramatic striking of the breast and melodramatic emphasis of certain words. A set act of contrition is not absolutely necessary. All that is strictly necessary is that the penitent is truly sorry in his will and shows his sorrow in some way by words or actions. There is no need to worry, therefore, if:

1. You get tongue-tied and mixed-up and only say half the act of contrition; or
2. If, in your confusion, you say the Confiteor by mistake—a mistake by no means uncommon; or
3. You are *entirely distracted* and do not think of what you are saying whilst you repeat the act of contrition.

Provided you were truly sorry before you entered the confessional and that your sorrow endures in the will, all is well. Your sorrow must endure, unless you deliberately retracted it, which you could not possibly have done whilst distracted and therefore thinking of something quite different. Do not fuss and worry about the act of contrition, as though everything depended on saying it with verbal exactitude. God reads the heart and He knows when the heart is in the right place. Confession is neither a test of composure of spirit nor of memory, nor is it an examination in grammar and grace of diction.

BE GONE

The catechism says: "You will say the act of contrition and *afterwards leave the confessional,*" i.e. be gone! Do not delay the proceedings, especially if others are waiting.

The formalities of Confession were introduced to enable us to make our confessions with ease, composure, reverence and devotion. We shall defeat their purpose if we allow ourselves to become slaves of a form. The Pharisees made the letter of the law more important than the spirit and purpose of it and were soundly berated by our Divine Master. Be careful to approach the Sacrament of Penance like a true disciple of Christ and not like a Pharisee of the Pharisees.

XVIII

The Divine Confessor

WE SHALL never approach Confession properly unless we have the right attitude towards the Divine Confessor. We must not allow Father John or Father Tom to obscure the Great High Priest, Our Lord Jesus Christ, in Whose Name and by Whose power alone he is able to forgive sin. "Who can forgive sins but God only?" The priest is only the instrumental cause of forgiveness; the efficient cause is Jesus. *"Christus absolvit,"* says St. Augustine—"Christ absolves."

Forgetfulness of this truth is the main cause of most of the worries and scruples of penitents. If they went to confession to Jesus in person, they would have neither doubts nor fears. "Why are ye fearful, O ye of little faith?"[1] Do we not always go to Confession to Jesus in person? By whose power do we imagine that we are forgiven?

Penitents must be careful to make their confessions to Jesus of Nazareth and not to a mirage of themselves. The danger of penitents really confessing to themselves is a subtle one which is hardly ever recognized. The first effect of sin is to make us distrustful of God and disgusted with ourselves. When our sin has been particularly heinous or shamefully petty and mean, we cannot disguise from ourselves how entirely unlovable we are. We find it hard to imagine any-

[1] Matt. 8:26.

one knowing us and loving us; and because we know ourselves, we find it hard to love ourselves. The next step in our thoughts is easy and almost automatic, we begin to imagine that others do not love us, or, at any rate, love us only because they do not know us. God knows us, therefore, concludes the mind unconsciously—He cannot love us. If we go to Confession in this frame of mind, we shall unwittingly be confessing to a mirage of our disgusted selves. If we could see Jesus of Nazareth as He really is, we should find Him still infinitely patient, infinitely forgiving, infinitely loving. But this consoling and true picture of Him is obscured and hidden from us by the false picture which has been conjured up by our distraught imagination. In consequence, we do not confess to the real Christ but to a fictitious and false Christ who is in reality only a projected mirage of ourselves. This is a very real and subtle danger, which we cannot be too careful to avoid.

We should spare no pains to form a true mental picture of the Divine Confessor, because without it we cannot possibly approach Confession in the right spirit. A true mental picture of Christ, the Confessor, cannot be formed without an attentive study of the Gospels and of the amazing liberality of the Divine forgiveness in Confession.

We must be careful not to take the Sacrament of Penance for granted. It is possible that we should value this sacrament more if Our Lord had made approach to it more difficult. There is in human nature a fatal tendency to take for granted and fail to appreciate things which are given easily and without stint. "Easy come, easy goes," as the proverb says. If absolution were given rarely or on difficult terms, possibly it would be more appreciated. It will be worth while to consider some of the conditions of which Our Saviour could have exacted fulfilment as the price of absolution. The actual terms could not possibly be easier, but it might be well to remind ourselves that they might reasonably have been very much more difficult.

The power to give absolution might have been reserved to the Pope or to the Bishops, or to a few penitentiaries in each diocese. In any of these cases, we should have had to scheme and plan and make considerable sacrifices in order to get to Confession at all. Confession would then have entailed a considerable expense of time and money, but whatever sacrifices we had to make would be a very small price to pay for absolution from our sins. Perhaps we should realize better what we get, if it cost us more! Must we reproach Our Lord with having, in the excess of His Mercy and Divine Liberality, made His pardon too cheap? A common fallacy outside the Church is that we have to pay for absolution. If we had to pay, no price could possibly be sufficient.

Our Lord might have limited the number of sins we may confess or the number of times we may be forgiven, and such limits might have made us more careful about sin. Instead, He forgives us to seventy times seven times, that is, indefinitely, and lest we should be tempted to despair, assures us in advance of His indefinite forgiveness. He risks His Mercy being taken advantage of, rather than leave us in any doubt about His willingness to forgive. God grant that His amazing goodness may not blind us to the amazing realities of the confessional.

If you have ever been privileged to go to Lourdes, you may have witnessed a miraculous cure; perhaps you saw vacant eyes suddenly light up and flash as sight was restored to them, or the lame fling away their supports and shout praises of God for very joy, or broken wrecks of humanity suddenly restored to health and vigour. If once you have seen such a sight, you will never forget it. Without a doubt that cure will have left an indelible impression on your mind.

During our Divine Lord's life on earth such happenings occurred wherever He went, for "laying His hands on every one of them, He healed them all." It is not surprising that the people went delirious with joy and recognized a power and goodness such as had never been seen before on this earth.

In our confessionals, still greater marvels are worked, and greater proofs are given of mercy and love. Alas, however, we have but a dim perception of what really takes place there, and the only reason why we are not made delirious with joy by it is because we are so deadly dull and uncomprehending.

One of the greatest miracles of Our Lord's earthly life was the raising from the dead of Lazarus, whose corpse had already begun to corrupt. "Lord," said Martha, "he stinketh." The raising of a soul from the death of sin to the divine life of grace is a still greater marvel and miracle. No bodily corruption can compare with the spiritual corruption of a soul in the state of mortal sin; a spiritual corpse is far more repulsive than a physical corpse. The spiritual degradation of a soul in mortal sin is indescribable, but even more indescribable is the transcendent beauty of a soul in grace. To transform a sinner from the loathsome corruption of spiritual death to the dazzling beauty of participated divine life is a work of power and mercy which even the angels cannot fully understand. Compare the first condition of the sinner (*terminus a quo*) with the last (*terminus ad quem*) and you will begin to realize the extent and marvel of that transformation. And such amazing transformations are regular daily events in the confessional!

The regeneration of a sinner is an incomparably greater marvel than the raising of Lazarus; in fact, as St. Thomas points out, it is a greater work than an act of creation. In creation there is no resisting subject-matter, such as there is in regeneration, and the life produced is not divine.

If only once we had seen Our Saviour in His goodness and compassion raise the dead to life, we should never forget the event and we should henceforth find it impossible not to trust and love Him. What a tragedy it is that still greater miracles of love, repeated so often in the confessional, leave us cold and unimpressed! The miracles of Our Divine Saviour during His earthly life were not so wonderful or so startling to the angels, as those which He works daily on human souls in the Sacrament of Penance—not so wonderful, not such collossal proofs of love or such motives for praising and thanking and loving God. A visible miracle of healing would send us into an ecstasy of love and admiration, and yet millions—yes, millions—of far more stupendous miracles in human souls pass almost unnoticed. We can come to only one conclusion, and that is that our spiritual sight is defective and our faith slumbering. How appalling is the contrast between the incessant, tireless, attentive, wonder-working love of God and human indifference and dullness! Jesus is still with us, working greater miracles than ever He worked during His life on earth, "He is daily with us in the temple"—in the confessional—"and we do not know Him!" The Sacrament of Penance is a tremendous proof of love too little understood, too little appreciated. If proof were needed, Confession is a standing proof that Jesus is "yesterday, today and the same for ever," still "the friend of publicans and sinners, Who came not to call the just but sinners to repentance."

To approach the Sacrament of Penance with becoming trust, we must understand the spirit of the Divine Confessor Who awaits us on the other side of the grille. It is inevitable that we should frequently go to Confession in anything but a happy and tranquil frame of mind and should tend to see only a mirage of ourselves and not the Master. It is instructive to find that the Apostles made this same mistake, and it is consoling to know what happened when they really did see the Master.

On the day of the Resurrection the Apostles were a very dispirited lot; how dispirited is clearly proved by the fact that the announcement of such an unheard-of event did not enliven them.

One can easily imagine their utter dejection. They had failed the Master; they had abandoned Him in His need; they had been cowards. Despite all their boasts that they would never abandon Him, they had fled at the first signs of danger. They had not done a single thing to save Him; something might have been done if they had made a vigorous protest at the Court of Pilate—that was left to Pilate's wife. They had not even had the courage to attempt to save His dead Body from desecration—that was left to Joseph and Nicodemus. Even now, although they had proof of His

Resurrection, they had not the courage to go out into the streets, and were gathered together behind closed doors for fear of the Jews. Worse, however, than their feeling of personal vileness was the consciousness of guilt. They had betrayed the Son of God. They had been chosen as the friends and intimates of the greatest of the prophets, One greater than a prophet, and they had done nothing to prevent His destruction.

A sense of utter despair seemed to pulverize them. The Holy Women said that Our Divine Lord had risen from the dead, and had requested the Disciples to go down into Galilee where He would appear to them. They did not go. They seemed to have lost all faith in the Resurrection, though Our Divine Lord had repeatedly foretold it. In any case, even if He had risen from the dead, what could they hope for from Him; what sort of a reception would He give them? If Peter in a moment of realization of His Divinity had exclaimed, "Depart from me for I am a sinful man, O Lord," how could they, vile sinners, face Him now glorious and transcendent?

It is easy to imagine the disciples sitting there in a moody silence, each nursing his own bitter thoughts, helpless, hopeless, the sun gone out of their lives, their hopes blighted.

"And Jesus came and stood in the midst." He seemed in a hurry to institute this Sacrament of Mercy. He could not bear to leave them in such a state of dejection. He would prove to them that He is "Jesus, yesterday, today, and the same for ever," that man's malice had not embittered or changed Him, since it was to repair the effects of that malice that He had died. "And Jesus came and stood in the midst and said: Peace be to you. And when He had said this, He showed them His Hands and His Side." He showed them the price and cause of their peace, recalling the words of Isaiah: "The chastisement of our peace was upon Him and by His bruises are we healed. God hath laid on Him the iniquities of us all."

"The disciples therefore were glad when they saw the Lord. He said therefore to them again: Peace be to you. As the Father hath sent Me, I also send you. When He had said this, He breathed on them, and He said to them: Receive ye the Holy Ghost." They were to go forth in the name of the Father, and of the Son and of the Holy Ghost, commissioned by the Father and Himself and in the power of the Holy Ghost, to restore unto men the joy of His Salvation for all time and in every place wherever there was need. His Divine Compassion, "reaching from end to end mightily," embraced all those who would ever find themselves in a similar predicament and with the same need for pardon. Not merely did He forgive the Apostles, He gave them power to forgive others. His understanding Compassion extended to all those who would ever need reassurance of His pardon and His enduring love. "When He had said this, He breathed on them and said to them: Receive ye the Holy Ghost: whose sins you shall forgive, they are forgiven them, and whose sins you shall retain, they are retained."

Peace! Pardon! Power to pardon! And to such men! Not a syllable about their cowardice and desertion, not a single word of reproof, not the slightest reference to their fall—what divine gentleness and refinement of feeling! what a revelation of the goodness and kindness of Jesus, Our Saviour!

This is the Master to Whom we present ourselves in the confessional. Whatever else we do, let us not dishonour such infinite goodness and mercy by distrust and implicit refusal to believe in it. What a pity it is that the devil succeeds so well in distorting this Sacrament in the eyes of so many of our fellow-men. Let us take good care that we do not allow him to distort it in our eyes.

To the Sacrament of Penance all Catholics owe more than they have ever realized or ever will realize this side of the grave. This statement admits of no exceptions and applies to the comparatively sinless even more than to the sinners.

Perhaps you have never committed a mortal sin, and so have never had absolute need of this Sacrament. For you it has been a Sacrament of prevention rather than of cure. God alone knows, however, how many mortal sins you might have committed but for its saving influence. God's grace has preserved you, not your strength; and you owe a greater debt of gratitude to God than those who have fallen and been reclaimed.

Perhaps you are not certain of ever having committed a mortal sin but have been sometimes in serious doubt. Recall those periods of doubt and mental torture, and how the Sacrament of Penance restored unto you the joy of His Salvation. How different life would have been if you had never been able to rid yourself of that gnawing uncertainty! You, too, owe the Divine Confessor an immense amount of gratitude.

Perhaps you have committed mortal sin; and possibly not once, but many times, you have had to call on Jesus for mercy and pardon. "To whom much is forgiven, he loveth much." You owe the Divine Confessor an immense debt of gratitude and love for His persevering mercy, and for the amazing transformations which He has caused in your soul. If you had been the recipient of a first-class miracle at Lourdes, if sight had suddenly been restored to you, or you had been raised from death to life, you would not fail to recognize your indebtedness to the goodness of God and your duty of unending thanksgiving. God has done more than that for you, since time and time again He has raised you from the death of sin to the life of grace; and it is impossible to state or exaggerate the degree of gratitude which you owe to Him.

Let us all thank God for this great Sacrament! How much poorer our lives would have been without it! How much of our lightness of heart we owe to it!

Throughout this book great insistence has been placed on the ease with which the validity of the Sacrament of Penance can be guaranteed. There is just a danger that this information may have a bad effect on penitents, because human nature tends to stop short at the minimum effort which is strictly necessary. Many spend a considerable time in anxious preparation for Confession because they fancy that such an effort is rigidly necessary. When they find out their mistake, there is a danger that they may relax their efforts and go to Confession in a careless, slipshod manner, giving to it the minimum of time and attention.

The ease of Confession has been emphasized so that we may dispense with worry and distrust, not that we may dispense with effort. The more time we give to preparation and thanksgiving for Confession the better, provided our devotion is prompted by love and not by Jansenistic fear. We should approach Confession with care and reverence but without a trace of nerves or uneasiness. Panic is a sure sign that we do not realize Who is waiting for us on the other side of the grille. If we knew Him, we could not distrust Him.

Do not be content to receive the Sacrament of Penance validly, but try to receive it perfectly. It is designed to do far more than take away sin; it is designed to increase the beauty of your soul, to fill it with grace and to bring it nearer and make it dearer to Jesus. The fervent use Confession frequently to reassure themselves that there is nothing in their souls displeasing to the Master's gaze.

The Holy Father desires that we should go to Confession frequently. Of course, there is no obligation, but why should we always wait for commands and, if we find there is no obligation, relax our efforts? Let us not be craven and mercenary. Let us approach this sacrament out of love and primarily to give pleasure to Jesus, not solely to feel safer and more at peace.

Fix a definite plan—once a week, once a fortnight, or once a month. Fortnightly confession will suffice to enable you to gain all the plenary indulgences for which confession is a condition.

Life is given to us that we may prepare ourselves to stand in the blinding Presence of God, "in Whose sight the angels themselves are not pure." The Sacrament of Penance, perfectly received, has power to prepare us for the immediate embrace of God, and to enable us to stand without blinking in the blinding Presence of God. Let us use Confession as a preparation for death. We should strive to preserve such habitual purity of soul that we may be ready to die at any time. Prepare for each Confession as though it were to be your last, your final preparation for Eternity. Each night before retiring put yourself in the dispositions in which you desire to be found at the hour of death, and renew those dispositions at each Confession. The person who is not afraid to die is able to live fully and courageously. In this life we are not likely to avoid all semi-deliberate venial sin; but we have the means at hand to obliterate all traces of sin, renew our strength and refresh our souls, so let us use this Divine assistance to the full.

Approach this Sacrament in a spirit of tranquillity and boundless trust. You are not going to an Ogpu or Gestapo inquisitor, but to your Divine Friend of Friends, Who only asks you to lay bare your wounds that He may heal them. A drop of the Precious Blood is, as it were, about to fall on your soul and "though your sins be as scarlet, they shall become white as snow." He is overjoyed that you are coming to Him—you must believe that. "There is joy before the angels of God upon one sinner that doth penance, more than upon the ninety-nine just who need not penance." "Let us eat and make merry," says the father of the prodigal, "because this my son was dead, and is come to life again; was lost and is found." Forget your shame in contemplating His joy, and the peace of Christ, which surpasses all understanding, will possess your heart and you will call His Name Jesus because He has saved you—His child—from your sins

Appendices

A

What Will He Think?

Considerations for those who are afraid what the priest will say or think:

1. "O! How priests must marvel at the mercies of God! And how the ever-recurring sight of His clemency towards the sinner must help them to be gentle and forgiving themselves."[1]
2. The priest has to go to Confession himself. He knows how one feels on the other side of the grille.
3. A friend of St. Francis of Sales, who had been to confession to him, said:

   "You can no longer esteem such a sinner as I am."

   The saint replied: "I should be a Pharisee indeed if I felt you were a big sinner after you have received absolution. I love you tenfold, you are white as snow in my sight, pure as Naaman when he had washed in the Jordan."

   The same saint once replied to a penitent who had said to him: "What must you think of me now that you know my ignominies?"—"Why do you place me in the number of the Pharisees who regarded Magdalene, after she was forgiven, as a sinner? I regard you as a vessel of election."

[1] Louis Veuillot.

4. Another saint made a similar reply to a penitent: "I am bound not to think of it at all. How could I dwell upon what is for ever done away and blotted out in God's sight? Put all uneasiness as to what I think out of your mind; my only thought is to praise and thank God and to join the angels who rejoice at your repentance. The tears in my eyes are tears of joy over your resurrection to grace."
5. Nothing can show the priest better that you are an object of divine love than your present conversion.
6. The priest is sure to think more of your present dispositions than of your past weakness. Your sorrow and humility will strike him more than your sins.
7. You are now a friend of God, so how can he despise you? Shall what makes you glorious in the sight of God, make you contemptible to him who is in the place of God?
8. The ancients said that there was nothing so pure as snow. We know of something purer—a soul washed with the Precious Blood of the Lamb unspotted and undefiled. "Though your sins be as scarlet, they shall become white as snow"—and whiter; the words of Sacred Scripture are an understatement. The priest believes that, so how can he despise you? Give the priest credit for faith.
9. The priest spends his life searching for the lost sheep. Is he to spend his life searching for you and then be unkind to you when he has found you? Your humble confession will be a source of joy to him. Your conversion will console him, your trust flatter him, your joy encourage him.

   Every "fisher of men" is pleased when he lands a big fish. The worse you have been, the greater will be the consolation of the priest. Give the priest credit for commonsense.
10. St. Francis of Sales used to say, as a sinner left his confessional: "There goes Francis of Sales, but for the grace of God." The priest is mindful of his own frailty. Give him credit for elementary humility.

11. If he happens to be suffering from gout or depression and is not as kind as he ought to be—offer it up. He will be sorry for it afterwards and will despise himself, not you; and he may be induced to say special prayers for you in reparation.
12. Misery is the magnet of mercy, both human and divine. How would you react if someone bared his soul to you and gave you humiliating and shameful confidences? The more difficult the confidences, the more the priest will love you with a special love.
13. There is joy in doing good. What man does not rejoice in restoring peace and giving happiness to his fellow-man? "There is joy before the angels of God upon one sinner that doth penance, more than upon the ninety-nine just who need not penance." Joy before God and His angels and none before His priest who has been privileged to be the giver of joy?
14. If you meant so much to Jesus that He thought you worth dying for, how can the priest think little of you?
15. "He that shall persevere to the end, he shall be saved." You may end up a saint and the priest a sinner. It is the end that matters and the end is not yet. The priest will not want to tempt God to withdraw His grace in punishment for his unkindness towards you.
16. Perhaps you imagine that your case is unique. Not at all. The priest has heard similar and probably much worse cases before, so you won't surprise or shock him—he is "hard boiled." Probably *you* will be shocked by the calm, matter-of-fact way he takes it. Try it and see.
17. If you are afraid of yourself, say so to the priest and he will help you.
18. Ask for courage. Jesus will give it to you if you ask Him. You won't find confessing nearly so difficult as you imagine; and when it is all over, and even before that, your joy will be overwhelming. Reflect what this Sacrament cost Him! It is much easier to go to Confession than to hang and die on the Cross! The price *you* have to pay cannot bear comparison with the price He had to pay.

"You have not yet resisted unto blood . . . He loved you and delivered Himself for you." Won't you do this for Him? What does it matter what the priest says or thinks, if the Sacred Heart of Jesus is made to thrill and throb with joy?

B

Why Confess Sins Again?

I

Quite a number of good Catholics are puzzled by the doctrine of the legitimacy of re-confessing past sins.

The question is often asked: "How can sins be forgiven twice?" The simple answer is that they are not forgiven twice. Then, what is the point of confessing them?

All the Sacraments, besides conferring or increasing sanctifying grace, also confer special sacramental grace, according to the purpose for which the Sacraments were instituted. Confirmation, for example, confers the grace of fortitude; Matrimony and Orders, the grace to sanctify the performance of the duties of the respective states of life. Penance confers a title or right to *actual graces* which will enable us to combat sin more vigorously. Of such graces we can never have too many, or even enough.

II

Sometimes the difficulty takes another form. "How," it is asked, "can sins already forgiven provide sufficient *matter* for absolution?"

Well, first of all, sins do not provide the matter for absolution. They provide what the theologians call the *remote matter*. What is necessary for absolution (at least as a condition *sine qua non*) is that there should be on the part of the penitent, confession, contrition and acceptance of the penance.

These three acts of the penitent obviously presuppose sin: but not necessarily the present actual guilt of sin. One can be sorry for and confess past sin, and the utility of doing so has been explained in the answer to the first difficulty.

In other words, to be a valid candidate for absolution, it is not necessary that one should be burdened with the *actual guilt* of sin. If this were necessary, the validity of many confessions of devotion would be extremely doubtful; and, as one is not allowed to risk the validity of the Sacrament, such doubtful confessions would be illicit.

We have already seen that the guilt of venial sins may be removed without confession, and it is to be hoped that the majority of fervent souls generally approach the sacrament of forgiveness without the actual guilt of sin on their souls. It would be absurd to suppose that fervent souls are excluded from the benefits of the sacrament by their very fervour.

St. Philip Neri and other saints who confessed every day obviously did not always find certain unforgiven sin to confess.

We must always approach the Sacrament of Penance as *sinners*, i.e., with contrition and in a spirit of penance; it is not necessary that we should approach *in* sin. Sin may be in the past tense, contrition must always be in the present tense.

What the theologians, who insist on the necessity of finding sufficient matter for confession, are really preoccupied about is the danger of not having genuine effective contrition. About our hardy habituals there is always a danger that we may be merely remorseful.

Provided we have no necessary matter to confess, any sort of sin will do for confession; but any sort of contrition will not do for absolution. Therefore, it is a wise safeguard to renew our contrition for some sin or sins of which we are certainly sorry.

C

Practical Cases

I

As X. is preparing for confession, he remembers certain *venial* sins which he has a peculiar reluctance to tell at all or to tell to this particular priest who knows him well. He feels unable to force himself to confess them and, uncertain what to do, wonders if it would not be advisable to delay confession until he has got the grace to overcome himself. He is afraid that it would be sinful deliberately to omit to mention certain venial sins through shyness or shame. What is he to do?

Several things are immediately obvious:

1. His reluctance presents him with a glorious opportunity of making real atonement for his sins and delivering a serious blow to his self-love. Therefore, he should pray for grace and strive valiantly to overcome himself.

2. If he fails to overcome himself, he will lose a precious opportunity of increasing in grace and deprive himself of a glowing relief of mind.

3. His weakness presents a strong reason for humility, gives a clue to his defects of character and points the direction of his particular examen.

4. There is no obligation to confess any venial sins at all, and, therefore, there is no obligation to confess these specific

ones. Reluctance to confess does not create an obligation to confess. A penitent is not obliged to confess sins simply because he doesn't want to confess them. The penitent is advised to confess humiliating sins by preference, but counsel and precept are two different things. The validity of the sacrament is not in any way endangered.

5. If he is truly sorry for his sins, they are included in the absolution, even if he does not confess them.

If, after prayer, he is still unable to overcome himself, it would be folly to stay away from Confession on that account, because his weakness should give him an added incentive to make use of the grace of the sacrament. He need not approach Confession with misgiving, because his omission constitutes an imperfection not a sin. He should discuss his weakness with the Master and prove his trust in His understanding and compassion; he should cultivate greater humility and resolve to overcome those inhibitions that fetter him so firmly; and after that he should approach Confession like one sick going to the physician to receive treatment for his ailments.

II

A somewhat similar case arises if a penitent is aware of an inveterate habit of venial sin, which he has the wish but not the will to reform.

1. Such sins are *not* included in the absolution and diminish the grace of the sacrament.

2. Omitting to confess them does not invalidate the sacrament; in fact, to confess them in those circumstances would be hypocrisy.

3. It would be folly to omit confession because of such defective dispositions. The penitent should humbly apologize to the Master for his imperfect disposition, and offer the reception of the sacrament as a humble petition for the grace to convert his wish into effective will.

4. Voluntary attachment to venial sin is no impediment to worthy Communion, and according to the decree of Pope

Pius X, the cessation of the attachment should be a fruit of daily Communion. If we may approach worthily the great Sacrament of the living whilst still attached to venial sin, obviously we may approach this Sacrament of the dead with no better dispositions.

5. If this were not the case, few of us could ever go to Confession. If we think that we have no attachments to venial sin, we are either saints or the victims of self-deception.